The Liturgical
Revolution

Michael Moriarty

The Liturgical Revolution

Prayer Book Revision and Associated Parishes:
A Generation of Change in the Episcopal Church

The Church Hymnal Corporation
New York

Library of Congress Card Catalog Number: 96-71102

The Church Hymnal Corporation
445 Fifth Avenue
New York, NY 10016

5 4 3 2 1

In memory of
Henry Hurd Breul
(1924–1996)
Guide, healer, friend

Contents

Abbreviations   x

Acknowledgments   xi

Preface   xiii

Introduction
A Revolution in Episcopal Worship   1

Chapter One
The Last Cranmerian Liturgy   13
   Muhlenberg, Huntington, and the 1892 Prayer Book   14
   The 1928 Prayer Book   18
   William Palmer Ladd: Catalyst for the Liturgical Movement   21
   Liturgical Awakening in Seminaries Before World War II   28
   Preparing for Prayer Book Revision: *Prayer Book
      Studies* 1950–1963   30
   Ecumenical Cross Currents   35

Chapter Two
Associated Parishes' Divine Discontent   40
   John O. Patterson   41
   Cincinnati: "Why Not Do Something?"   42
   Washington, D.C.: A.P. Is Born   44
   A.P. Gets to Work   52
   A.P. Meets with Dom Gregory Dix, A.G. Hebert   54

Chapter Three

The Shape of Things to Come   58

The Breakdown of Cranmer's Synthesis   59
A.P.'s Debate: Liturgical Leader or Leaven?   61
"This Is What We Mean:" A.P.'s Publications   64
A.P.'s Liturgical Conferences: 1958, 1959, 1962   77
Social Action and Liturgical Worship   82
The Changing Liturgical Context   88

Chapter Four

The Turning Point   101

A.P. Opens Its Membership   103
Trial Use Begins: *The Liturgy of the Lord's Supper*   109
Analysis of *The Liturgy of the Lord's Supper*   113
Reaction to Trial Use   117
A.P. Backs *The Liturgy of the Lord's Supper*   122
The Crisis: A.P. Mobilizes for a New Prayer Book   125
A.P. Members on the SLC and Drafting Committees   130
A.P.'s Regional Liturgical Conferences   133
Open   135
A.P. Considers Merging with the Liturgical Conference   137
Special General Convention 1969   139
A.P.'s Liturgical Experiments   145
Beyond *The Liturgy of the Lord's Supper*   150

Chapter Five

The Creation of the 1979 Prayer Book   156

An Overview of Developments from 1970 to 1976   156
The Controversy About the Rites of Initiation   162
The Problem of Initiation: Background to PBS 18   162
The Reform of Baptism: From PBS 18 *to 1979 Prayer Book*   166
Popular Reaction to PBS 18   175
1970 To 1976: A Time of Transition in A.P.   179
A.P. Membership   179
Create and Celebrate   181
A.P.'s National Liturgical Consultant   182
A.P. and Women's Ordination   185

Ecumenism and Lay Leadership for A.P. 187
A.P. and the Diocesan Liturgical Commissions 188
The Work of A.P. in Introducing the 1979 Prayer Book 191
Learning to Live the New Prayer Book: A.P.'s New Brochures 192
Inclusive Language in the Prayer Book 205
The Next Prayer Book 206

Chapter Six
A Prayer Book for a Post-Christendom Church 209

Notes 221

Bibliography 261

Abbreviations

A.P.   Associated Parishes for Liturgy and Mission

BCP   Book of Common Prayer

JGC   *Journal of the General Convention of the Episcopal Church*

PBS   *Prayer Book Studies*

SLC   Standing Liturgical Commission

TLC   *The Living Church*

Acknowledgments

Unless otherwise noted, all of the material relating to Associated Parishes cited in this book—minutes of A.P. meetings, correspondence, publications, and so on—is housed in A.P.'s archives, which are now located in Fort Worth, Texas, but at the time I researched them were in Alexandria, Virginia, a subway ride across the Potomac from Washington, D.C. The Council of Associated Parishes gave me complete access to all A.P.'s materials. Mr. Arthur Jenkins, A.P.'s treasurer and office coordinator at the time, gave of his time and resources as I ferreted through filing cabinets and cupboards stuffed with the uncatalogued history of Associated Parishes. The Rev. Dr. Samuel E. West—a founding member of A.P. who in his fifty years' association with the group has held every elective office but treasurer—generously put at my disposal his typewritten reminiscences of episodes in A.P.'s history. For some key incidents, such as A.P.'s meetings with Dom Gregory Dix, O.S.B., and A.G. Hebert, S.S.M., West's unpublished eighty-page collection is the only remaining written evidence. Files pertaining to A.P. as well as all the papers of Massey H. Shepherd, Jr., at the Archives of the Episcopal Church, USA, in Austin, Texas, also were examined.

The Rev. Dr. Henry H. Breul introduced me to A.P. and at his nomination I served on its Council from 1980 until my resignation in 1985 (though I continue as a member of A.P.). I first knew Henry when I became a parishioner at St. Thomas' Church in Washington, D.C. For twenty-six years there as rector, and before that in parishes in Connecticut and Kansas, Henry put into practice the liturgical ideals of A.P. Henry was an "active, hopeful, expectant vigilante," in the words of the Rev. James C. Holmes, who preached his funeral sermon. There was nothing small-scale about Henry. His was an abundance of intellect, culture, good humor, and zeal, as well as of stubbornness and impatience, and he spent of his abundance generously. As Sally, his wife of twenty-two years, remarked, Henry occupied a vast psychological space in one's life. His friendship was a turning point for me, and I am still spending the power of his presence.

This book grew out of doctoral work at the University of Notre Dame under the Rev. Dr. James F. White, a generous scholar and friend. The painstaking editorial skill and liturgical expertise of the Rev. Dr. Byron D. Stuhlman has helped to make this a better book, and I am grateful to him.

To my teammates of the Notre Dame Rugby Football Club, I owe thanks of deep joy. May each of them find in his life what they have given me.

MICHAEL MORIARTY
South Bend, Indiana, June 1996

Preface

Gertrude Stein once wrote: "Wars are a sign of change that has already taken place." This was certainly true of what I call the World War, Part I and Part II, 1914–1945. The social, ideological, linguistic, psychological/sociological changes were even present in the arts before 1914, and sensitive people within the churches were relating to it before the turn of the century. Percy Dearmer, A.G. Hebert, and William Palmer Ladd were the harbingers of this in Anglicanism. Between Part I and Part II of the World War, liturgical interests were beginning to come to the fore. When Associated Parishes began in 1946, the impacts of the World War were so profound that it was clear that the old ways of doing things were in serious trouble. Radio and films had already dazzled the eyes and ears of our society, and television would soon immerse society in the visual and auricular maelstrom by putting it in everyone's living room. Associated Parishes and its sister organization in the Roman Catholic Church—the Liturgical Conference—were both responding to the deep confusion in the churches about the usual Sunday morning service which was perceived as deadly dull and irrelevant to contemporary concerns.

When I was a senior at the General Seminary in 1951, A.P.'s first brochure, *The Parish Eucharist*, was put in our mail boxes. It was a revelation. We had heard and read Dom Gregory Dix. We had all seen his demonstration eucharist at St. George's Church in Manhattan, but here was an American group trying to reform worship.

It was exciting. Eleven years later I became a member of the A.P. council after having used A.P. material and policies in two parishes. I arrived at a moment of change when the old guard was being assaulted by the "Young Turks" whom I joined. There were stormy meetings as we new members pushed for more social involvement —particularly in the movement toward racial integration. One of our most strident meetings was in Oshkosh in the midst of George Wallace's racist campaign for President. We had to pass the "Wallace for President" office every time we went to our hotel rooms so the issue was ever in our midst. As time and events went by, A.P. had many more crises and severe disagreements but managed to carry on the central task of liturgical reform.

Michael Moriarty has written a brilliant chronicle and interpretation of A.P.'s nearly 50 years, outlining our mistakes as well as our victories. This book will lay to rest much of the paranoia the radical conservatives have felt about A.P.'s "secret plot" to undermine the Episcopal Church, and at the same time will show that in a very real sense A.P. was the spark plug that set off the operation which led to the 1979 Book of Common Prayer.

Hundreds of clergy and laity have passed through A.P., some lasting only one meeting—a few never showing up after being voted as members of the council. There has been a constant flow of new blood into the organization which speaks well for its vitality and poorly of its mode of functioning, which can be quite off-putting to the less resilient. However, the council members were often very supportive and caring for its members in their time of personal and parochial crises.

Now I am a member of the "Old Guard" looking at the new "Young Turks" with alarm, feeling uncomfortable with the new jargon and suspecting that the baby is about to hit the drain. And so it goes.

HENRY H. BREUL
Chestertown, Maryland, June 1995

Introduction

A Revolution in Episcopal Worship

Episcopalians love the Prayer Book.

In a way that is true for no other church, Episcopalians define themselves by their liturgy. What other churches find in confessional statements or in magisterial authority, the Episcopal Church locates in its liturgy. The Prayer Book is not only a grammar for the church's conversation with God, but an arbiter of doctrine and polity, a definer of corporate identity, and a *vade mecum* for the individual soul's journey. Three times since the first American Book of Common Prayer was adopted in 1789 it has been revised—in 1892, 1928, and 1979. The versions through 1928 moved in the orbit of Thomas Cranmer's original sixteenth-century work. The book of 1979, however, abandoned a Tudor worldview and the liturgical and theological context of the Reformation, and embraced

1

the language, values, and insights of the twentieth-century liturgical movement. In the fifty years between the books of 1928 and 1979 a revolution had taken place.

One group in particular, the Associated Parishes for Liturgy and Mission, founded in 1946, was a catalyst for the creation of the 1979 Prayer Book. A.P. did not cause Prayer Book revision. It did not have to. Prayer Book revision was an ongoing process; preparation for the 1979 Prayer Book began the day after General Convention passed the 1928 Prayer Book. A.P.'s genius was to draw into its orbit and form the outlook of most of the people responsible for producing the 1979 Prayer Book. So much so, that the 1979 book may be seen as a tangible fruit of thirty years of work by A.P.[1]

When A.P. began its work, Episcopalians still had the habit of linking the word "liturgy" with "our incomparable." The Prayer Book represented the quintessence of reformed yet catholic religion. Its services presented essential primitive Christianity while avoiding the extremes of either Rome or Geneva. In moderation, reasonableness, beauty, and piety, the Prayer Book stood second to none. Its intrinsic worth had recommended it to other Christian bodies and helped mold the devotion of English-speaking Christians— Methodist, Presbyterian, Lutheran, Reformed Episcopal, even the Unitarian-Universalist liturgy of King's Chapel, Boston. The incomparable Prayer Book held a mediating, reconciling position among the Christian churches and was strategically placed to promote Christian unity and influence the future shape of Christian worship. It seemed that the perspectives of the sixteenth century had constellated a permanently valid liturgical universe.

The Prayer Book of 1979 exploded that Ptolemaic system. The 1979 book did not merely modernize the language of worship or rearrange the ritual furniture. With this book, the church declared that the middle ages finally were over. Rites for the eucharist, initiation, daily prayer, reconciliation, ordination, marriage, and burial, as well as the shape of the Christian calendar, which had stood largely unchanged for 400 years, now returned to earlier liturgical models for their inspiration. The liturgical movement transformed the worship of American churches in the twentieth century.[2] From the 1960s to the 1990s, various churches underwent their own versions of liturgical renewal and issued new service books that revolutionized how these churches saw who they are and who they want to be. The new liturgies of Episcopalians, Roman Catholics, Lutherans, Methodists, and Presbyterians describe a shift in the understanding of "church," a shift from church as coterminous with society to church as set apart from society in a pluralistic culture which no longer looks to the church as a unifying force in society or as a source of common wisdom.

This shift began in the 1830s with the first stirrings of the liturgical movement. Its causes were complex, but the liturgical revival of the nineteenth century owed something to Romanticism; to a concern with a return to origins; to reaction to Enlightenment rationalism, to Liberalism, and to state establishment of churches; and to the social tensions produced by a shift from agricultural to industrial society. At the heart of the revived interest in liturgy, however, was a rediscovered interest in the nature of the church. Protestants and Roman Catholics alike in Europe and the United States in the decade of the 1830s expressed their concern liturgically by seeking to restore the eucharist to the center of religious experience.

Coincidentally, the nineteenth-century phase of the movement in Anglicanism and in Roman Catholicism began independently of one another in the same year, 1832—among Anglicans with the publication of William Palmer's (1803–1885) *Origines Liturgicae*,[3] an inquiry into the sources of the Book of Common Prayer, which awakened the Church of England to liturgical and ecclesiological issues; and, among Roman Catholics, the purchase in that same year of the abandoned property of Solesmes, France, by Prosper Guéranger (1805–1875) and the revival of Benedictine monastic life there in 1833.[4]

Palmer's work helped inform the aspirations of John Keble (1792–1866), Edward Bouverie Pusey (1800–1882), and John Henry Newman (1801–1890), who launched the Oxford Movement (1833–1845), with its theological emphasis on the sacramental life of the church. The counterpart of the Oxford Movement in architecture and the arts centered on Cambridge University and the Cambridge Camden Society (later the Ecclesiological Society), founded in 1839, which championed a revived Gothic architecture as the only setting for a revived Catholic worship.[5] The Oxford Movement's theological ideas, embodied in architecture and the arts by the Cambridge Movement, carried into the liturgical field to stimulate "ritualism" beginning in the 1840s, when individual priests acting independently began to graft medieval and contemporary Roman Catholic ceremonial onto Prayer Book services.[6]

Guéranger was the first to use the term "liturgical movement" to describe the revival of interest in liturgical studies and the growing interest in understanding and improving liturgical practice. His liturgical theology, embodied in *Institutions liturgiques* (1840, 1841, and 1851) and in *L'Année liturgique* (1841), as well as the liturgical practice he fostered at Solesmes, focused the liturgical issue for Roman Catholics and had a profound influence in his own church and beyond.

Two theologians at the University of Tubingen in particular greatly influenced nineteenth-century leaders of the liturgical movement. Johann Adam Möhler (1796–1838), in his books *The Unity of the Church* (1825) and *Symbolism* (1832), pioneered a paradigm shift in ecclesiology based on an organic conception of the church as the Body of Christ (as opposed to a juridical conception of church as hierarchy with pope and clergy exercising viceregal authority from God over the people). Möhler also fostered an ecumenical openness to learning from the insights of Protestant theologians. Matthias Joseph Scheeben (1835–1888), building on Möhler's thought, helped redefine the responsibilities of membership in the church in light of new insights emerging in biblical and patristic scholarship (*Nature and Grace*, 1861; *Mysteries of Christianity*, 1865).

Among Lutherans in Bavaria, Wilhelm Loehe (1808–1872) led a sacramental revival in the decade of the 1830s, with the eucharist at the center of his ecclesiology. Nikolai F.S. Grundtvig (1783–1872) started a reforming movement in the Danish Lutheran church that emphasized the role of sacraments in Christian life and fostered a new understanding of church.

Among American churches in the Reformed tradition, the Mercersburg theology of John W. Nevin (1803–1886) and Philip Schaff (1819–1893) stressed the need for liturgical renewal and sought a return to John Calvin's objective and Christ-centered sacramental theology. The first enduring success in making the weekly communion of the congregation the norm for worship since the fourth century was achieved on the American frontier by the Disciples of Christ, formed in 1831.

The nineteenth-century liturgical movement was heavily colored by its European political and social context, where religious institutions were under assault. The movement understood the social dimension of its work as a matter of the re-Christianization of western culture—of the church showing the way to a recovery of common faith and a God-centered social life. The nineteenth-century movement idealized the middle ages as a time when church and society formed a cohesive whole, and proposed a romantic reimagining of a medieval past as a basis for the regeneration of industrial society.

That analysis of the cultural context and the prescription for remedying the situation began to shift as the liturgical movement entered the twentieth century and as it traveled to an American setting. Virgil Michel, O.S.B. (1890–1938), who introduced the liturgical movement into the United States in 1926, was one of those who sensed that the church was riding the crest of a profound cultural change. He wrote in 1938:

We are definitely at the end of an era of human history. One of its characteristics is—or is this a universal mark of such times?—that an alarmingly large number of both the secular and spiritual leaders of today still seem blissfully unaware of the fact of its vast significance. . . .

We are living in extraordinarily important times; . . . our days are in a special sense big with the human destinies of the future, and . . . we are witnessing the complete breakdown of the ideals of a civilization that had been building up for a whole period of history.[7]

Writing in the closing decades of the twentieth century, Henry H. Breul, onetime president of Associated Parishes, analyzed the cultural shift in sociological terms of the difference between short-term (300 years) and long-term (1,500–2,000 years) change.

What is happening to us now is extraordinary in that we are at the common ending of a long-term and a short-term change in society. It may well be that this "one-two punch" has never happened before in human history. To a sailor it would be like having a heavy ground swell with a severe chop on it and a flukey wind—one tends to ignore the ground swell.

We are at the end of the Western culture formed in the crucible of the late Roman Empire when Christian love was added to the Roman law. We are also at the end of the Industrial Revolution. Therefore nineteenth century answers to late twentieth century problems give us all a queasy feeling that something is terribly wrong.

The upheavals of peoples and the displacement of structures of society that occurred at the end of the Roman Empire and at the beginning of the Industrial Revolution have hit us head on and all at once. . . .

The Church must look to the 2,000-year cycle and realize that it is the only institution to have survived the last upheaval of the "ground swell" and is indeed in the process of recovering its "survival kit."[8]

American leaders of the twentieth-century liturgical movement were not minded to rebuild Christendom stone by stone. Instead of erecting a liturgical folly by making individuals and societies fit themselves to an idealized medieval liturgy, the liturgical movement in the twentieth century shifted to making the liturgy fit the realities of people no longer situated in Christendom.

The liturgical movement was just that—a movement, not an organization. It had no single point of origin, no unanimous program, no leaders empowered to set policy and exact obedience. As they confronted common issues, the churches of Europe and America began to reach simultaneously new points of view, different from their inherited historical positions. There evolved a meeting of minds—a common language, agreed perceptions of common problems, and consensus on the shape of solutions. Across the theological disciplines—in biblical studies, systematics, liturgy, ecclesiology—scholars moved away from the medieval synthesis.

By returning the liturgy to its sources in the bible and early tradition, the liturgical movement rediscovered not only a broader tradition but also a grammar for engaging contemporary issues. Active participation in and comprehension of the liturgy, it was thought, would renew the structures of the church as well as create a new consciousness in individuals, who in turn would affect the structures of society by living out the implications of liturgy.

Primary among the movement's theological insights was a rediscovery of the liturgical priesthood of the people, and a concern for their full, conscious, and active participation in the liturgy. A concern for society, ecumenism, a rediscovery of the church as Body of Christ, a renewed awareness of the Bible, new assessments by scholars of liturgical sources, and what we have come to call inculturation of the liturgy characterized the twentieth-century movement's response to cultural crisis.

The difference between the liturgical movement and other renewal movements of the twentieth century (biblical, social, ecumenical) was the level at which it saw the problem of renewal. The liturgical movement claimed to be working at depth. Sooner or later these other movements must "turn to the praise of God in the liturgy as their fulfillment. ... The liturgy is quite simply the climactic expression in this world of our incorporation into Christ."[9]

The eucharist, in particular, was the initial vehicle for the liturgical movement's teaching and hopes for renewal. The eucharist offered a pattern for Christian community and for human society. The self-giving celebrated in the Holy Communion not only was the model for the church's life, but also was to be extended in social, political, and economic communion. Baptism began to attract more attention from liturgists only in the late 1950s, and became the major focus of liturgical renewal in late 1960s. But leaders like Virgil Michel already had begun in the 1930s to speak of the recovery of a social, as opposed to an individualistic soul-saving, sense of baptism.

The recovery of the problematic document known as *Apostolic Tradition*[10] in the early twentieth century had the profoundest effect on the course of the movement. First identified in 1910 by Eduard Schwartz and independently by R.H. Connolly in 1916, the document, which is generally supposed to have been written circa 215 C.E. by the Roman presbyter Hippolytus, appeared to give scholars the earliest surviving text of a eucharistic prayer as well as unprecedented insight into pre-Constantinian liturgies for baptism, ordination, and daily prayer.

It seemed to echo contemporary concerns, such as the corporate nature of the church and the active participation of the laity in liturgy. But most fundamentally, the document resonated with the modern church's experience of standing outside the structures and values of the surrounding culture in the position of a minority. Whatever the influence of *Apostolic Tradition* in the third century, its hold on the twentieth-century liturgical imagination has been enormous. Every major reform of liturgical books in America in the past thirty years—Roman Catholic, Episcopal, Methodist, Lutheran, Presbyterian—has been shaped by it; Hippolytus is on every page of the 1979 Prayer Book's rites of initiation, eucharist, and ordination.[11]

When A.P. formed immediately after the Second World War, the liturgical movement already had been percolating into the Episcopal Church's consciousness for a decade. Seminaries had begun to teach it, books began to appear about it. But there was no one to show the ordinary parish how to do it.

For twenty years, until the late 1960s, A.P. showed parishes how to take the living liturgy of their time, the 1928 Prayer Book and *The Hymnal 1940,* and make it speak in the accents of the liturgical movement. In 1947, Dom Gregory Dix, O.S.B., called A.P. the first group he knew of to take the liturgical movement seriously by putting it into practice in parishes.[12]

Through publications that reached into parishes in virtually every state and Canada and through sponsorship of three major national liturgical conferences in 1958, 1959, and 1962, A.P. galvanized the liturgical consciousness of the church and gained recognition as a spokesman for the liturgical movement. A.P.'s experience in interpreting the 1928 Prayer Book also exposed willy-nilly the deficiencies of that book and helped create a body of opinion in favor of Prayer Book reform. When General Convention called for Prayer Book revision in 1964, A.P. members served on the Standing Liturgical Commission and on the drafting committees that drew up the new rites. A.P. was recognized officially as an agent of trial use when that began in 1967; its publications promoting trial use were commended by the chairman of the SLC and the Custodian of the Standard Book of Common Prayer.

At the General Conventions of 1969, 1970, 1973, 1976, and 1979, A.P. was there to focus liturgical issues, define, educate, and lobby. From 1965 to 1969, A.P. held regional liturgical conferences around the country which drew hundreds to the insights of liturgical renewal. A.P.'s sponsorship of the first annual meetings of chairmen of Diocesan Liturgical Commissions, beginning in 1970, and A.P.'s cooperation with the National Center for the Diaconate, beginning in 1977, aided in the creation of new forums for reflection, education, and support for Prayer Book revision. In the late 1960s, A.P. opened its membership to all comers, giving direction and focus to popular interest in and enthusiasm for liturgical renewal.

A.P. was unique in the American church. It began as a group of twelve clergymen who drew up a specific plan for introducing the liturgical movement into their own parishes. It was an unofficial, voluntary group, free from official constraints. It grew into a kind of town meeting of the liturgical movement, a place where parish clergy, laity, seminary educators, bishops, and church administrators could think and talk together and find mutual support. It became a source of influence in its own right, and it flourished in the specific political structures of the church which provided toeholds for the exercise of influence.

The Episcopal Church's experience of the liturgical movement was channeled in courses dug by the Reformation, American political experience, and a history of periodic Prayer Book revision. The fact that the liturgical movement made its bid in this context of a church whose government was constitutional and representative at every level—parish, diocesan, and national—is fundamental. A participatory structure was in place which allowed change to happen at the same time that it directed that change.

The church's highest authority was not a bishop or group of clergy but a bicameral legislative assembly of a house of elected laity and priests and a house of bishops. No one bloc had final control of church affairs. It was a government of shared power and popular participation created by men who had read John Locke and the American Constitution as well as the New Testament and the Church Fathers. Within the framework of the spiritual authority vested by constitution and canons in bishops and clergy, the church offered a political context that took for granted open, public advocacy of causes. And because the government provided for the participation of the governed, advocacy could not only change minds but change practice.

This is not to overestimate the potential of representative government, which is as amenable to obstructing change as fostering it, or to ignore factors such as the race, class, and gender of those operating the system. The point is, a participatory political machinery was at hand and it colored people's presuppositions, perceptions, and expectations of what was possible.

The political configuration of the local parish offered a specific location of influence for the liturgical movement. Since the 1630s, the church in America had developed a powerful sphere of local parish autonomy, as well as lay political power, in the institution of the parish vestry, where laity governed the parish jointly with the rector. The parish, relatively independent of episcopal control, was precisely where local leaders of the liturgical movement could operate with some degree of authority and some hope of real change.

The 1928 Prayer Book itself offered a toehold for the liturgical movement. Change in the texts of the church's liturgy could come about only by action of General Convention. But short of that, the Prayer Book's rubrics at least were patient of a variety of ceremonies, vestments, church furnishings, music, and of theological interpretation. The liturgical movement capitalized on this open-endedness. It was possible to be loyal to the Prayer Book, the movement suggested, and yet understand and celebrate the liturgy in a way that caught the accent of modern concerns.

Revision of the Prayer Book was not unthinkable, either. The book was not a legal document voted by a parliament with sanctions and penalties attached; nor was it a missal imposed by an absolute ecclesiastical authority. The American church already had revised its liturgy three times, and latent in the Preface to the American book, as well as in articles XX and XXXIV of the Articles of Religion, was the combustible stuff which said the church had authority to alter its liturgy "according to the various exigency of times and occasions" as seemed necessary or expedient.[13] And since 1928, the church had in the Standing Liturgical Commission an agency specifically charged with receiving and developing recommendations for revisions to the Prayer Book.

Many who opposed Prayer Book revision rightly perceived that it challenged the status quo. The Prayer Book, after all, is more than a text. The liturgical movement struck at the very root of personal and corporate identity when it talked about reform of the liturgy. But the particular circumstances in this church meant that proponents of liturgical renewal could be perceived as acting within the ethos and politics of their church and could present their work as part of an ongoing Anglican phenomenon. The theological and ecclesiological ideals of the liturgical movement funneled into something familiar to Episcopalians—Prayer Book revision.

Chapter One

The Last Cranmerian Liturgy

Episcopal worship patterns were changing in the century and a half leading up to the 1979 Prayer Book as the church responded to cultural shift. From 1799 to 1877, several changes and additions affected the Prayer Book, even though the book itself was not revised between 1789 and 1892.[1] Services for the Consecration of a Church (1799), for the Institution of Ministers (1804), and various forms of prayers for particular occasions were added. General Convention authorized translations of the Prayer Book into French (1832), German (1835), and Welsh (1850), and proposed a translation into Greek as well (1868), to meet the needs of a burgeoning immigrant population.

The cry of both evangelicals and ritualists for "flexibility" in adapting Prayer Book services, particularly by shortening services, was a *leitmotif* of the century's liturgical debates; its persistence was a sign that all was not well. The concern for "uniformity" was the other side of the continued call for flexibility in convention after convention; its persistence reflected alarm that in parishes across the land priests were making their own adaptations of the Prayer Book in response to perceived pastoral needs. Convention's designation in 1832 of a standard edition of the Prayer Book as a touchstone for legitimate liturgical practice is a measure of the anxiety felt about the adequacy of the church's liturgy.

Muhlenberg, Huntington, and the 1892 Prayer Book

By the middle of the century it was plain that the church's liturgical arrangements were not meeting the needs of the times. A pioneer of liturgical renewal, William Augustus Muhlenberg (1796–1877), experimented with the liturgy to adapt the services at the Church of the Holy Communion in New York to the urban masses he was trying to reach. In his social and pastoral concerns, he anticipated the spirit of the later liturgical movement. Both Muhlenberg and nineteenth-century Anglo-Catholics got their ideas about ritual from contact with Roman Catholic services (as well as Lutheran tradition in Muhlenberg's case). But while Anglo-Catholics used ritual to express an emphasis on the authority of the church, the priesthood, and the sacramental system, Muhlenberg pragmatically adapted ritual to practically invent modern urban ministry.

Muhlenberg introduced the custom of singing parts of the service, chanting the psalter, letting music and decorations reflect the seasons of the church year, an altar with cross and flowers, the altar in a central position with the pulpit at the side instead of in the center—and most significantly, a weekly celebration of the Holy

Communion. Muhlenberg achieved weekly communion by innovating boldly and breaking up the long, drawn out Sunday service of Morning Prayer, Litany, Ante-Communion, and sermon. Neither Prayer Book nor canons required all three services together on Sunday mornings, but the arrangement had the authority of long-standing custom. Separation of the services made it possible to have more frequent celebrations of the eucharist and enabled working people to attend and be active communicants.[2]

In the Muhlenberg Memorial of 1853, Muhlenberg and the co-signers asked General Convention to consider whether the church's "fixed and invariable modes of public worship" were competent to answering the needs of people "in this land and in this age." Though the memorial had goals that encompassed ministry, mission, and ecumenism, as well as liturgy, its immediate result was permission from the House of Bishops in the Convention of 1856 to use Morning Prayer, the Litany, and the Holy Communion (or Ante-Communion) with sermon as separate services on Sundays and feasts.[3]

As a result of the Muhlenberg Memorial a pattern had evolved in the majority of Episcopal parishes by the end of the nineteenth century that carried well into the next century: communion as the main service on the first Sunday of the month, and Morning Prayer as the main service on the other Sundays with an "early celebration" of the communion for those who desired it. In Anglo-Catholic parishes, on the other hand, the main service each Sunday was the eucharist. Monthly communion represented an enormous increase over the quarterly communion common in the eighteenth century.

But this shift in worship patterns also had unforeseen consequences that set the agenda for part of the liturgical movement's task in the next century. The most significant consequence was the fragmentation of the parish community. Instead of worshiping together week by week, people followed their personal preference in choosing among several services of various kinds.[4] Depending on which service one chose, one might go from year's end to year's end and not hear the psalms or Old Testament read, or a sermon, or prayer for the world, or have one's attention drawn to the doctrines of creation, incarnation, or atonement.[5]

When the nineteenth-century church did revise the Prayer Book in an attempt to respond liturgically to the thought and sensibilities of its age, the result was a liturgy *manqué*, the Prayer Book of 1892,[6] which the church outgrew within a single generation. The 1892 revision, which was largely the work of William Reed Huntington (1838–1909), did, however, begin to frame the terms of the question for modern liturgical revision: the relation of worship to the circumstances of contemporary life—in this case, massive immigration, missions to blacks and to native Americans, evangelization of the frontier, urbanization and the growth of city slums, and ecumenical relations.

The church's liturgy gained in flexibility by further provisions for the shortening of Morning and Evening Prayer, the Litany, and the Holy Communion on occasion, and by the adoption of a rubric that made explicit the bishops' permission of 1856 for separate use of services on Sundays and feasts.

In significant ways, the 1892 Prayer Book showed the church beginning to respond liturgically to modern sensibilities. It recognized pastoral needs by a revised lectionary which provided certain options; more proper psalms and selections of psalms; provision for an additional, early celebration of the eucharist on Christmas and Easter; provision of a Penitential Office for Ash Wednesday (an adaptation of the English Commination service without its curses or its opening address); and new prayers For Unity and For Missions that reflected a new awareness of the Episcopal Church in relation to other churches and society.

The newly confirmed now were by rubric urged to come to the Lord's Supper; the commendatory prayer in the Visitation of the Sick was made less ominous and more humane; a new collect in the office for the Visitation of Prisoners shifted the emphasis from deserved punishment to divine forgiveness; the Communion of the Sick could be shortened in cases of disease or extreme weakness, and the service also could be used for the aged or bedridden with the substitution of the eucharistic propers of the day.

But the 1892 book's real achievement was that it raised the question of liturgical revision for Episcopalians, helped to destroy the fetish of uniformity, and afforded the church an education in liturgical principles during the twelve years the work was in progress—insights that were not lost on the revisers of the 1928 Prayer Book who further adapted the church's worship to new knowledge and new needs.[7]

The Oxford Movement and ritualism were part of the background of the formation of the 1892 and 1928 Prayer Books. Though neither movement issued directly in Prayer Book revision, in a general way ritualism answered a growing desire for beauty in and enrichment of worship. It led to an appreciation of the comprehensiveness of the Anglican tradition and a wider experience of Christian worship. It also drew attention to the shortcomings of an overly intellectual, didactic kind of worship, and fostered a new interest in the study of liturgy. But factors other than ritualism had more effect on the formation of the 1892 and 1928 Prayer Books— things like the stirrings of ecumenical interests, the awakening of the church to the social gospel and a wider missionary outreach, and the contact of Anglican missions with cultures that were not even western, much less Anglo-Saxon.[8]

The 1928 Prayer Book

No one regarded the 1892 Prayer Book as final, and some of the unfinished agenda of 1892 was taken up in the 1928 book,[9] the most thorough revision of the American church's liturgy since the first Prayer Book of 1789. Edward Lambe Parsons (1868–1960), more than any other person, was in the forefront of those responsible for the 1928 book.[10] Parsons' knowledge of and interest in liturgics stemmed directly from his early association with Huntington.[11]

Parsons officially initiated the revision process in the 1913 General Convention when he presented the memorials from the dioceses of California and Arizona asking convention to appoint a joint commission to revise and enrich the Prayer Book. Parsons guided discussions and debate on the floor of successive General Conventions, from 1913 in the House of Deputies, and then in the House of Bishops after his election as bishop of California in 1924. He was a member of the Standing Liturgical Commission from its formation in 1928 and was its chairman from 1930 to 1946. After his retirement from his see in 1941, Parsons was professor of theology and liturgy at Church Divinity School of the Pacific until 1948. Parsons' colleagues in General Convention remembered him for his "broadmindedness" in carrying the 1928 revision through and his carefulness and fairness in "protecting and preserving the comprehensive tradition of our Church in doctrine and worship."[12]

Whole spheres of modern life found expression for the first time in the 1928 Prayer Book. New prayers for social justice, for the family of nations, and the collect for Independence Day were all written by Parsons. The book expressed a connection between liturgy and social justice in new prayers for "every man in his work," for prisoners, for "faithfulness in the use of this world's goods," for "all poor, homeless and neglected folk," for "those in mental darkness," and for "the families of the land." The marriage service dropped the word "obey" from the wife's vows, making the man's and woman's promises equal, and included prayers for children and for the home. The derogatory reference to the Jews in the third collect for Good Friday was expunged, and the prayer expressed a new vision of Christian unity as encompassed, not in one *fold*, but as members of one *flock*. In the Visitation of the Sick, the suggestion of imminent death was dropped, and psalms and prayers spoke of hope and recovery. Most significantly, the church began to think about what "healing" might mean given the facts of modern psychology and medical technology: new prayers for the despondent and for healing, and a form for anointing the sick brought the liturgy into touch with modern experience and questions.

The 1928 book also quietly abandoned a pre-critical attitude toward the bible and accepted the critical view of holy scripture which was one of the great intellectual accomplishments of the nineteenth century.[13] The older view regarded scripture as all of a piece, all equally inspired and equally valuable. But the 1928 book appointed special psalms for Sundays and deleted psalms or verses that called down the curses of heaven on enemies. The apocrypha was appointed to be read more frequently. Passages of scripture for the eucharistic propers were taken from the Revised Version of 1881–1895, which represented current biblical scholarship, and in many cases the marginal renderings correcting the biblical text were accepted in the Prayer Book.

A continuing desire for shorter services and for flexibility was provided for by rubrics and by the inclusion of more alternative texts in Morning and Evening Prayer and in the Holy Communion. The 1928 book introduced the possibility of an unheard-of degree of flexibility by allowing the use of newly drawn up services, under the bishop's direction, in place of Morning and Evening Prayer— or in addition to Morning and Evening Prayer, the Litany, and the Holy Communion—"when the edification of the Congregation so requires."[14]

Though the 1928 Prayer Book introduced elements of catholic practice, this was due more to contemporary need and pragmatism than to any preoccupation with Rome or the diffusion of Anglo-Catholic principles. The revisers of 1928 shaped the rite of Holy Communion, for example, into closer accord with ancient and more universal patterns, but broadly speaking their approach built on the inheritance of the Non-jurors as brought up to date by contemporary English and Scottish scholarship.[15] Anglo-Catholic desiderata like the *Agnus Dei* and *Benedictus qui venit* and adoption of a rubric to permit reservation of the sacrament for the sick—practices which Anglo-Catholics interpreted as implying a particular doctrine of real presence in the sacramental species—were rejected.

The 1928 book also introduced propers for celebrations of the eucharist at marriages and burials, as well as prayers for the dead, which at first strike the eye as imitation of catholic practice. But as E. Clowes Chorley wrote in a commentary on the new Prayer Book in 1929, "The old objection to these particular services that they were Roman in character has been worn down in later years. The Church is glad to take devotions of proved value from whatever source they come."[16] Americans who had lost husbands, fathers, lovers, and friends in World War I were ready to abandon any lingering Reformation inhibitions about offering specific petitions for the souls of the dead, which are scattered through the 1928 book. The war also pointed up the need for a more pastoral orientation in prayers for the sick, wounded, and dying, and for the doctors and nurses who cared for them.

The 1928 Prayer Book reflected new emphases that had appeared in the life and thought of modern people and subtly repudiated the Reformation context as the standard for liturgical practice. Yet because many of the new attitudes were subtle or tucked away in seldom-used collects or services, they could be invisible to most church people. And since, after all, the shift was clothed in Cranmerian language it still was possible to perceive "our liturgy" as being as "incomparable" as ever. Most people did not notice that the 1928 Prayer Book had begun to use modern English—for example, in the parts of the Offices of Instruction where the people are addressed by "you" and "your" and with modern verb forms and syntax; and in the prayer For a Birthday, "when *he* stands," not standeth.[17] The church was demonstrating some important principles in adopting the 1928 book. It demonstrated an openness to the modern world and its intellectual currents; a certain pragmatism in being willing to adopt both ancient and modern elements for the sake of meeting present needs; and most fundamentally, that change was normal.

By the last third of the century, however, the limitations of the book's assumptions seemed more evident. The Prayer Book of 1928 was part of a phase of ritual revisions that many Protestant liturgically oriented churches underwent in the 1920s—including Anglican revisions in England (a book never adopted officially), Scotland, Canada, and South Africa. These books

> were solid enrichments based on the liturgical studies and interests of the nineteenth century; but they were only tangentially touched by the new stirrings in the European liturgical movement. ... [T]hey were unable to envisage and free themselves from the idea of a Christendom well-established in Western civilization whose benefits were available to the rest of the world. Only the "shaking of the foundations" following World War II would bring to naught this fantasy.[18]

William Palmer Ladd: Catalyst for the Liturgical Movement

William Palmer Ladd (1870–1941) was the conduit to Episcopalians for the new stirrings in the liturgical movement.[19] Ladd was the first in the Episcopal Church to see that the liturgical movement presented his church with means to respond to a cultural crisis and to plead with it to seize the moment to enter intelligently and wholeheartedly into the movement. By reforming its worship, Ladd argued, the church could prepare itself to speak credibly to a culture that no longer looked to the church as a unifying force in society or as a source of wisdom or tradition.[20]

Ladd taught for thirty-seven years at Berkeley Divinity School in New Haven, Connecticut, as Professor of Church History from 1904 to 1918 and as dean from 1918 to 1941. He was in touch with European leaders in liturgical renewal like the Roman Catholic Benedictine abbey at Maria Laach, Germany. He brought to Episcopalians' attention the importance of the work of scholars like Ildefons Herwegen (1874–1946) and Odo Casel (1886–1948) at Maria Laach; the abbey's "indispensable" publications *Ecclesia Orans* and *Jahrbuch für Liturgiewissenschaft* were among the texts he recommended to his students. In this country, Ladd recommended the liturgical publications of the Benedictines of St. John's Abbey, Collegeville, Minnesota, and especially their journal *Orate Fratres*, founded in 1926 and renamed *Worship* in 1951.[21]

Ladd also helped introduce to Americans several overseas Anglicans who were concerned about the social implications of liturgy. He brought A.G. Hebert (1886–1963) and Percy Dearmer (1867–1936) to lecture at Berkeley. Hebert's 1935 *Liturgy and Society*[22] was one of the first books to alert Anglicans to the new winds blowing in the European liturgical movement and to the relation of liturgy to the problems of modern society. Dearmer was perhaps best known for *The Parson's Handbook*, but he also was one of the first members of the Christian Social Union, founded in 1889 as part of the Church of England's attempt to meet the challenges of the industrialization and urbanization of modern society.[23]

Ladd was part of a generation of scholars who, through the church's seminaries, had begun to shape a climate of liturgical opinion. Scholars like Burton Scott Easton in New Testament and patristics, Parsons in Prayer Book studies, Bayard Hale Jones in historical liturgiology, and Charles Winfred Douglas in church music spread news of the coalescence of new insights and perspectives in liturgical studies. But Ladd was the catalyst for the liturgical movement in the Episcopal Church. He was the first to grasp its significance for a church no longer located in Christendom and to point out the movement's relation to social justice, ecumenism, and Christian art.

Ladd's written legacy and prophecy was some eighty essays on the liturgy, where he argued for a revolution in the church's liturgical consciousness. The essays—witty, candid, impatient with obscurantism and pretense, and passionate for the genuine and relevant—began appearing in church magazines in 1938. During his final illness, Ladd began collecting his essays into *Prayer Book Interleaves* because, he said, he wanted those "who have the liturgical destiny of the Church in their hands" to "seriously consider the facts and ideas" he so urgently argued.[24] *Prayer Book Interleaves*, published in 1942, is a milestone in the liturgical history of the Episcopal Church. The book was reissued in 1957; the church was only then beginning to realize the full import of Ladd's work.

"Nothing is more important than that the liturgical movement should take the right direction in this country at the present time," Ladd wrote. In plain English, that meant "adapting our inherited forms of worship to the modern situation" so that the church could be prepared "to meet the needs of a generation it has done so much to mislead and to alienate."[25]

Given the "eruption of paganism and barbarism in the World War and since," said Ladd, the urgent question facing the church was whether "the modern world will ever again listen to the gospel of Jesus Christ."[26] In the face of what he called "our new polytheism" of commercialism and humanism in America, and fascism, communism, nationalism, and totalitarianism in Europe, Ladd pleaded for a recovery of the bonds of community centered in God the Father and in Christ and sacramentalized in the eucharist.[27]

Liturgy must speak to the situations of men and women today.

But it must not just talk to people, said Ladd. As a response to the command to "do this," it must allow them to *do*, to experience their lives as part of something larger, something possessing a universal and urgent human appeal, the millennial drama of redemption. If it did not, people would look to other compelling liturgies, of sports or politics, and the church would become increasingly irrelevant to the longings and questions of modern society.[28]

Ladd rejected both Anglo-Catholic and Roman Catholic liturgical practice as foundations to build on. He accused both of a certain measure of unreality in failing to cultivate a living liturgical tradition that arose out of and responded to the lived circumstances of contemporary life.[29] To Ladd's mind, the liturgical movement offered an opportunity for "evangelically-minded churchmen"[30] to carry a step forward the liturgical ideals of the Reformation—ideals like the place of the laity in worship, frequent communion, criticism of individualism in worship, an appeal to the liturgical usage of the ancient church, and worship in a language "understanded of the people."[31]

Ladd took as his starting point the 1928 Book of Common Prayer, the living liturgy of his time. He understood the book's shortcomings and the need for the church to move beyond it to a liturgy that was "primitive and ... modern,"[32] but his genius was that he offered a way to find in the realities at hand of parish and Prayer Book a renewal for the here and now. In the final analysis, though, he realized there was no single ideal of liturgy. What makes liturgy good is how well it adapts to conditions of place, time, and circumstance, Ladd wrote.[33] Only as the church conserves and constantly reinterprets its past does it become competent to deal in the present with live issues and new problems, he said.[34] Antiquity is a good thing, Ladd would say, "but not too much of it at any one time." Excessive devotion to it makes a church "ineffective, and even a bit ridiculous."[35] A shrewd Yankee appreciation of "the good sense to disregard precedent" sometimes in order to meet the needs at hand tempered Ladd's regard for tradition.[36]

The only reason for studying past history is that we may learn how to live now. ... It should not chain us to the past, or supply arguments for outworn ideas, or spread content with the *status quo*.[37]

Ladd regarded reform of the eucharist as "the heart of the whole liturgical problem."[38] Facing an indifferent or hostile world, the eucharist was where the church ought to concentrate its energies because that is where it can most plainly communicate the gospel and show its own mind—as the primitive church did until paganism surrendered.[39] Ladd produced a sample rite of "The Holy Eucharist Simplified" for study and discussion which demonstrated many of his liturgical ideals. He even proposed that the beginning of his simplified service might be led by "laymen," the priest going to the altar only at the offertory.[40] Though he did not discuss explicitly a theology of the priesthood of the laity, Ladd was adamant that liturgy was "of, by, and for the people. The wretched medieval idea, sanctioned, alas, to some extent in our Prayer Book, that services are the monopoly of the priest, must be dropped."[41]

Tradition as well as present need indicated to Ladd that the eucharist ought to be the chief service every Sunday. Since Episcopalians had inherited a custom of monthly late communion on the first Sunday of the month, Ladd urged clergy to take it as a starting point for building up a parish eucharist that "appeals and attracts" and would be the highlight of parish life every month. The newly confirmed should make their first communion at this service, "and it is the proper time for adult baptisms." Taking a cue from "our Protestant brethren," the monthly communion could become a special "dedication service" to Christian work and witness in the world and the first Sunday of each month a "rally Sunday." Social concerns that the liturgy made no provision for—such as the parish's high school graduates, missionaries from the parish, labor disputes, the city council, the sick and well of the parish—could be brought into relation with the liturgy through special prayers and thanksgivings.[42] A renewed eucharistic worship must inevitably have social consequences, Ladd believed.[43] Despite the name, Ladd's parish communion had a different spirit than its contemporary English counterpart. The English project was a weekly event each Sunday, a compromise born of the tension between Anglo-Catholic and Evangelical worship patterns.[44] Ladd's starting point was different. Ladd began with the existing American Episcopal realities and borrowed from Protestant examples as well as the contemporary liturgical movement.

Ladd saw at issue in baptism nothing less than modern Christianity's re-encounter with an alien culture. He was scandalized by practices that denied baptism's social implications, like baptizing privately or as a Sunday School event, and trivialization of the sacrament by "negligible" baptismal fonts. He wanted the sacrament celebrated so that the whole congregation could witness the admission of new members to their fellowship, and he wanted the ceremony dignified with processions, lights, music, and burning of a paschal candle during Eastertide.[45] "We may smile" at the idea of demons and exorcism which early Christians associated with baptism, said Ladd, but at least the church of that period did actually overcome paganism; "how far are we getting with our easy-going ideas about baptism and church membership?"[46]

Ladd's ideas about the eucharist and baptism, as well as on calendar and lectionary reform, anticipated what would emerge in the next generation as major accomplishments of the liturgical movement. The calendar of saints' days should be revised to include examples of holiness relevant to modern people, Ladd said, the redundant season of pre-Lent eliminated, and the joyful nature of the "great fifty days of Eastertide" emphasized by having the people stand for the preface of the eucharistic prayer.[47] And there should be a revised eucharistic lectionary, drawn up "with the help of modern Biblical scholarship," to allow for an Old Testament lesson and a better selection of other scripture.[48] Ladd not only made the liturgical movement speak to modern needs, he made it think like a modern. He built on the standards of the primitive church, the Reformation, and the American Prayer Book, but his pragmatic eye was on ways to adapt the liturgy to meet revolutionary social changes and to connect liturgy with a vital social gospel. By critically evaluating the current situation, imagining alternatives, and encouraging study and discussion, Ladd helped lay a foundation for the next phase of liturgical reform.

Like his nineteenth-century counterparts in Prayer Book liturgics, Muhlenberg and Huntington, Ladd tried to make the Prayer Book respond to modern life. But Ladd was far more successful than they; in a sense, Ladd is on every page of the Prayer Book today. A line of influence descends from Ladd to one of his foremost liturgical disciples, Massey H. Shepherd, Jr. (1913–1990), an architect of the 1979 Prayer Book who helped to found Associated Parishes in 1946.

Shepherd and Ladd were "very close" and there is "no question of the impact of the personality and thought of Ladd upon the guiding spirit of liturgical reform in the Episcopal Church."[49] According to one friend who had known Shepherd for nearly fifty years, Ladd "greatly influenced" Shepherd's "thinking and his liturgical style."[50]

Shepherd said his friendship with Ladd "began in the winter of 1938 and grew in intimacy until his [Ladd's] death."[51] The twenty-five-year-old Shepherd, fresh from earning his Ph.D. at the University of Chicago in 1937, already had read the Roman Catholic liturgical scholars Romano Guardini (1885–1968) and Odo Casel, and had become a convert to the ideals of the liturgical movement. Shepherd had written to Ladd about making a visit to New Haven and received from him "a letter of urgent welcome (he always wanted to know young people)."[52] Shepherd went into residence at New Haven periodically from 1938 to 1941 and spent six months studying and lecturing there near the end of Ladd's life in 1941.

What Shepherd found "remarkable" about Ladd was his "very progressive ... outlook" coupled with a strong and accurate scholar's sense of history.[53] Shepherd was particularly impressed by two chapels in New Haven, "chapels unlike any others I have ever seen,"[54] that epitomized the relevancy, simplicity, and straightforwardness of Ladd's teaching and resonated with Shepherd's own developing view of liturgy. One chapel was "the inimitable 'upper room' of the seminary, where one discovered a worship formal without formality and artful without artificiality. In it we sang plainsong and prayed for social justice ... ," Shepherd recalled.[55] The other chapel was the reconstruction in the Yale Art Museum of the earliest known Christian church, with its frescoes, from third-century Dura Europos in Syria. "Dean Ladd literally made all his visitors go to see it," Shepherd said. "The two chapels, so distant in age and clime, united to describe the Church as the home of the family of God."[56]

Theodore O. Wedel (1892–1970) was another of the young men who "heard that there was resident in New Haven an expert in liturgical learning" and "made bold to ask for an interview."[57] A series of dialogue sessions followed and Wedel began to read liturgy under Ladd's guidance, which led him to "a major, even revolutionary, event in my imaginative understanding of the Eucharist."[58] As a result of his commitment to the liturgical movement, Wedel in 1946 invited Associated Parishes to hold its founding meeting at the College of Preachers in Washington, D.C., where he was warden. Wedel was A.P.'s friend, encourager, and frequent host for the rest of his life.

Liturgical Awakening in Seminaries Before World War II

Ladd was the harbinger of the liturgical movement, but he was not alone in the liturgical awakening of the Episcopal Church. In 1943, a book by an American Episcopalian was hailed as "the most important contribution made to liturgy thus far in America."[59] The book was Canon Charles Winfred Douglas's (1867–1944) *Church Music in History and Practice*,[60] published in 1937, that aimed to teach clergy, seminarians, and organists the principles of liturgical worship, especially the centrality of the priestly participation of the people in worship.

At the heart of Douglas's musicianship was the conviction that "each member of the Mystical Body of Christ" must "actively participate ... with heart and mind and voice"[61] in the liturgy. Douglas argued that historical evidence shows that "the Congregation was never considered as other than an essential factor at the Eucharist. ... The very framework of the Eucharist is the ordered series of invitations from the Celebrant and responses from the Congregation, which indicate that both together do the work of worship in the Lord."[62]

The issue was more than simply getting everyone to stand and sing; at stake was the creation of liturgy itself by the whole worshiping community. By teaching the integrity of the musical experience at worship, Douglas contributed to a fundamental shift in perceptions of liturgy. Douglas served on the Joint Commission on the Revision of the Hymnal which produced *The Hymnal 1940*. The 1940 hymnal reflected the liturgical movement's emphasis on the priestly participation of the people. It provided musical settings for the Holy Communion and for the daily offices which were designed for congregational singing, as opposed to choir performance, and it enriched and elevated the experience of liturgy by a selection of hymns ranging from the medieval to the modern. Through his scholarship and his work on the hymnal, Douglas "almost single-handedly reshaped the practice and taste of the Church in liturgical music."[63]

The same year that Douglas's book appeared, another book which was a force in the liturgical awakening and which became a common seminary text was published. *The American Prayer Book*[64] by Edward Lambe Parsons and Bayard Hale Jones (1887–1957) interpreted the very latest liturgical scholarship and helped shape the liturgical perceptions of a generation of future leaders of worship. Jones taught liturgy at Church Divinity School of the Pacific in Berkeley, California. Like Parsons, Jones served on the Standing Liturgical Commission, from 1934 to 1957. And, as with Parsons, his colleagues on the SLC praised his commitment in liturgical matters to the principle of comprehensiveness in the church.[65]

Parsons and Jones spread through the church's seminaries an awareness of the general revision in received opinions that had occurred as a result of the liturgical studies of the previous twenty years.[66] Their book began to raise the question of the desirability of further specific changes in the liturgy—for example, in the wording of the Prayer of Consecration[67]—and declared frankly that the recent 1928 revision of the Prayer Book demonstrated that the church had "at last" recognized that "liturgical change is inevitable" and that "[f]urther revision is inevitable."[68]

Preparing for Prayer Book Revision: Prayer Book Studies 1950–1963

The 1928 General Convention had created the Standing Liturgical Commission, composed of laity and clergy, as an outgrowth of the 1928 Prayer Book revision committee. The SLC's mandate was to preserve and study all matters relating to the Prayer Book "with the idea of developing and conserving for some possible future use the Liturgical experience and scholarship of the Church."[69] It was a remarkable step; the church was saying, in effect, that 1928 was not the last word. No other General Convention ever had taken so open-ended a view of the Prayer Book by building into the church a structure for ongoing liturgical reform. Succeeding triennial General Conventions continued to authorize the existence of the SLC; in 1940, convention took the significant step, at the SLC's request, of granting it canonical status, making the SLC a permanent agency in the church for liturgical self-reflection and revision.

The SLC at first was cautious about the need for Prayer Book revision. It reported to the 1940 General Convention that when the time came for a future revision, "the continued familiarity ... [of the SLC] with the problems and suggestions will be invaluable." At the same time, the members of the commission said they did "not believe, and they are sure that their judgment is that of the General Convention, that the time has come for the opening of the Prayer Book to further revision." But the "increasing lawlessness in the conduct of worship" was one of the reasons it cited for continuing the process of liturgical investigation at the most official level.[70]

Demand for a shorter, simpler rite of the Holy Communion prompted the SLC to propose a rubric permitting shortening of the service on special occasions when authorized by the bishop, but the 1940 General Convention did not approve it.[71] In subtle ways, though, the church began to recognize that the old forms were no longer sufficient to meet modern social needs and that some change was inevitable.

The all-sufficiency of the Prayer Book was implicitly challenged in 1940 with the SLC's production of the first official *Book of Offices*, containing optional services for which the Prayer Book made no provision.[72] Subsequent editions reflected the changing social patterns which surrounded the church by providing liturgies for adoption of children and for the blessing of persons already married. Provision of special services for Holy Week and other occasions in the church year recognized another growing pastoral need. The SLC also produced a new lectionary for Morning and Evening Prayer. Trial use of the lectionary began in 1935, and General Convention approved it in 1943.

By 1943, the "lawlessness" the SLC had perceived just three years earlier looked more like "many and varied experiments being made by individuals" which "although unauthorized, furnish further indication of needs which the present Prayer Book does not meet." What struck the commission now about the suggestions it continued to receive for Prayer Book revision was "their number and ... their cogency."[73]

"We feel that the time is ripe for a more systematic and complete revision than has been possible heretofore," the commission reported to the 1943 General Convention.[74] Besides the mounting pastoral evidence of the need for liturgical reform, the SLC pointed to "the rich stores of liturgical knowledge contributed by recent research," as well as the experience of other churches of the Anglican communion which had revised their Prayer Books since 1928. The commission proposed that it present a draft book to the church by 1949, the 400th anniversary of the first Book of Common Prayer.[75]

General Convention, however, reflecting the general disinterest of the church at large in liturgical reform, refused the request. By 1946, the SLC had come to agree that full-scale revision was "inopportune." Too many other issues, like union discussions with the Presbyterian Church in the U.S.A. which engaged the church from 1937 to 1946, occupied the church's attention, and the SLC agreed that the remaining three years before 1949 was too short a time to do justice to such an extensive project.[76]

But the SLC remained convinced that an eventual revision of the Prayer Book was "inevitable." The issue was how to avoid the formidable processes of the 1892 and 1928 revision when the two Houses of General Convention sat as virtual committees of the whole "to work out the problems of revision in painful detail; only finally to cut short the process in sheer weariness, in an incomplete and unsatisfactory state."[77] Part of the difficulty lay in the church's constitutional provisions for Prayer Book revision. There was no allowance for experimentation and testing of proposed rites; once a proposal passed both Houses in two successive General Conventions (and both the 1892 and 1928 revisions labored through many more than two conventions), it became part of the Prayer Book. If it turned out to be a mistake, it could only be removed from the Prayer Book by starting the constitutional round of revision all over again.

Borrowing from the pioneering experience of the South African church from 1929 to 1954, which was being followed by the Canadian, Indian, and Japanese churches, the SLC proposed to the 1946 General Convention the publication of a series of *Prayer Book Studies* comprised of the proposed texts of revised services from the Prayer Book with explanatory introductions. The booklets at first would be only for study and free discussion, then for experimental use and revision, and only then for adoption.[78]

So low was General Convention's interest, though, that it gave no consideration to *Prayer Book Studies* until 1949, when it agreed to finance publication.[79] General Convention's attitude reflected the mood of the church at large. Church growth and church education programs seemed more important just then. The 1949 convention asked the SLC to survey the dioceses and report in 1952 on what interest there was in Prayer Book revision. Only thirteen dioceses responded; ten were against revision now, two were in favor (Michigan and Los Angeles), and one said neither yes nor no (New York).[80]

The sixteen volumes of *Prayer Book Studies* that appeared between 1950 and 1963[81] incorporated some of the insights of new liturgical scholarship and showed some sensitivity to modern need, but in their continued use of Tudor English and their limited sense of what was possible, they still moved within the orbit of Cranmer. Their very appearance reflected the cautious tenor of their contents. Uniform in size, about six by four inches, with dull blue covers, the studies even were set in the same unalarming format and typeface as the 1928 Prayer Book.

Sales of the studies were only moderate[82] but the proposed revision of the eucharistic rite published in 1953 as *Prayer Book Studies*

IV: The Eucharistic Liturgy caught the church's eye and it consistently outsold all the other studies in the series.[83] Sometime in the mid- or late 1950s, the SLC prepared a 316-page, single-spaced, typewritten document summarizing more than 150 responses it had received on *PBS IV*.[84] The document did not evaluate the responses, but aimed to give the SLC and other interested persons an overview of the reaction to *PBS IV*. The general tenor of response favored the "principal directions of the changes proposed," the SLC said, but "there was not a sufficient consensus, except for a few details of formulary and ceremony, to suggest that the proposed draft of Study IV would receive a widespread and enthusiastic acceptance."[85]

The eucharistic rite of *PBS IV* is thought to be chiefly the work of Bayard Hale Jones, who was the SLC's vice chairman at the time and signed the study's preface. Jones has been characterized as a man who "believed that the best of all worlds had been achieved in the English Reformation."[86] *PBS IV* reflected that lineage.

Bernard J. Wigan, a prominent liturgist of the Church of England, was invited to criticize *PBS IV*. He faulted the rite for not having the courage of its convictions, for staying within the framework of Cranmer's scholarship, both for the whole rite and particularly for the eucharistic prayer, when the drafters should have known better. He accused the SLC of

> sacrificing 'great principles ... in order to produce a rite which seems likely to be readily acceptable to the majority.' Instead, they should have forthrightly submitted a draft—let the criticisms fall where they may—that takes more seriously into account the two principles that 'must be the basis of any revision of the liturgy which is to measure up to its evangelical purpose: that our Lord's prayer at the Last Supper was a Jewish thanksgiving-blessing, and that the essential structure of the rite consists of taking, blessing, breaking, giving—in that order.'[87]

The eucharistic rite of *PBS IV* was the last of its genus, a relic of a stage in liturgical evolution. Already signs were appearing among Anglican scholars and in the liturgical experiments of other churches that pointed to a whole new species of liturgical revision. More and more, it was looking to concerned church people as if it were time to move beyond Cranmer.

Ecumenical Cross Currents

A movement can influence in several ways: by direct contact, whether official or private, or by osmosis, the mutual currents that are set up and have their way subtly. The liturgical movement had no central office with certain ideology, membership criteria, or strategy. Its story in each of the churches affected by it differed according to each one's particular complex of circumstances and problems.[88]

Dialogues at an official level came after the mid-1960s. From the late 1930s until the mid-1960s, contact between Episcopal liturgists and the liturgical stirrings in other churches was through a web of private individuals of goodwill sharing mutual interests, through personal contacts, and through scholarly publications, what Massey Shepherd described to a 1958 Associated Parishes' audience as "an indefinable free play of ideas and personal acquaintances."[89] Chief among the avenues of intercourse were the books and journals of scholars, as well as the popular literature, which were shifting the base of liturgical science from medieval to patristic standards.[90]

The researches of Roman Catholic, Lutheran, and Anglican scholars contributed to what Shepherd called an

[e]xact scholarship ... not bounded by ecclesiastical commitments. There is a community of scholars that transcends confessional loyalties. ... It is impossible to estimate what the Liturgical Movement owes to the pure and disinterested research of liturgiologists.[91]

Gerald Ellard (1894–1963), a leader among American Roman Catholic liturgical scholars, likened the liturgical movement in 1948 to a "leaven" acting to produce the ecumenical worship of the future among Christians in the United States and Europe.[92] He hailed Evelyn Underhill's 1936 book *Worship*[93] as "very influential" among churches in the English-speaking world and as a "real herald of worship-reform."[94] Of her book *The Mystery of Sacrifice*,[95] Ellard said that he "more than once ... recalls seeing it, as the sole book by a non-Catholic author, in Catholic book displays. ... One would wish for millions of users of this little booklet."[96]

Virgil Michel, that pioneer of the liturgical movement in American Roman Catholicism, read "avidly" the works of Church of England members like A.G. Hebert interested in the Christian social reconstruction of society based on liturgical renewal.[97]

William Palmer Ladd was passionately committed to promoting ecumenical dialogue about the eucharist, which he saw as offering the means of repairing the breaches among the churches and drawing them closer together around the sacrament of unity, so that they could make the eucharist the symbol and instrument of unity for the world.

Ladd organized an interdenominational Liturgical League in New Haven in the late 1930s to popularize the eucharist among young people, which had "great success" and "the hearty cooperation of the local ministers."[98] The league discussed biblical and ecumenical aspects of the eucharist as well as its social implications and even compared Anglican, Roman, Orthodox, and various Protestant eucharistic liturgies.[99] Ladd's conviction that the reunion of the churches must center in the eucharist, not in questions of the ministry, was an approach that later ecumenical dialogues found to be a fruitful way forward, beginning with the formation of the World Council of Churches in 1948 and its several commissions on ways of worship. It reflected a fundamental insight of the liturgical movement of church as people gathered to worship, not hierarchy.

Interchurch communion held "little appeal" for Ladd as an avenue to reunion;[100] it smacked too much of a quick and easy cure for a deep-seated disease. Instead, he suggested Episcopalians and others follow the Presbyterian lead (Episcopalians at the time were in the midst of serious unity talks with the Presbyterian Church in the U.S.A.), which was taken up by the (then) Federal Council of Churches, for a communion in all churches throughout the nation on the first Sunday of October. This day, said Ladd, "might grow on American soil into an ecumenical festival, a new *Corpus Christi* day, and one of far greater significance than that inaugurated in the XIII century by the medieval church."[101]

Ladd credited the American Prayer Book with stimulating among American Roman Catholics a desire for a vernacular liturgy. It also had had an enormous influence on the worship of Protestant churches.[102] Within the ecumenical framework, Ladd saw the Episcopal Church, with its Prayer Book and its mediating position, as strategically placed to take a leading part in the unity of the churches by a return to the liturgical tradition of the first centuries.[103] But as the liturgical movement gathered momentum within the various churches, they found less need to look to the Episcopal Church for mediation of the fruits of research into the worship of the first centuries or for an emerging consensus on the common direction of liturgical reform.

Shepherd acknowledged frankly to his 1958 Associated Parishes audience that "the ideals and practices of liturgical renewal in the Roman Catholic Church have exercised a predominant influence upon the thinking and programs of liturgical leaders in other Christian Churches."

> Yet because of its policy of nonco-operation with other Christian bodies, at least officially, the Roman Catholic Church has largely excluded from all its several activities in liturgical revival the active participation of members of other Churches who are deeply interested in the movement.[104]

There had been, of course, friendly conversations and exchanges of a personal nature, Shepherd noted, and Benedictine monasteries that were harbingers of liturgical renewal in Europe and the United

States had extended their customary hospitality to non-Roman Catholics who wanted to study the liturgical movement close-up.

> But the fact remains that the impact of the liturgical revival in the Roman Catholic Church upon other Christian Churches has been indirect and undirected. Its progress and goals have of necessity to be studied from the outside, so to speak, through the initiative of individuals who are interested.[105]

Contributing to this distancing, Shepherd said, were the internal pastoral and political issues which Roman Catholics faced. Roman Catholic leaders had to give attention to problems peculiar to that church, such as "extensive discussions concerning the use of vernacular in the liturgy, ... the complications of adjusting liturgical experiment to the intricate corpus of canon law, and ... the restrictions laid about theological speculation by the rigid dogmatic structure of the Roman Church."[106] The tenor of relations changed only with the Roman Catholic Church's entry into the ecumenical movement in the mid-1960s.

Despite their differences, the liturgical movement in American Roman Catholicism operated in the same social environment as the movement in the Episcopal Church, which allowed the two to resonate with each other. The liturgical movement in the Church of England, on the other hand, touched the American scene through its important liturgical writings, but it was not an importable model because it did not fit American realities.

The problems, from an American point of view, of the English liturgical movement are summed up in the history of the Parish and People Movement, which was founded three years after Associated Parishes. From 1949 to 1970, Parish and People worked to revive the principles of corporate worship in the Church of England, primarily through advocacy of the parish communion.[107]

Though Parish and People was generally well-regarded in the English church, it expired because it was unable to link its advocacy of parish communions and offertory processions with the deeper issues of the liturgical movement. The parish communion proved to be widely popular—but Parish and People did not seem to have the same success in articulating a theological and liturgical rationale for the centrality of the eucharist, nor was it able to work out the connections between liturgy and society.[108]

Nor could the Prayer Book serve as a focus of unity for the English movement when one part of the Church of England repudiated the book and all it stood for, while the other part practically equated it with the ark of the Lord. Parish and People reflected this division between Anglo-Catholic and Evangelical interests in that it had no clear position on the Prayer Book and its authority and teaching, and none, therefore, on the future direction of liturgical reform.[109]

Associated Parishes maintained a nodding acquaintance with Parish and People from about 1950 until that group's demise in 1970. The complex of circumstances and problems that defined Parish and People, however, accurately measures the gulf between the English movement and the American, even if they had common ideals and goals.

Americans who had been reading Hebert, Ladd, and Parsons and Jones were eager to get on with the job of liturgical renewal. But a question remained. How does an interested priest make liturgical renewal work in an ordinary American parish? Who was there to show the Episcopal Church how to put the liturgical movement into effect, given the realities at hand of Prayer Book, hymnal, and parish?

Chapter Two

Associated Parishes' Divine Discontent

"Associated Parishes was founded in 1946 by a group of clergy who were in despair over eleven o'clock Sunday morning," according to Henry H. Breul, one-time president of the organization.

> The reign of *Solemn Morning Prayer* was in place, but a titanic war had shuffled peoples' value structures so that static-intellectual worship no longer carried the faith along. The Liturgical Movement had come to fruition in the publishing of Dix's *The Shape of the Liturgy* in 1945 and dramatic changes were in the wind. A.P.'s despair led to years of effort culminating in the Book of Common Prayer 1979.... [1]

The story of A.P.'s founding and its work—its temperament, what it was trying to do and why, its self-perception vis-a-vis the church at large—shows specifically how the liturgical movement began to take concrete form in the context of the actual worship of Episcopal parishes, not just in theory. The particulars of the actors and the organization that helped make liturgical renewal happen, their motivations, voices, and tone, contribute to an understanding of the Episcopal Church's experience of the age of liturgical reform, one of the most profoundly important events in the history of the church.

John O. Patterson

John Oliver Patterson (1908–1988) was one of the people sensitive to the changes that were in the wind. Patterson had set out in life to be an architect and started studies at Massachusetts Institute of Technology, but moved from that field to the priesthood.[2] Perhaps a sense of scale and priorities is what disturbed Patterson about the disproportion between Christian ideals and Christians' effect on society, which caused him to see in the liturgical movement a way of restructuring a relationship between worship and world.

Already at Grace Church, Madison, Wisconsin, where he was rector from 1941 to 1949, Patterson had begun to make a mark in liturgical renewal. His parish "became more and more the symbol of the depths of the liturgical movement, with the establishment of the Parish Eucharist, the greater training and use of the ministry of the laity and all that it implied."[3]

His associate at Grace Church from 1947 to 1949 and a co-founder of A.P., Samuel E. West (b. 1915), remembers that Patterson "always had the driving force of a construction engineer to get a job done, done well, and on time to meet reasonable deadlines. His staff was never allowed to drag feet, or to give up."[4] Nor did Patterson's architectural expertise go for naught. As a priest promoting the liturgical movement he often designed or redesigned altars or whole buildings for parishes and schools.

For years, Patterson had been talking with clerical friends who shared his frustration with entrenched attitudes in the church and his sense of what the liturgical movement could mean for renewal. He was "looking for some organization that was interested in bringing the Church alive with the dynamics of the liturgical revival and the centrality of the eucharist."[5]

> Finally, Betty Patterson, John's wife, said, "Why not do something more instead of talking; get a group together and make a plan!"[6]

Cincinnati: "Why Not Do Something?"

Sometime in the late spring or summer of 1946, the core of what was to become A.P. met in Cincinnati to talk, think, plan, pray, "and hope that something would come from this four-day unstructured meeting."[7] Patterson had invited three colleagues to meet at the Netherlands Plaza Hotel. They were Massey Shepherd, who had been teaching liturgics, early and medieval church history, and church music since 1940 at Episcopal Theological School, Cambridge, Massachusetts; John H. Keene (1904–1958), rector of Christ Church, West Englewood, New Jersey, Patterson's good friend who shared his liturgical concerns; and West, who was then rector of Trinity Church, Atchison, Kansas.

Patterson and Keene had talked to Shepherd some time before the Cincinnati meeting to sound him out on his interest in such a venture.[8] At the time, neither Patterson nor Shepherd knew each other very well, though each admired and respected the other.

> Each not only had enormous talent and experience, but each had at times a personal mannerism or mode of expression that increased among observers a sense of the formidable. Those who came to know each over a period of time, however, realized that each was indeed very shy! Each possessed a warm personality and charm that became apparent when given a chance to engage persons individually.[9]

At the end of four days of brainstorming, a plan emerged. The four men agreed to contact other people who shared their convictions about the liturgical revival and the centrality of the eucharist to

Christian life and mission to see if something could be done. After further talk with Shepherd and Keene, Patterson sent a letter to sympathetic clergymen outlining their objectives and calling for a "corporate venture" to bring the liturgical movement to life in their parishes.[10]

> We are convinced that the Church is not making the impact it might upon our world today. ... We are disturbed by the gap which exists between our Christian ideals and their expression in the lives of individuals and parishes. ... We believe that the Holy Spirit is at work in that movement known as the "Liturgical Revival" and that our own Church has a rare opportunity to apply the principles behind that movement.[11]

The issue was not what kind of ceremonial a parish ought to observe or how many kinds of organizations a parish provides, the letter said, but a more fundamental question of the nature of worship and of how parish organizations relate their work to the altar, and how that work of the parish relates to mission to the world.

Characteristically, Patterson and his associates linked the liturgical revival to a wider social dimension. Even in embryo, A.P. was not absorbed with narrow ceremonial questions, but with the fundamental relation between liturgy and society. Their focus was the individual parishes of the Episcopal Church. The altar and the corporate life of worship and work centered on it was their theological framework. Each parish should be a center of worship and work, a place where people could rediscover the nature of the church and their liturgical priesthood in order to turn around and minister to the world in God's name.

Having stated the problem and offered a vision of a solution, Patterson outlined in his letter what a practical parish liturgical movement might encompass: 1) Worship in the parish: what should be a parish's schedule of services and what sort of ceremonial best manifests the significance of worship? 2) Organization of the parish: how can the parish be organized to manifest the church as

"Body of Christ" and "Family of God"? How can groups and jobs in the parish be manifested as extensions of what goes on at the altar? 3) Evangelism by the parish: what is the most effective appeal to the unchurched? How can parishioners be brought to a fuller understanding of the ministry of the laity? 4) Study in the parish: can Christian education become part of parish life for adults as well as children? Are clergy, through church schools and sermons, meeting their prophetic charge?

The recipients of Patterson's letter were invited to think about the whole proposal and then to meet in November to see whether they could evolve a program that would work in their own parishes.

> We are anxious to seek out and to apply these principles as a corporate venture, for we are convinced that we will find wisdom and strength from a group working together towards such a common goal.
>
> We desire to share such a venture with you—first discussing, then applying mutually agreed upon activities for our respective parishes. As we achieve some measure of success together, we can then seek means of furthering such accomplishments throughout the Church.[12]

Washington, D.C.: A.P. Is Born

In the common room of the College of Preachers, Washington, D.C., on the evening of November 6, 1946, A.P. was born. A two-page legal document, incorporating A.P. under the laws of New Jersey, was ratified that night and signed the next day by A.P.'s legal trustees, Patterson, Shepherd, Keene, and West. "Our job," said Patterson, "is to stir up divine discontent with things as they are."[13]

Patterson had summoned twelve clergy[14] to meet at the college on the grounds of Washington Cathedral at the invitation of the college's warden, Theodore O. Wedel, whose own understanding of liturgy had been revolutionized by study with William Palmer Ladd. None of the twelve knew personally all of the other members. They were chosen from a range of pastoral experience, age, and "churchmanship" orientations, as their seminary backgrounds indicated. A.P. could not be accused of a particular partisan position. Attempts to label A.P. soon proved fruitless, Shepherd said.[15]

The founding members of A.P. spent their entire first morning in a two-and-a-half hour meditation led by Bishop Noble Powell of Maryland. Over the course of their five-day meeting, they attended the Holy Communion each morning in the cathedral, and prayed daily morning and evening prayer. They heard presentations on the liturgical movement, organization of the parish, worship in the parish, Christian education, evangelism, and the liturgical arts. On the concluding two days of the meeting, Patterson outlined the projected organization of A.P. Articles of incorporation, a constitution, bylaws, and an "Accepted Corporate Program," embodying the basic aims of A.P., had been prepared before the meeting with Shepherd's help.[16] With their adoption, A.P. acquired an identity and a concrete plan of action.

Underlying the superstructure was a simple idea. These twelve priests would begin to put the liturgical movement into effect in their parishes, first by restoring the eucharist as central to the life of the parish. They would keep in touch with one another for mutual accountability and support. When they had some concrete results, they could think about sharing their experiment with other parishes of the church.

A.P.'s name "was not chosen whimsically," according to Patterson, though there is no record of whose idea it was. A.P. did not intend to be Associated Theologians, or Liturgists, or Pamphleteers; its practical focus was the parish church and its liturgy. At the same time, these founders were pragmatic enough to see that the local parish, relatively independent of episcopal control and governed jointly by rector and laity, was precisely where they could operate with some degree of authority and some real hope of change.[17]

Forty years later—after the satisfaction of seeing the 1979 Prayer Book adopted and all that A.P. stood for recognized by the whole church—Patterson recalled for a new generation of A.P. members what those early days were like.

> To some degree A.P. was organized to aid and serve battered clergy who had perhaps found that by themselves they were making little progress against firmly entrenched attitudes in what Julian Bartlett once called "incestuous" parishes. So also A.P. was organized to aid and serve battered parishes in which concerned laity were making little progress against status-quo entrenched clergy. It worked both ways!
>
> It is fair to say that, for many clergy and laity, Associated Parishes offered a secure sense of belonging to something larger, wiser, stronger than they themselves were. The group offered the parishes of the Church a witness and testimony saying in effect: "Look, this is what we are doing and at least this part of it works."[18]

A.P. was "fully aware" it was not called to supersede the church, or to be a new agency of the Holy Spirit, or to be a confessional group. It had "no particular wisdom, charisma, or new revelation. We tried to deal with existing realities of Scripture, Creed, Church, Prayer Book, as we worked in the existing reality of such-and-such a parish."[19]

None of the founding members "could ... have thought of our parishes—of whatever stripe of 'churchmanship'—as seedbeds or ripe fruits" of liturgical renewal, Patterson said.[20] But they were convinced that at hand was a time, a place, and an act where they as parish priests could make a beginning. The time was now. They were not to seek a revival of the past or dream up a renewal for the future. Their obligation was to today, now. The place was the parish, that outward and visible sign of the church. Their object was to find techniques, methods, and policies that would join the spirit of liturgical renewal to the routine activities of the parish. The act was the eucharist. They were convinced that all that went on in a parish must be related to the altar and express the Christian teaching that all of life is to be offered to God for its redemption. The Accepted Corporate Program, which represented a constantly sought liturgical and organizational goal rather than a fact of life in A.P. parishes, laid out an itemized program for putting the liturgical movement into practice, building on the foundation stones of today, the parish, the eucharist. The Accepted Corporate Program answered the practical question, "What does A.P. stand for and what does it do?" It covered: 1) Liturgical Worship; 2) Parish Organization; 3) Christian Education; 4) Evangelism; and 5) Liturgical Arts. In 1947, sections on social action and on pastoral ministrations were added.[21]

A.P.'s starting point was the people. The parish communion would be the main service on Sunday in an A.P. parish. The ceremonial would serve the people and foster a sense of community: offertory processions, reading the gospel in the midst of the people, banning choir processions and recessions, choosing service music which the people could join in—all aimed at enhancing the people's sense of participating in the great action of self-offering, the eucharist.

Altars ought to be of the "liturgical" kind, though it is not clear what this meant. Perhaps it meant free-standing, so that priest and people could face one another; at least it meant free of clutter and bric-a-brac. Church art and architecture ought to be clear, joyful, and simple. Daily Morning and Evening Prayer ought to be said publicly, and baptisms, marriages, and funerals be celebrated as public services in the presence of the parish, not as private rites.

An A.P. parish would use only the authorized liturgy of the church, the Prayer Book and hymnal. The rubrics of the 1928 Prayer Book at least were patient of ceremonies like offertory processions and altars facing the people, arrangements which suggested that priest and people were co-offerers in the eucharist, offering themselves through symbolic gifts and facing one another in dialogue across the table of offering.

The Accepted Corporate Program indicated how the experience of authentic fellowship around the altar was to be spelled out in parish life. In addition to the canonically established vestry, A.P. parishes were to have a parish council with committees responsible for evangelism, education, worship, stewardship, and house and grounds. Informing the organizational structure was a fundamental theological conviction about the nature of Christian life and Christian priesthood.

> The members of the Council thus say to the Parish, "Here is a job for all of us. All of us, clergy and laity alike, share a royal priesthood differing not in importance but only in function. Our job is to make manifest the divine fellowship in this parish, to relate all that we do, all our thoughts, words, and deeds, to the worship of the Holy Trinity and to carry into every phase of life the Grace of God given to us."[22]

An A.P. education program for all members of the parish, based on the Sunday liturgy, was to be developed to link liturgy with mission to the world. The relation between liturgy and the surrounding culture was crucial in Patterson's thinking about the kind of movement he wanted to introduce into the church. At the crux of liturgy and world stood the parish, that outward sign of the church's divine life.

> It is foolish to talk about going forth into the world with a mission, or to talk about worship, until we have faced squarely and fairly the function of the parish. Liturgy is primarily: "We are gathered together—let us pray." And until there has come to the front a very real sense of the church as God's family, there is going to be very little response to the words, "Let us pray."[23]

At the same time, Patterson respected the limits of what the liturgical movement was capable of. An A.P. parish council should not try to duplicate or compete in its programs with civic organizations. Every project of the council must be checked against the questions, "Is it in accord with the Church's goal? Is it related to the altar? Is it assisting the Church to be the Church?" The function of the church is religious; all activities of the council must be religious.[24]

The goal of the liturgical movement in a local parish is to shape perceptions and motives, Patterson implied, not to prescribe solutions for the ills of the world out of the wisdom engendered by the liturgical movement. A.P. was not out to define "the" Christian position on anything. At the same time, one of A.P.'s strengths was that it was able to forge links between a recovered understanding of liturgy and issues of property, economics, politics, and race. A.P. saw its task as forming priestly Christians who drew their sustenance from the parish community gathered around the altar, so that they could turn around to do justice in the world. Not that Christians mustn't have social service agencies of their own—but the liturgical movement was not one of them.

A.P. deliberately set itself some limitations on its corporate action. Its focus was the liturgy. Homing on that time and again saved A.P. from dying a death of a hundred good intentions. It took, Patterson said, frequent meditation on Luke 14:31 and Matthew 4:1 ("Or what king, going out to wage war against another king, will not sit down and first consider whether he is able with ten thousand to oppose the one who comes against him with twenty thousand," and "Then Jesus was led up by the Spirit into the wilderness to be tempted by the devil") to keep A.P. on track.[25]

According to Patterson, it was Shepherd who kept calling A.P. back to three basic theological convictions that undergirded A.P.'s liturgical activity: 1) Jesus Christ is Lord; loyalty to him must transcend all other loyalties; 2) the church is the earnest of his kingdom; through the Holy Spirit Christians are to seek to realize on earth what they will be when Christ appears in glory; 3) the eucharist is the great action of the church; it is both the pleading of and the showing forth here and now of the accomplished fact of redemption.[26]

A.P.'s loyalty to the Prayer Book as the standard of teaching and practice put it solidly within the church's ethos and later lent it credibility in Prayer Book revision. A.P.'s early members were anything but Prayer Book jingoists, however.[27] Certainly, nothing in A.P.'s official pronouncements or publications of the time suggested that the current liturgical situation might be improved by revising the Prayer Book. But from the perspective of forty years later, Patterson denied that A.P.'s intention was to reinforce the status quo. A.P.'s founders did not think of the 1928 Prayer Book as "presenting the ideal liturgy of the ages," he said. The fact was, the Prayer Book was one of the realities A.P. had to deal with if it was to seek a liturgical revival in the here and now.[28]

That many parishes failed to use the book in its wholeness was obvious. And it is true A.P. believed that a more exact adherence to the rubrics might improve worship by letting the Prayer Book's priorities come to light. But it also is true that by carefully using the book as it was intended to be used, A.P. parishes were able to surface some weaknesses of the 1928 Prayer Book and, by taking advantage of advances in scholarship, had concrete suggestions for revision when the time came.[29]

A.P. stood for something more than reorganization of ceremonies. Its purpose was not merely to encourage the church to a better standard of liturgy—a more esthetically pleasing or more historically "correct" liturgy. At its core, the mission of A.P. was theological—to reform the church by reminding it of its reason for being the church, of what was at the basis of all Christian activity—the worship of God in the liturgy. The best way for A.P. to do that, the early members thought, was to use their own parishes as laboratories and, when they had some concrete results, to go public. In the meanwhile, they agreed that A.P. "should not be discussed until the work is further established and advanced."[30]

Behind this reserve was a desire to see whether this voluntary band of clergy with no official mandate from the church could in fact make the liturgical movement work in their own parishes. A.P. decided it needed to test the validity of its own convictions about the liturgical movement and demonstrate that it could be productive before it knew whether it had something of substance to say to the church. From the beginning, as the "founding letter" from Patterson and records of the founding meeting at the College of Preachers makes clear, A.P. was discussing, arguing, planning, and organizing for a public mission to the church.[31]

From its founding until 1963, A.P. was a closed, self-perpetuating corporation with a membership that eventually grew to about thirty. No one could propose himself for membership. These arrangements contributed to a perception of A.P. as a *sub rosa* organization in its earliest years. But selectivity helped A.P. cohere. A limit on the size of the working membership also was essential just for good management. The early membership of A.P. was a tightly knit group; anyone accepted into it would have to be able to work with the personalities involved. One negative vote was enough to eliminate a candidate for membership. The way A.P. got its work done was by gathering everyone face-to-face in a room twice a year, and having at it. The sound of A.P. at work is the sound of discussion, reasoned argument, theological acumen, methodological insight, convolutions, outbursts, injured feelings, heroic stands on principle, and laughter of a roomful of able people who are not reluctant to let their views be known. It was not an atmosphere for the thin-shelled.

Looking back forty years later on the movement he helped found, Patterson recalled nothing in particular that made 1946 seem an auspicious moment to launch A.P. But perhaps the end of a cataclysmic war coupled with the cultural shift it signified alerted some people's sensitivities to the realization that the time to make an attempt at preparing the church to address a culture in transition was now, with the materials at hand—parishes, Prayer Books, and all.

A.P. Gets to Work

Their ideals were grand, their vision wide. They had a program and an organization. Now they had to make it work. For the first several years of its life, A.P. concentrated on sweeping and garnishing its own house as it prepared for a public role.

Patterson served as chairman of A.P. until 1948, after which he seems never to have held elected office again. The officers (president, vice-president, secretary, treasurer) at first were elected annually, and later biannually, but there never was a cult of the founding father about Patterson.

At the very first meeting after the founding meeting, in May 1947, the members already were beginning to look beyond the original circle of twelve and approved a procedure for nominating and voting on new members.[32] They particularly were on the lookout for laity to include in their membership. Francis F. Bowman, Jr., was the first layperson elected to A.P. Bowman was an active parishioner at Patterson's Grace Church. Immediately on being elected in November 1947 he was given the job of executive secretary to raise money for the educational, evangelistic, and promotional work of A.P.[33] As A.P.'s treasurer until 1970, Bowman kept the group's hand-to-mouth finances (mostly from members' dues, grants and gifts, and eventually from publications) on an even keel. When he died in 1975, he was sorely missed as one of the living links with A.P.'s beginnings.

A single sentence in A.P.'s records offers an insight into one problem A.P. faced as it expanded its membership. In 1970 A.P. rescinded "a motion of about 1957 barring curates from membership."[34] This is the only reference to the matter in any of A.P.'s records. Why curates had been persona non grata is not explained; apparently in the late 1950s A.P. had to stem the entrance of unqualified members who had been nominated by their rectors.

A pattern of meeting for a week twice a year—in May to handle business and in November for the "annual meeting," when the liturgical agenda had the floor—served A.P. until 1970. In the spring of 1971 A.P. began to combine the business and annual meetings into a five-day, once-a-year event—partly because of rising expense; and partly because, as the church's program of official liturgical revision went into high gear, A.P. members who were sitting on the SLC, on drafting committees, and in other ways were involved in Prayer Book revision, could not afford the time twice a year.

A.P. also began to define its social vision at the same time that it was developing its internal organization. Just one year after its founding, in November 1947, A.P. added a new section on social action to its Accepted Corporate Program.[35] It was a significant development, both because it linked A.P.'s liturgical mission in a specific way to society, and also because it characterized what was to be A.P.'s stance on social issues.

The six-point social agenda committed A.P. members to self-education and to participation in organizations working for social justice. Members were to set up programs in their parishes, or use existing parish programs, to address specific social problems in light of the gospel. Not exactly a call to the barricades, perhaps, but it takes only a little imagination to see how combustible this provision might be if the subject were, say, racial discrimination:

> Members will instruct their congregations to recognize their Christian duty to engage in redemptive activity in the field of social relationships, and where possible will suggest specific fields of actions.[36]

The social action portion of the Accepted Corporate Program committed individual A.P. members to education and action, but without championing specific causes. There was no attempt to define "the" Christian position on anything. What A.P. affirmed was that there was a relationship between liturgy and social action; but the program implicitly recognized that the liturgical movement had no panacea. In this way, individual members and their parishes, inspired by A.P.'s liturgical ideals, were free to define the issues and their response, while A.P. itself remained identified with its liturgical mission.

The distinction was never a given, however, in A.P.'s experience; it had to be constantly renegotiated and reappropriated. But in the end, the group always came down along the lines of Patterson's insight at the founding meeting of 1946: the liturgy, the primary function of the parish and the church, was the arena for A.P.'s energy and talents.

How well did member parishes fulfill the Accepted Corporate Program? What sort of impact was A.P.'s vision making on the handful of parishes that constituted A.P. as it began to take its first steps? The members were to have reported annually on their progress; unfortunately, no written reports exist in A.P.'s records. But an undated newsletter circulated to A.P. members around 1950 or 1951 reported that "analysis showed members had reached the halfway mark in the program or 50% efficiency."[37] Which fifty percent is only one of the unanswered questions.

A.P. Meets with Dom Gregory Dix, A.G. Hebert

Once it was launched, A.P. lost no time in meeting face-to-face with leaders in Anglican liturgical scholarship. A.P. was clear about its mission and its area of operation, the local parish, but its context was the wider liturgical movement and it engaged the best liturgical thinking available. The group met with Dom Gregory Dix, O.S.B., in 1947 and A.G. Hebert, S.S.M., in 1948 for several days of conversation and debate with each.

A.P., said Dix, was the first group he knew of to take the liturgical revival seriously by putting it into practice in parishes.[38] It probably would be more profitable for him and for A.P., Dix said, not to hear him lecture, for he really had no more insights to offer, but to have several days of conversation. Other than the daily offices and a celebration of the eucharist, there was no agenda. The meeting took place August 5–7, 1947, at St. Barnabas House near Gibsonia, Pennsylvania, where Dix was visiting while traveling around the country lecturing to raise money to help found an Episcopal Benedictine house in the United States.

The heart of the three days' conversational give-and-take was the "delightful and challenging intensities" of some "heated arguments" between Dix and Shepherd, as Shepherd challenged some of Dix's resources and conclusions in *The Shape of the Liturgy.*[39] A.P. was willing to learn, but it was not uncritical, and it possessed in Shepherd a scholar of the first rank who helped channel the group's specifically Episcopal appropriation of the ecumenical liturgical movement. The celebration of the eucharist at that meeting was a lesson in the meaning of liturgy, Samuel West recalled.

We had decided to join with the Brothers, Dom Gregory as celebrant. He entered the medieval chapel, his monk's cowl over his head, and was flanked by two brothers as acolytes. The Mass opened with the *Confiteor* at the foot of the Altar, most of the English missal, rite and ceremonial, was used, and it closed with the "Last Gospel." Afterward we asked Dom Gregory about this seeming contradiction in rite and ceremonial with all he professed in his writing. But his answer was plausible enough. He was still under obedience to the [Benedictine] order which, up to then, had made no changes, and he wanted also to respect what those of St. Barnabas might expect of him out of older tradition.

The other side of the story was the context of that Eucharist. The work and life of St. Barnabas order was certainly offered. Those not too ill, who were cared for by the Brothers, were brought in on rolling cots or in wheelchairs, crowding the aisles of the chapel, some in very weakened state. Those unable to be brought in heard the full rite over a homemade public address system, the speakers placed in all infirmary wards. Then, for the administration of the Sacrament, Dom Gregory proceeded in and beyond the Chapel to minister Holy Communion to the entire community, sick and well, a memorable enough testimony at that time, in that place.[40]

The year after meeting with Dix, A.P. met for a week of discussion with A.G. Hebert, whose books had awakened many in the Episcopal Church to liturgical renewal. The November 1–5, 1948, meeting in the common room of the College of Preachers, Washington, D.C.—the tall, lanky Hebert in his monastic habit curled up on a couch and A.P. seated around—was a lesson in some of the deficiencies of the 1928 Prayer Book and the dawning of the realization that a new Prayer Book was the answer.[41]

The liturgical movement was a crossroad of the twentieth-century church renewal that encompassed the biblical, the social, and the ecumenical movements. From the start, A.P. was trying to integrate aspects of the whole, particularly critical scholarship of the bible, and to find ways to bring them to bear on parish worship.

How could modern people, who had largely lost touch with a biblical frame of reference, grasp the daily and Sunday lessons read in church as a living word of God addressed to them in their own day, was the question A.P. posed to Hebert.[42] More particularly, A.P. wanted to benefit from Hebert's biblical and liturgical insights as it tried to create a parish educational curriculum based on the eucharistic propers of the 1928 Prayer Book. A.P. believed that "the Liturgy of the Word is an essential, constituent part of the Holy Eucharist and intends recognition that the Holy Bible is a vital essential in liturgical renewal," Samuel West said in his memoir of the meeting with Hebert.[43]

Hebert embodied the fruit of his reflection on the week's discussion in a new book, *The Bible From Within*. For A.P., the deficiencies of the 1928 Prayer Book's eucharistic lectionary began to seem more evident after its meeting with Hebert and after several more years of trying to fit the square peg of the 1928 lectionary into the round hole of a coordinated, thematic educational curriculum. That realization, and the accompanying conviction that a completely new approach to Prayer Book lectionaries was needed, came only gradually over years. But surfacing the deficiencies of the 1928

Prayer Book was a step towards the 1979 Prayer Book. An important tributary to that stream was the practical question asked by A.P. about how the men and women of its parishes could grasp the implications of the liturgy for their lives today.

Beginning in 1948, minutes of meetings and letters between A.P. members reflect growing disenchantment and frustration with devising a parish education course based on the 1928 eucharistic lectionary. By 1952, only three courses were in use—by three A.P. member parishes.[44] The reference to "long and vigorous discussion" which appeared in the minutes of the November 1954 meeting veils a floundering for direction and a rising exasperation.[45] By 1956, six A.P. parishes were teaching four A.P. courses. But that meant that fewer than half of A.P.'s member parishes were using the material, "which again raises the point as to how far we all are committed to use them," John H. Keene said.[46]

Discussion on the education program at the November 1956 meeting "was long, involved, and gave expression to many opinions," as the minutes diplomatically put it. After twenty years of trying to develop a parish education program based on the liturgy, A.P. in 1966 carefully considered the whole project, thanked everyone involved for their work, recognized their serious effort, and shelved it.[47] By then, A.P. was moving more directly into liturgical education of the church at large through encouragement of trial use of the new rites that began to appear.

Despite the blind alley it had been, the instincts guiding A.P.'s efforts at liturgical education had been sound. Full participation in the church's life, not knowledge about the church's life, was the goal of A.P.'s educational efforts. The eucharist with its propers and sermon was the source of the gospel and of Christian experience. A.P. aimed not at teaching people about the liturgy, nor at piggybacking other issues onto the liturgy, but at expressing the conviction that the eucharist summed up and manifested Christian life, and at drawing out the implications of eucharistic living.

Chapter Three

The Shape of
Things to Come

Real liturgical change began to look possible by the 1950s and 1960s. The liturgical insights that had grown up since World War II had begun to coalesce. To leaders in the liturgical movement, if not yet to the church at large, the shape of the liturgical changes that lay just over the horizon began to be discernible.

Eyes were on the Church of South India, formed in 1947, when it issued its new eucharistic liturgy in 1950. By the end of the decade, other experiments with eucharistic rites by Anglicans and Protestants began to put into practice what so far had only been talked about, attracting ecumenical attention and commentary. A vast and ever-growing literature by scholars of all churches in all aspects of liturgics—biblical, historical, and theological—expanded understanding of the nature and meaning of Christian worship and therefore of the future direction of reform. Faculty in Episcopal seminaries mediated this ferment in liturgical thought to their students and helped prepare the church for liturgical change.

The Breakdown of Cranmer's Synthesis

A.P.'s public stance from its founding through the early 1960s was one of uncritical loyalty to the Prayer Book. A.P. tried to make the most of the Prayer Book as it stood and treaded carefully among the rubrics when it encouraged liturgical experimentation. A.P.'s publications did not even hint that a revision of the Prayer Book might be desirable. A.P. saw its task as educating the church for liturgical renewal. To A.P.'s mind that did not mean publicly critiquing the liturgy or arguing for change. Even in the privacy of its meetings, the records show, A.P. did not consider crafting a strategy for Prayer Book revision.

In a statement printed in its publications during the 1950s, A.P. declared that its purpose was to use the church's "rich inheritance of 'common prayer' ... to set forward this [liturgical] movement by applying its basic principles" in the parishes, while disclaiming any "interest in promoting any rigid, uniform schedule of parochial life, whether in worship or in organization."[1] A.P.'s caution mirrored the temper of the church as a whole during the 1950s and early 1960s. During the same period, the Standing Liturgical Commission engaged in one last attempt to reappropriate Cranmer through the Prayer Book Studies that appeared between 1950 and 1963.

Yet A.P. effected real liturgical change in the two decades preceding Prayer Book revision. Through seminary faculty who were members of A.P., through its brochures beginning in 1950, a quarterly journal begun in 1954, liturgical books published in 1956 and 1958, and three major national liturgical conferences in 1958, 1959, and 1962, A.P. offered new ways of thinking about and experiencing the liturgy. A.P. showed parishes how to implement liturgical renewal at their altars, encouraged imaginative use of the Prayer Book, and raised expectations by offering a model of what liturgical renewal might mean for the church. At the same time, A.P. worked out the implications of liturgy against the background of live issues of the day—racial desegregation, capitalism versus socialism, and anti-communism.

In 1946 Massey Shepherd still could argue that reinterpreting the 1928 Prayer Book in light of the liturgical movement was all that was needed to reinvigorate the church's mission to and action in the world.[2] More and more, though, it was apparent that there was a conflict between the worldview of the Prayer Book and modern reality.

As Shepherd himself acknowledged, the Prayer Book's assumption that church and state were still coterminous had been a "fiction" in England for three hundred years past and an "absurd anachronism" in America. The petition for Christian rulers in the Holy Communion, for example, was an "enigma" for many people, with its assumption that secular government is Christian and part of its task is to foster the church. The prayer for Congress, an optional element in Morning or Evening Prayer, assumed that part of the legislature's duty is to advance the good of the church, religion, and piety. These sentiments "would be more suitable nowadays as a prayer for the General Convention," Shepherd said.[3]

And was it the case that bad weather is God's punishment for human sin, as the prayer in time of dearth and famine said? Or that sickness is God's chastisement, as the Order for the Visitation of the Sick suggested? Even in 1946 it was clear that the perception of the world presented by the Prayer Book, a world in which the church is "a leaven gradually and quietly working for the amelioration of human society and comforting world-weary and none-too-world-weary sinners with the ultimate hope of heaven beyond the skies," was at odds with the eschatological and ecclesiological insights focused in the liturgical movement.[4]

At the risk of becoming again "strangers and pilgrims" upon the earth in the primitive Christian sense the Church must revive within itself the consciousness that it is a community of the redeemed in and through whom the Lordship of Christ is made presently operative, because by Him and with Him it has entered into the new realm of life of His Kingdom.[5]

As A.P. tried to teach Cranmer to speak in the accents of Hippolytus, it came to several realizations. The Tudor underlay of the Holy Communion vitiated attempts to image a communal model of eucharistic celebration in the parish eucharist; the Prayer Book's ecclesiology was ordination-oriented rather than baptism-centered, modeling church as clergy-hierarchy rather than as community in the Body of Christ; and try as A.P. might to construe the Prayer Book in terms of the modern liturgical movement, the Prayer Book's assumptions and expectations spoke out of and to a world that had vanished.

That the 1928 Prayer Book still could be the vehicle for heartfelt devotion was not the issue. The point was that this was not the sixteenth century anymore. A.P. was loyal to the liturgy of the church, but "all of us, at the same time, became frustrated a thousand times over" with the shortcomings of the 1928 book, according to onetime A.P. President Paul Z. Hoornstra, and that "thrust us very soon into revision" of the Prayer Book.[6]

A.P.'s Debate: Liturgical Leader or Leaven?

As early as 1948, treasurer Frank Bowman was telling A.P. it simply had to make itself better, and more accurately, known. It had to set out the issues of the liturgical movement and the principles of A.P. "to clarify [the] false impression that A.P. might be promoting party ideas."[7] A.P. began debating strategy for its role in the liturgical renewal of the church in 1949: should A.P. be a leaven for renewal by working solely in its own parishes, or should it try to be a public presence with a program for educating the whole church in liturgical values?

The danger of going public, some members thought, was that A.P. might "unhappily and inadvertently become a party or mere pressure group." Giving the impression that A.P. was "the" liturgical revival "would be erroneous from any standpoint," said Samuel West.[8] But after three years of existence, some members felt it was time to take bolder steps. At its May 1949 meeting the group discussed the idea of a "liturgical center" to serve as a clearinghouse of information and as an agency for liturgical education in the church. The idea lingered, and the following Spring A.P. examined several alternative plans to make A.P. a public liturgical leader in the church.

Should they 1) hire a part-time secretary to work under the direction of an A.P. priest; 2) hire a priest to work part-time for A.P. and part-time for an A.P. parish; 3) hire a priest to work full-time for A.P., writing, editing, and publishing A.P. materials; 4) or buy a farm to be used as an A.P. conference center with a priest in charge, the land rented out for farming and the buildings used for A.P. conferences and meetings? The members voted to accept plan three.[9] It apparently never was implemented, but the discussion does offer a reading of some members' sense of A.P.'s development by 1950 and its potential.

"[T]o a layman A.P. seems to be on the track and moving," Bowman wrote to A.P. members in 1952.

> We have passed through the excitement of birth, we have survived the inevitable doubts of early existence, we have taken form and we are becoming known throughout the church.[10]

"Where do we go from here?" was on members' minds a year later. Massey Shepherd acknowledged there had been change in the years since A.P.'s founding and a growing desire to reach out; but he doubted A.P., with its limited resources and members who could give A.P. only part-time attention, was ready for the larger program of educating the whole church. The basic task as he saw it still was in A.P.'s own member parishes.[11]

By 1956, A.P. members like Frederick W. Putnam were convinced the time had come "to think about A.P. becoming a movement in the Church, and to move ahead." But the majority still argued that "we should influence the Church—permeate its thinking—but should not become a pressure group fighting or opposing it."[12]

By 1957, A.P. was soliciting grants to support a full-time priest-teacher for five years, who was to develop church school courses, write brochures, organize regional liturgical conferences, be available to preach on the liturgical movement, and oversee the distribution of A.P. literature.[13] Though nothing came of the proposal, it does take the measure of A.P.'s maturing sense of its own mission and of its leadership in "experimentation and instruction in the adoption of the Liturgy to daily life."[14] Some members, at least, thought that with financial backing A.P. was ready to rapidly expand its role and become a leader in the liturgical movement within the church.[15]

By 1959, after A.P. had sponsored two of its three major national liturgical conferences, people's appetites were whetted for more information about A.P. and about becoming a member of the group. A.P. was wrestling with the issue of extending its membership, but did not yet see its way clear to expanding beyond its small working group size. A.P. was still debating whether it ought to be a public leader of liturgical renewal or a leaven in the church working through its own member parishes.

In a 1959 article in *Sharers*, Shepherd suggested some guidelines for parishes and clergy who wanted to extend A.P.'s ideals and aims: 1) loyalty to the Prayer Book and study of its rationale and teaching; 2) use of A.P.'s brochures and its liturgical quarterly, *Sharers*; 3) financially supporting A.P.'s work; 4) use of A.P. members to lead conferences, which might lead local clergy to band together to promote the liturgical movement; 5) institution of the parish eucharist as the chief Sunday service.[16]

Whatever the ferment within A.P., its first public foray into the marketplace of ideas at General Convention was cautious, qualified, and understated. A.P. rented a booth in the exhibition area for the first time at the 1961 convention in Detroit. A.P.'s exhibit was a tastefully arranged Jacobean altar with bread and wine on it which A.P. said "was quite effective and drew much favorable comment." But A.P. felt compelled to explain to inquirers at General Convention that A.P. was not intending to put its imprimatur on Jacobean frontals; in fact, A.P. hastened to add, it did not regard this or any particular type of altar as best suited for a "liturgical movement parish."

By its own description, A.P.'s presence was passive. It handed out back copies of its publications and answered questions about itself and about the liturgical movement, but did not recruit, promote, or argue a cause. But by A.P.'s assessment, the attention the booth attracted and the questions people asked "showed us that many people, clergy and lay people, alike, have great respect for the collective opinion of the Associated Parishes group."[17]

"This Is What We Mean:" A.P.'s Publications

Four years after its birth, A.P. felt confident enough to begin sharing the results of its experiment with the rest of the church. Beginning in 1950 and continuing to 1963, A.P. published a series of brochures which gave parishes practical and specific guidance in liturgical renewal by applying the theological and ecclesiological insights of the liturgical movement to the rites of the 1928 Prayer Book.[18] That very act, though, began to put more strain on the sixteenth-century liturgy than it could bear. A.P.'s experience exposed willy-nilly the deficiencies of the 1928 Prayer Book and contributed to critical self-reflection in the church and a body of opinion in favor of reform.

By 1960, a total of 938 Episcopal parishes in every state (except Delaware and South Dakota) and in the District of Columbia, as well as thirty-one Canadian parishes, were using A.P.'s brochures.[19] Even some Lutheran, Methodist, and Presbyterian churches had begun to trust and use them.[20]

Taken together, the brochures were agents for the spread of "state-of-the-art" liturgical thinking in the church at the "grass roots." What the brochures did not do was criticize the liturgies or argue for Prayer Book reform. Nor did the brochures mandate particular ceremonial or vesture. A.P. attempted to appeal within the realities of liturgical life in the church as it found them, even as it tried to educate. Nor were the brochures concerned with historical education, itemizing the when, where, and how of the liturgy's formation.

A.P.'s interest lay in reappropriating the inner meaning of the rites and bringing them to address people's contemporary situation. The format of the brochures typically encompassed two facing pages —the left page headed "This Is What We Do," walking through the sequence of prayers and actions in the liturgy, and the right page headed "This Is What We Mean," offering theological commentary and practical applications.

The text of each brochure was the result of a consensus among all A.P. members. A topic would be assigned to a member who would prepare a draft. One of A.P.'s semi-annual meetings would function as an editorial committee of the whole, debating the draft, proposing revisions, discussing illustrations, and voting on the text for publication. The brochures were published without any author's name; they were presented simply as "Prepared by the clergy and laity of the Associated Parishes, Inc."

A.P.'s first venture into print apparently was a five-cent tract called *What I Promise As a Sponsor in Baptism*. The only evidence of it that survives is a brief review in *The Living Church* for October 8, 1950, which calls it A.P.'s "first publishing effort." No copies of the tract or record of it exists in A.P.'s archives. The tract explained the duties of a godparent "in the light of the theology of baptism and confirmation and the facts of spiritual growth."[21]

A.P.'s first brochure, *The Parish Eucharist* (1950), proved to be one of its most popular. A.P. gave permission for its translation into Japanese (1955), Portuguese (for use in Brazil, 1956), and Spanish (1961) at the request of overseas clergy. An Australian edition appeared in 1960.[22] This brochure was one of the ways Episcopalians began to reevaluate the eucharist in categories provided by the liturgical movement and to restore it to the center of their religious experience. The brochure also reflected both the strengths and the limits of A.P.'s appropriation of liturgical movement theology during this period.

Parishioners studying *The Parish Eucharist* learned a fundamental understanding of baptismal priesthood and of the eucharist as an action with social implications. A reader of the brochure carried away the understanding that the beginning of building human community in the world was the formation of holy fellowship with God at the eucharist in the parish.

The brochure linked receiving communion to building up "true community" by working for "Good Government, Social and Welfare Agencies, Wholesome Recreational Facilities, Improvement of Housing and Working Conditions, Schools and Colleges, Cooperation with other Parishes and Christian Bodies. In every area of human activity, political, economic, social and cultural, we must extend the Holy Fellowship of the Altar." To the extent that the parish exhibited eucharistic living among its own members, it could be an agent for change in the world.[23]

A.P. staked out a theological position on eucharistic sacrifice that ran counter to a position common among Roman Catholics and some Anglo-Catholics at the time. Readers of *The Parish Eucharist* learned that the true meaning of sacrifice is the offering of one's self and the whole of life to God. The sacrifice of the parish's offering of its life is linked to the eucharistic bread and wine, but the eucharistic sacrifice is not a sacrifice of the consecrated elements, an unbloody representation of Calvary, as contemporary Roman Catholic thought held. A.P. also struck a distinctively Anglican note when it refused to baldly equate the eucharistic bread and wine with the body and blood of Christ; it left open different possibilities for articulating eucharistic presence. The elements are "the means whereby we can receive His power," A.P. said; in the action of the sacrament Christ's presence "is real through the medium of Bread and Wine."[24]

Yet *The Parish Eucharist* made little out of one of the most distinctive elements in the 1928 prayer of consecration, the invocation of Word and Holy Spirit on bread and wine. Aside from calling it "one of the glories of our liturgy,"[25] the brochure did not discuss the invocation, or epiclesis, to offer a specific Episcopal contribution, arising out of this church's praying experience, to the liturgical movement's thinking about eucharistic sacrifice, consecration, eucharistic presence, or participation in and union with Christ's life. It might have been possible, for example, to examine the invocation as a counterweight to current theories of consecration by repeating a formula of words, whether words of institution or of epiclesis; the 1928 form skillfully avoids the implication that the invocation makes or changes bread and wine into the body and blood of Christ. Or it might have been possible to suggest that the point of eucharistic praying was to hallow the communicants or the church no less than the bread and wine; the 1928 form suggests that by receiving and remembering, the communicants are made partakers in Christ's life.

The brochure also ignored one of the most important elements in Episcopal eucharistic praying, the offering to God of "our selves, our souls and bodies, to be a reasonable, holy, and living sacrifice unto thee." Such a theology, in the heart of the Scottish-American eucharistic prayer, would seem tailor-made for the liturgical movement's teaching about sacrifice, self-oblation, and the meaning of the eucharist. (In the 1662 English rite, self-oblation is expressed not in the prayer of consecration but after communion in only the first of two alternative post-communion prayers.) Everything A.P.'s brochure had to say about self-oblation was said in connection with the offertory and offertory processions. A little creative reading of the 1928 offertory rubrics legitimated a people's offertory procession with alms, bread, and wine. A stricter reading allowed for only a procession of alms, without the bread and wine which were the instruments for associating together the people's offering of themselves, Christ's offering of himself, and participation in Christ's life. "'Ourselves, [sic] our souls and bodies' are offered as we present our oblations of bread and wine," A.P.'s brochure said, and it noted that "Today, in many parishes, representatives of the congregation bring these offerings reverently in procession to the celebrant."[26]

The Parish Eucharist could have linked the people's oblation of themselves more directly to Christ's own offering of himself, which in fact is what the concluding paragraph of the 1928 prayer of consecration does, as Shepherd pointed out in 1950 in his definitive commentary on the 1928 Prayer Book, *The Oxford American Prayer Book Commentary*. In this prayer, Shepherd said,

> We not only memorialize Christ's oblation; we unite our offering of ourselves to His. ... [T]he gifts of bread and wine symbolize not only our Lord's oblation of his Body and Blood; they also represent our own life and labor and all that we possess. ... Thus ... the Eucharist unites the memorial of our Lord's sacrifice in His Incarnate Body, the re-presentation of that sacrifice in His sacramental Body, and the continual offering of His sacrifice in His mystical Body, which is the Church.[27]

By linking self-offering with the offertory, A.P. missed an opportunity to relate the more scriptural and theologically more significant movement of self-oblation found in Anglican eucharistic praying with one of the deepest themes of the liturgical movement. But offertory processions were part of the liturgical movement's repertory and were attractive because they were a visible expression of its theology. They provided people a ritual way to express self-offering, an element which remained only a verbal movement in the prayer of consecration. Dom Gregory Dix had begun to teach Anglicans to think of liturgy as an action, something done, rather than something said. A merely verbal self-offering may have seemed inadequate.

Ceremonially, *The Parish Eucharist* took a sober approach. Gospel and offertory processions were mentioned as sometimes taking place in parishes, but it was left at that. The celebrant might elevate the elements at the end of the prayer of consecration. The fraction might take place after the prayer of humble access instead of just before the words of institution as the 1928 Prayer Book required. The "peace" might be spoken by priest and congregation, but there was no suggestion that it be enacted. Saying "amen" at reception of communion "would be a laudable custom for our day," but there was no urging of the case.[28] The illustrations sometimes depicted priests vested in surplice and stole, sometimes in chasuble, but vestments received no mention in the text.

A.P.'s brochures on Christian initiation—*Holy Baptism* (1953) and *Confirmation* (1954)—broke no new ground regarding the structure of the rites of initiation, nor did they touch the question of adult versus infant baptism. But, against privatizing interpretations, they did teach parishes a crucial new perspective on baptism by arguing for the public, corporate nature of the sacrament and its social consequences.

A.P. accepted the Prayer Book's separation of water baptism, confirmation, and holy communion. The tension between historical evidence for a unified rite of baptism-anointing-eucharist and the Prayer Book practice landed the brochures in what would later be seen as some unresolved contradictions. But baptism only began to attract the attention of liturgical scholars in the late 1950s. The church as a whole had not yet identified initiation as an issue. A.P. at this stage did not argue for a change but simply took the rites as they stood and worked from there.

The two brochures asserted that baptism confers the Holy Spirit and membership in the church. But almost in the next breath, baptism was said to be but the first stage in full initiation, which must be completed by a mature profession of faith and reception of the strengthening gifts of the Spirit in confirmation.[29] The issue of adult versus infant baptism, with its accompanying theological and social implications, did not even arise as a matter of debate. Infant baptism was accepted as the norm.

But A.P. emphasized the corporate, social nature of baptism in several ways. Baptism was to be administered on a Sunday or holy day at the eucharist or at Morning or Evening Prayer. The congregation was singled out as an important party to baptism, representing the community of the church through the ages and around the world into which the candidate was brought.

Holy Baptism taught that "the Christian in renouncing evil, promises to resist it not only in his personal life, but also in the corporate life of society." Parishes using A.P.'s brochure learned that the sacrament was the means of sharing in Christ's healing of humanity's separation from God and of the selfishness and discord that exists in individuals and society. Baptism commissioned Christians to evangelism, both as individuals and as a parish.[30]

A.P. suggested no ceremonial elaborations of the rite, such as giving the newly baptized candles or white garments. The brochure noted that baptism could be by dipping or immersion according to the Prayer Book's rubrics, but made no argument for the richer sign-value of immersion.

"In Newness of Life:" A Guide for Self-Examination (1954), illustrated by Allan Rohan Crite, offered a practical way for individuals to link

eucharistic worship with eucharistic living by guiding the user through an examination of conscience based on the structure of the eucharistic liturgy itself. The pamphlet built creatively on the Prayer Book's exhortation to those troubled in conscience to seek priestly counsel. Since the Prayer Book provided no form for sacramental confession, the brochure printed the rite from the South African Prayer Book as a suggestion.

A.P.'s *Christian Burial* (1955) and *Holy Matrimony and the Christian Family* (1960), with its striking illustrations by H. Boone Porter, tried to rein in cultural customs and extravagances that conflicted with Christian values, in addition to providing a commentary informed by the liturgical movement on a major cycle of Prayer Book liturgies which touched people at critical moments in their lives when they were apt to be receptive. *The Daily Office* (1963) attempted to make the discipline of daily liturgical prayer more popularly available.

The brochures reflected A.P.'s cautious public tenor through the 1950s and into the next decade. A.P. did not criticize the text of the Prayer Book, though it did criticize practice. A.P. focused on teaching parishes how to make the most of the liturgy as it stood; it tried to revivify the symbols by teaching what the symbols were grounded in; and it tried to represent liturgy not as creating an alternative to the reality of the secular world, but as the ritual representation of what Christians ought to be up to in the world. But neither the church as a whole nor A.P. was yet willing to act on the mounting historical and pastoral evidence that the old forms would have to change.

In 1954 A.P. launched a quarterly journal that showed what renewed liturgical consciousness might mean for the church in relation to art, architecture, social relations, parish organization, personal devotion, and Christian education. *Sharers* evolved from some newsletters that shared news and ideas solely among the A.P. members into a quarterly review that kept open a line of communication in the church among those interested in practical liturgical renewal in the parishes.[31]

Its circulation was small, only 488 subscribers at its peak. Prohibitive printing costs finally drove it out of business in 1962, to be succeeded by A.P.'s current newsletter, Open, in 1968.[32] But during a crucial period in the development of liturgical awareness in the church, Sharers was the only publication of its kind, presenting articles of help and interest to the parishes of the church interested in liturgical renewal, as well as offering a distinctly Episcopal viewpoint on and contribution to the liturgical movement.

The articles in Sharers generally were pastoral in tone, written by local rectors or laity who had some liturgical knowledge. Scholars like Massey Shepherd, H. Boone Porter, professor at Nashotah House and then at General Theological Seminary, William H. Nes, professor at Seabury-Western Theological Seminary, and others wrote articles that backed up pastoral advice with scholarship.

Social issues appeared as early as 1955, with the article "Segregation and the Eucharist," which argued from the liturgy of the Holy Communion against discrimination. Articles on urban and industrial issues, the social implications of, for example, the prayer for the whole state of Christ's church, and the congregation's mission in the world made specific the connections between liturgy and society.[33]

Art and architecture, especially the renovation of church buildings to accommodate altars facing the people, drew some practical guidance from A.P., as well as a theological rationale for liturgical space. Henry H. Breul, then rector of the newly built St. David's Church, Topeka, Kansas, reported, "We are rethinking everything we do liturgically, for what made sense in the old building does not necessarily do so in the new one"—which was exactly the kind of realization A.P. wanted to encourage: change the furniture around and you begin to change perceptions and behavior.[34]

Sharers kept readers in touch with liturgical developments on the ecumenical scene. Alfred R. Shands reported on the movement in

Europe. H. Boone Porter's 1960 description of participating in the liturgy of the Church of South India showed Episcopalians something of what they themselves would be doing in seven years.[35]

Sharers reported on the need for the liturgical movement in Australia, carried news of the 1961 Pan-Orthodox Conference where the Episcopal Church was the only American church represented, and described the liturgy consummating the 1962 Concordat of Communion between the Episcopal Church and the Philippine Independent Church. The liturgical movement's effect on worldwide Anglicanism, the progress of Prayer Book revision in other countries, and new forms of Anglican church architecture were reported in editor Frederick W. Putnam's 1961 account of his globe-circling tour of Anglican churches and mission stations.[36]

Sharers did not neglect to offer practical help on parish ceremonial, either. Massey Shepherd and Boone Porter, for instance, wrote on rubrical observance and how to make imaginative use of the elements of the Prayer Book to highlight theological emphases of the liturgical movement.* There were articles on Morning and

---

*Porter's article, "Commemorating Our Lord's Blessed Baptism," *Sharers* V (Fall 1959): 5-7, offers an insight into one of the ways in which A.P. during this period tried to make the Prayer Book speak in the accents of the liturgical movement.

Porter offered an ingenious way for "a normal, altar-centered parish, where the Prayer Book is loyally followed" to recover observance of the theologically rich feast of Christ's baptism, which in the 1928 Prayer Book was the gospel for the Second Sunday after Epiphany.

Porter suggested that:

1) The decoration of the church, music chosen, vestments, and so on, be festive.

2) With patience and luck, one could cull from *The Hymnal 1940* a few selections that had relevance to Christ's baptism, though not a single hymn was devoted primarily to this theme.

3) Where shortened Morning Prayer preceded the eucharist, the priest could invoke the "special occasions rubric" on p. viii of the Prayer Book and select a psalm and Old Testament lesson suited to the day.

(continued...)

Evening Prayer, the mechanics of offertory processions, and roga-
tion processions. Howard R. Kunkle described how his Fort Scott,
Kansas, parish experimented with an observance of Pentecost by a
project of evangelism to lapsed members and the unchurched and of
community-building within the parish. For several years, *Sharers* ran
a column called "Parish Music for the Holy Communion" which
recommended hymns and service music suited to the liturgical
seasons. With these and similar articles, A.P. shared experience
among parishes, broadened awareness of the ceremonial possibilities
of the Prayer Book, and encouraged experimentation.[37]

The ministry of the laity, use of oil in baptism and confirmation
(which A.P.'s brochures did not mention), the parish eucharist,
youth ministry, sickness and healing, and a host of other issues testify
to the breadth of the liturgical movement A.P. helped bring to bear
on the church.[38]

A.P. fostered liturgical renewal beyond its own member parishes
in the late 1950s with an important book of Holy Week services

---

*(...continued)

4) Public baptism could be celebrated "with maximum dignity."

5) If there was no baptism, a procession could be made to the font after the
creed. On the basis of the rubric on p. 71 of the Prayer Book allowing "the
Bidding Prayer, or other authorized prayers and intercessions" at this point, the
priest could lead the congregation in: a) the Trinity Sunday collect, as a thanksgiving for the revelation of the Trinity; b) as petitions for the worthy administration and reception of baptism and confirmation, the two prayers for this purpose
from the Form of Consecration of a Church or Chapel; c) and as a thanksgiving
for the congregation's own baptism, the concluding thanksgiving from the
baptismal rite, changing the appropriate words from singular to plural. Hymns
could be sung on the way to and from the font.

6) The significance of the occasion must be expounded in the sermon.

It took some gerrymandering, but the rite that resulted did no violence to
Prayer Book rubrics while encouraging an imaginative use of the book's elements. At the same time, it inevitably demonstrated the shortcomings and
frustrations of the 1928 Prayer Book. The 1979 Prayer Book and *The Hymnal
1982* have full provisions for observing this feast with appropriate psalms,
readings, songs, and renewal of baptismal vows, and it is one of the four times of
the year recommended for baptism.

and another book which encouraged celebrating the eucharist facing the people by offering practical ceremonial guidelines. A.P.'s books expanded the liturgical possibilities available to the whole church.

Before the Holy Table (1956), based on a paper Massey Shepherd presented to A.P., offered a flexible guide to offertory and gospel processions as well as celebrating the eucharist at altars facing the people—an art which was by no means self-evident.[39] More and more churches were building freestanding altars, A.P. noted, and some ceremonial guidance was urgently needed.[40]

A.P.'s *Holy Week Offices* (1958), which Shepherd edited, offered a round of services complementing those in the Prayer Book. The genius of *Holy Week Offices* was that its rites were designed not to replace the appointed public worship of the church but to fit "to the spirit and rhythm, no less than to the doctrine, of the Church's official liturgy." Almost the entire content of the book was drawn from scripture, the Prayer Book, and the hymnal.[41]

Holy Week Offices exemplified the kind of creative use A.P. made of the Prayer Book to promote liturgical renewal—in this case, the new "special devotions" rubric of the 1928 Prayer Book which allowed services in addition to Holy Communion, Morning and Evening Prayer, and the Litany or in place of Morning and Evening Prayer. With the authorization of their local bishops, A.P. said, it had used the offices in member parishes and now offered them for the enrichment of the wider church's liturgical life.[42]

By criticizing the Prayer Book's liturgies in imaginative ways, and supplementing them with other traditional services, A.P. provided parishes with a practical way to answer pastoral needs according to the genius of their own church's history and ethos, without displacing the Prayer Book with foreign rites whose temperament and theology were not always congruent with Anglicanism.

The book suggested several ways to combine Morning and Evening Prayer, the Litany, the Holy Communion, and Holy Baptism with the supplemental material A.P. provided. A.P. complemented the Prayer Book rites with a service of blessing of palms and procession for Palm Sunday; the way of the cross, using only those nine stations which could be substantiated from scripture; tenebrae for Wednesday, Thursday, and Friday of Holy Week; a Good Friday rite of ante-communion, bidding prayers and collects, and reproaches; and an Easter Even service of lighting of the paschal candle and a vigil. The book did not provide supplementary services for Maundy Thursday. The two obvious enrichments would have been foot-washing and reservation of the sacrament at an altar of repose for consumption on Good Friday. The 1928 Prayer Book's eucharistic gospel for Maundy Thursday presented a choice of either the Lukan passion account or the Johannine foot-washing story. Just two years before A.P.'s book, the restored Roman Catholic Holy Week rites of 1956 provided for a ceremony of washing feet in parishes, which until then had been restricted to cathedrals and abbeys. An added ceremony of foot-washing might have dove-tailed neatly with the Prayer Book, but perhaps the custom was still too foreign to Episcopal parish experience. Omission of reservation of the sacrament at an altar of repose for communion on Good Friday was more understandable given the dubious theological and legal status of reservation in Anglicanism. If Anglicans did reserve the sacrament, it was understood to be for communion of the sick and shut-ins, not for distribution to a congregation in church. Anglican custom in earlier centuries had been to celebrate the Holy Communion on Good Friday. The 1928 Prayer Book provided eucharistic propers for Good Friday, but such celebrations were practically unknown in the Episcopal Church by this time.

An important feature of the book was A.P.'s concern to restore the baptismal character of the Easter liturgy. Holy Baptism could form the climax of the various patterns offered for Easter Even.

Where the service is held at night, it may not be practicable to have the Baptism of Infants, but it is most appropriate at such a time to administer Baptism to adults. . . . When the Bishop is present, Confirmation may be administered [to adults] immediately after Holy Baptism.[43]

Though the schema A.P. offered still were a ways from articulating a coherent theology for the reintegration of the rites of initiation into the theological context of the paschal mystery, they were a step along the way. Many of A.P.'s Holy Week rites were incorporated into the third edition of the *Book of Offices* and ultimately into the 1979 Prayer Book.

A.P.'s Liturgical Conferences: 1958, 1959, 1962

In 1954 Arthur C. Lichtenberger, then bishop of Missouri and from 1958 to 1964 presiding bishop, asked A.P. to hold a conference with some of his clergy to educate them in the liturgical movement. For the first time, A.P. began to discuss seriously the possibility of holding liturgical conferences to raise awareness of the liturgical movement, spread an idea of what its theology might mean for the church, and inspire the church with a renewed ideal of liturgy, ecclesiology, and mission.[44]

Liturgical conferences were part and parcel of the movement's methodology. Roman Catholics in the United States had held liturgical days since 1929 and liturgical weeks since 1940.[45] William Palmer Ladd had organized an interdenominational Liturgical League "to promote the study of the Liturgy," which held several conferences at Berkeley Divinity School in the 1930s.[46] American Methodists in 1946 formed an association known as the Order of St. Luke (not to be confused with the Episcopal association of the same name involved in the healing ministry) to advance the cause of the liturgical movement in their church and began to hold annual convocations in 1948.[47] Lutherans began sponsoring liturgical institutes each year at Valparaiso University in Valparaiso, Indiana, in 1949.

A.P. co-sponsored three major national liturgical conferences—in 1958 with Grace Church, Madison, Wisconsin, the "mother church" of A.P.; in 1959 with St. Paul's Church, San Antonio, Texas; and in 1962 with St. James's Church, Wichita, Kansas. The conferences galvanized the attention of the whole Episcopal Church, drew ecumenical participation, and attracted hundreds of people to hear experts discuss the theology and practice of liturgical renewal. The conference papers were published, carrying the message of the liturgical movement to an even wider audience and bringing A.P. to prominence as a leader of the liturgical movement.[48]

More than 130 people attended the May 19–21, 1958, conference held in conjunction with Grace Church's centennial celebration, on "The Liturgical Renewal of the Church." Lichtenberger, who was elected presiding bishop the following October, delivered one of the conference's major papers, on the social implications of liturgical renewal.

Bishops supported and attended the conference, including Donald H.V. Hallock of Milwaukee, the conference's episcopal patron; William H. Brady of Fond du Lac; John P. Craine of Indianapolis; and Edward C. Turner of Kansas. All the participants in this conference were clergy except for nineteen laypeople, six of whom were women.[49]

A.P.'s old friend Theodore O. Wedel, speaking on the theology of the liturgical renewal, offered an important exposition of Dom Odo Casel's "mystery theology" of the eucharist, which he had learned under William Palmer Ladd's tutelage.[50] Casel's theology broke with medieval theological models and returned to patristic roots, opening up exhilarating possibilities for scholarly thought about such issues as eucharistic presence and sacrifice which bypassed many old points of division among churches. Casel articulated a vision of the liturgy as a continuation and appropriation in time of the saving action of the death and resurrection of Christ, the great sacrament or mystery. He anticipated the paschal understanding of the eucharist that became the common currency of liturgical thought a generation later. Because Casel wrote in German, his work was largely unavailable to English readers until its translation in 1962. Wedel applied Casel's theology to the Anglican context of common prayer and discussed how the new categories of thought Casel made available informed Episcopal thinking about the liturgy.

Massey Shepherd and Arthur C. Piepkorn of the Lutheran Church, Missouri Synod, set the liturgical movement in an ecumenical perspective. They discussed its progress among Roman Catholics, Lutherans, Presbyterians, Congregationalists, Reformed, Methodists, and Anglicans both in Europe and America. John O. Patterson brought the theology and principles of the liturgical movement down to the day-to-day life and work of Episcopal parishes, speaking on the pastoral implications of liturgical renewal. Patterson was not envisioning reform of structures of ministry or of the Prayer Book at this point, but his words bore significant implications for the future.

The success of the Madison conference was due largely to the organizing and directional skills of John H. Keene, then rector of Grace Church and one of the four co-founders of A.P. Keene died suddenly three months after the conference. Shepherd called his death a "great loss ... to the liturgical leadership of the Church."[51] The published volume of the conference's papers was dedicated to him.

So successful was the Madison conference that A.P. decided to do it again the following year. This time, some 700 clergy and laity attended the November 16–18, 1959, conference held in conjunction with the seventy-fifth anniversary of St. Paul's Church, San Antonio, Texas, on "The Eucharist and Liturgical Renewal." Participants heard about the implications of the eucharist for a theology of the church, the Bible, education, economic and social issues, and the ministry of the laity.[52]

The speakers at the first conference had been exclusively clerical. This time, the laity played a larger role. Dora P. Chaplin, assistant professor of pastoral theology at General Theological Seminary, spoke on the eucharist and education. Frank S. Cellier, a layman who began to teach liturgy at Seabury-Western Theological Seminary in 1959 as a nonstipendiary faculty member, discussed the ministry of the laity.

Alexander Schmemann, eminent liturgical scholar of the Orthodox Church, assessed how the Orthodox eucharistic liturgy exemplified the ideals of the liturgical movement. Bishop Stephen F. Bayne, Executive Officer of the Anglican Communion and former bishop of Olympia, argued for the centrality of the eucharist as the pattern of the church's worship and life through a recovery of a sense of the personal and social responsibility which is at the heart of the eucharist. John M. Holt, associate professor of Hebrew and Old Testament at the Episcopal Theological Seminary of the Southwest in Austin, Texas, discussed "The Eucharist and the Bible." Wilford O. Cross, professor of philosophy of religion and ethics at the University of the South, Sewanee, Tennessee, outlined the "Economic and Social Implications of the Eucharist." As at the Madison conference the year before, bishops supported the San Antonio conference and addressed its sessions. Everett H. Jones, bishop of West Texas, and his suffragan, R. Earl Dicus, were the conference's episcopal patrons. Jones gave a welcoming address. John P. Craine of Indianapolis preached on "The Eucharistic Life" at the conference's closing choral eucharist.

A new ecumenical and liturgical world was opening up by the time of A.P.'s November 5–7, 1962, liturgical conference in Wichita, Kansas. The Second Vatican Council had begun that year in Rome. It was too early to see exactly where Vatican II would lead, but it was clear that the liturgical scene was on the verge of momentous changes. A spirit of generosity, optimism, and confidence was abroad.

A.P. invited Roman Catholic leaders to the conference, and both Roman Catholic and Episcopal bishops encouraged their people to attend. Gerald Ellard, S.J. (1894–1963), one of the pioneers of the liturgical movement in Roman Catholicism, was present. The Roman Catholic Bishop of Wichita, Mark W. Carroll, attended a presentation on "The Liturgical Movement in the Roman Catholic Church" by Fr. Joseph T. Nolan, who had been active for many years as an author and speaker in his church's liturgical movement.

More than 950 people from forty-six states heard speakers explore the connection between liturgy and the urban, artistic, and scientific worlds.[53] Shepherd's keynote address "Liturgy and Mission" set the conference's theme. Bishop James A. Pike of California, already well-known through his books, lectures, and television appearances, preached on "The Liturgy and Work" at the conference's concluding choral eucharist. The church's mission to the artist, to a scientific culture, and to urban society were addressed. W. Moelwyn Merchant, head of the English department at Exeter University, England, spoke to the arts. William G. Pollard, executive director of the Oak Ridge Institute of Nuclear Studies in Tennessee, who had worked for two years on the Manhattan Project, which produced the atomic bomb, addressed scientific culture. C. Kilmer Myers, director of the Urban Training Center, Chicago, and a pioneer in inner-city ministry, spoke to urban concerns. The bishop of Kansas, Edward C. Turner, a long-time supporter of the liturgical movement who had attended A.P.'s two previous conferences, was the episcopal sponsor of the Wichita conference.

The 1962 conference was "an outstanding milestone in the liturgical thinking of the Church," in the estimation of Frank S. Cellier who edited the conference's papers for publication. A steadily expanding interest in the liturgy was a sign of the church's "desire to reassume the ancient kerygmatic obligation which it owes more than ever to the world of the later twentieth century," Cellier said.[54]

The letters of appreciation that A.P. president Frederick W.

Putnam received and the speakers who called it "the finest conference of its kind they had ever attended" made him feel "that we
have all been part of something quite significant in the life of the
Church."[55]

A.P.'s liturgical conferences succeeded because at a critical moment they focused comprehensive treatments of the theology and
activity of the liturgical movement and showed the movement's
connection to all aspects of life. What A.P. offered was a complete
re-thinking of the relation between church and world grounded in
a renewed theology of the church and expressed in the liturgy.
A.P.'s conferences gave the church a place to experience and reflect
on the revitalization of church life offered by liturgical renewal.

"It is very encouraging as I get about the Church to see the
growing liturgical awareness of more and more parishes," A.P.
member Arthur E. Walmsley wrote in 1961.

> It would be presumptuous to think that A.P. is the sole cause of this,
> but at the same time it is gratifying to know how much influence
> our group has had on liturgical revival in America.[56]

Social Action and Liturgical Worship

The tensions of the cold war with its fearful atmosphere of a world
divided East from West, the growth of a consumerist society, and
the early civil rights movement, which laid bare a society in crisis
but also pregnant with the possibility of change, were some of the
social realities A.P. faced as it worked out the relation between
liturgy and society in the 1950s and 1960s.

Politicians exploited the public's fear of communism in the late
1940s and 1950s. Hearings by the House Un-American Activities
Committee and by Senator Joseph R. McCarthy recklessly pursued
people deemed disloyal or subversive. Their tactics included use of
unidentified informers, the flimsiest evidence, pressure on witnesses
to name former associates, vague and sweeping accusations against

individuals, and the assumption of a person's guilt because of association with a suspect organization.

The Korean War (1950–1953) and the trial in 1951 and execution in 1953 of two American citizens, Julius and Ethel Rosenberg, on charges of passing top secret information on nuclear weapons to the Soviet Union during World War II gave substance to fears that the nation was engaged in a grave struggle with an alien ideology fomented by communists abroad and subversives at home.

The epithet of "subversive" could include anyone who questioned the capitalist economic system. A.P. had no direct confrontation with these political events. But in this volatile atmosphere, A.P. drew out the implications of liturgy to articulate some basic theological convictions about ownership, property, and the ultimate loyalty of workers during the 1950s. Capitalism did not win unqualified support.

In 1951, A.P. adopted its "Principles Concerning the Christian Use of Property," which were incorporated into the Accepted Corporate Program. A.P. committed itself to "teach and preach" that no one can lay claim to "*absolute* ownership or control of property" and that "every individual is entitled to the use of such a measure of property, for the material necessities of his existence, as will afford him personal security and freedom."[57]

Two theological convictions underlay A.P.'s economic principles: 1) God is Lord of all creation and humans are entrusted with a stewardship of property, for which they must ultimately give an account to God; 2) since humans are sinners "they cannot assure justice and peace among themselves, by any system either of collective or of private ownership of property." Private property is not contrary to the will of God, A.P. said, but it demands responsible use.[58]

It was not the church's job to define or impose economic or political systems on society, A.P. said. The church must "constantly proclaim" the "basic truths" of the lordship of God and sinfulness of humanity. On men and women fell the "responsibility of developing ways and means, political and economic, whereby these rights and responsibilities can be maintained."[59]

A.P. grappled with the Christian's attitude toward mass-producing, mass-consuming industrialized society, with its attendant abundance as well as alienation between consumers and producers and loss of individual control of decisions about one's own work, in its 1959 brochure *The Christian Meaning of Work*. A.P. did not advocate any economic system, capitalist, socialist, or communist in this brochure. "That society in which men enjoy the opportunities and rewards of their work is a better society than one in which work is frustrating or exploited." A.P. aimed not at changing economic systems, but the human heart. "The place where work goes wrong first is in the hearts of the men involved," the pamphlet said. "It is there that the change must be made."[60]

What distinguished A.P.'s approach was that it related its vision of an economically just society to the eucharist. Preeminently in the eucharist, redeemed humanity offered its work to God for blessing and redemption. The eucharist, A.P. taught, was the paradigm for economic justice. The eucharist was the reference point for the individual, in society with others, to find a meaning in work beyond expediency or mere conformity with laws and accepted morality by using one's skills and talents for good or evil under God's judgment.[61]

A.P. entered into one of the most volatile social justice issues of the day when it declared its commitment in November 1962 to work "for the accomplishment of cultural and racial unity in Parish and Diocese, open occupancy in neighborhoods and desegregation in public and church schools."[62] A.P. based itself on the liturgy. Since all races and cultures depend on Christ and are interdependent with one another, "we will do all in our power to extend the human unity of the altar rail into the streets and neighborhoods of the communities served by our parishes."[63]

Barely a month earlier, Martin Luther King, Jr., had excoriated white religious leaders for their "abysmal silence" during the crisis surrounding the entry of James Meredith into the University of Mississippi, when federal troops had quelled white rioters. "Where was the cry of the Lord's prophets?" King asked. Recalling the sight of churches set in a landscape of segregation, King said, "When I review the painful memory of the last week at Oxford [Mississippi] and cannot recall a single voice 'crying in the wilderness,' the questions are still the same: 'What kind of people worship there? Who is their God?'"[64]

Many white clergy remained unmoved by King's appeal in the early 1960s. As nonviolent demonstrations picked up across the South—and on the very eve of King's June 1963 "Letter From Birmingham City Jail" directed primarily to the conscience of American white churches—eight white clergy opposed King openly and said that demonstrations were "unwise and untimely." The signers included bishops in the Episcopal, Methodist, and Roman Catholic churches, a Presbyterian moderator, a Baptist pastor, and a rabbi.[65]

A.P.'s action in 1962 came just as the church was beginning to face up to its own segregation policies, which it had begun to dismantle in the late 1940s.[66] In 1962, John Burgess of Massachusetts was elected the first black suffragan bishop in the United States since 1918, and in 1970 he became the first black bishop of an American diocese. The 1964 General Convention prohibited racial discrimination in Episcopal parishes. Clergy and laity in the Episcopal Society for Cultural and Racial Unity (ESCRU), founded in 1958, as well as other clergy and laity from other churches who were strong supporters of civil rights, took part in sit-ins and participated in March 1965 with King in the second Selma-to-Montgomery march.[67]

A.P.'s commitment to desegregation was part of a thorough recasting of the Social Action section of the Accepted Corporate Program. The principles on use of property were reduced to two points, and new agendas were made matters of explicit A.P. policy: the obligation to work for a solution to chronic unemployment, responsibility to participate in the political party of one's choice, and desegregation.

The 1962 revision was not passed without what the minutes called *"fervent* discussion"[68] or what Samuel E. West more bluntly called "a great deal of rough talk and worry."[69] At issue was A.P.'s fundamental identity and mission. Agendas were beginning to conflict, the liturgical versus the social. A.P. was struggling to spell out what it owed to each, even as it tried to bring liturgy to the "cutting edge" of social change.

Bonnell Spencer, O.H.C., A.P.'s only monastic member, feared A.P. was letting a social action agenda take over its liturgical renewal program and commitment to liturgy, from which all other endeavors must grow. "This is the core responsibility which is ours," Spencer said. Carl Sayers, who as chairman of the Committee on Revision of the Corporate Program was responsible for the 1962 draft, "insisted on A.P. accepting the implications of his revision, so we can speak to the world beyond our own parishes."[70] A.P. compromised by agreeing not to release the new Accepted Corporate Program publicly until the full membership had reviewed it. Spencer withdrew his objection and the program was passed.[71]

The tension between liturgical worship and its consequences, and social action as the applied result of liturgical worship, had concerned A.P. for years, West said in a December 1962 letter to A.P. secretary James Joseph. One can't live without the other. But, he added, "I do think A.P. must avoid the arrogance of trying to be all things to all men." Coming off the heady success of its three national liturgical conferences with their "great stirring papers and startling people . . . we get tempted to solve or try to solve all the problems in the social order, right now!"[72]

One issue A.P. refused to have anything to do with was aligning the church with anti-communist crusades. Trevor Huddleston, C.R., Bishop of Masasi, Tanganyika, sketched for an A.P. audience at St. James's Church, Wichita, Kansas, on All Saints' Day 1961 a sense of black Africans' perspective on the cold war and the Christian churches' performance in Africa. Americans at the time had firsthand experience of the importance of third world countries in the cold war. Huddleston's talk came midway between the defeat of the Bay of Pigs invasion of Cuba in April 1961, which was prepared by the U.S. Central Intelligence Agency, and the Cuban missile crisis of October 1962 that brought a tense world to the edge of nuclear war.

Huddleston's remarks were printed in *Sharers*. His response to a questioner who asked about the danger of communism in Africa ran to two printed pages. "I'm not obsessed with this bogey of Communism as the only enemy," Huddleston said. "The only enemy is the reality that while two-thirds of the world are hungry, one-third has never had it so good—and in that third lies the bulk of the Christian Church."

> The Churches' job in Africa is not to fight Communism. Let me say this as strongly as I can say it. THE CHURCHES' JOB IN AFRICA IS NOT TO FIGHT COMMUNISM. It is to be faithful to the Lord Jesus Christ, and Communism can take care of itself.[73]

The editorial page of *Sharers* agreed with him. But, said editor Frederick W. Putnam, "many will misunderstand what he said. He was, of course, saying that the Church's greatest defense against Communism is an aggressive OFFENSE to preach and live the Gospel everywhere in the world. If we would do that, in his opinion, Communism would be put on the defensive and would eventually disappear."[74]

Whatever the merits or limits of A.P.'s political and economic insight, it was able to stand apart from and criticize its culture. It did so from a unique perspective within the Episcopal Church, the perspective of the day-by-day and week-by-week worship in parishes. By examining the assumptions and implications of the liturgy, A.P. helped create an idea of the social demands of the Prayer Book and was a force in the church's critical self-reflection.

A.P. spoke in a grammar Episcopalians could understand, whether they agreed with it or not, when it appealed to the Prayer Book and forged links between it and the social questions of the day. A.P. increased awareness that social action was a consequence of eucharistic worship and an inherent part of eucharistic living. The church as well as the individual must engage in redemptive activity by educating itself and by participating in local and national organizations that promoted the welfare of all people. The church could learn to live more nearly as it prayed, A.P. taught, by attending to the wellspring of redemptive activity, the liturgy.

By articulating a connection between liturgy and culture, A.P. was also a force for liturgical change since it raised the expectation that in the liturgy people should be able to catch the accent of the concerns and needs of their own time. A.P. helped the church define the connection between the offering of worship and the offering of life, between cult and culture, and the liturgical expression of that connection.

The Changing Liturgical Context

The new liturgies of the Church of South India in the 1950s were an index of the forces driving the liturgical movement on the eve of ecumenical reforms in western churches. The CSI was formed in 1947 by a union of Anglicans, Methodists, and a united church of former Presbyterians, Congregationalists, Reformed, and Lutherans. Its eucharistic liturgy attracted widespread attention when it first appeared in 1950. A confirmation rite also came out in 1950, baptism was first published in 1955, and other rites followed in a series of booklets. The rites were revised and collected in The Book of Common Worship in 1963.[75]

The South Indian experiment had three important implications for western churches. First, the CSI's rites represented a modern attempt to fashion a living liturgy growing out of the life and culture of the worshiping community, using the resources of the liturgical movement. Second, the church's liturgy aimed at ecumenical consensus by transcending the heritages of the uniting churches while still being in continuity with them. The liturgy intentionally borrowed Eastern Christian liturgical elements—such as a memorial acclamation in the eucharistic prayer—in a gesture toward appropriating classical liturgical forms. Third, and perhaps most significantly, its rites of eucharist and baptism were fashioned by a church which experienced itself as "only a small minority in the midst of a passively resisting, if not actively hostile, non-Christian environment."[76]

Most people in the Episcopal Church, however, flush with postwar optimism about the prospects for American society, either did not yet see the significance of or necessity for liturgical change, or thought the existing forms could supply what was needed. The 1953 eucharistic rite in *Prayer Book Studies IV*, as we have seen, was essentially backward-looking.

In many parishes, the family service became popular during the 1950s. The service furthered some of the practices of the liturgical movement, but its premise was fundamentally at odds with the aims of liturgical renewal. The family service was an outgrowth of the religious education movement which was part of the general resurgence in American church life after World War II.[77] The goal of the family service was not to restore the centrality of eucharistic worship, but to encourage family attendance at Sunday worship as integral to a parish education program. Some parishes instituted weekly parish communions as their family service, but others used Morning Prayer—though, significantly, many Morning Prayer parishes began to institute a eucharist for the family service.

From a liturgical point of view, the assumptions of the religious education movement reversed the priorities of, for example, A.P.'s parish education program. The religious education movement treated worship not as an end in itself but as a "resource" for another agenda, Christian education. How could A.P. teach the normative use of the parish eucharist and all that it implied in conjunction with a program that described worship as an adjunct, A.P. asked?[78] As Massey Shepherd put it at a 1956 A.P. meeting, instead of experiencing the Christian faith in the eucharist and using the classroom to draw out the meaning of the liturgy, the religious education movement took the classroom as the experience and used liturgy to explain that experience. The religious education movement also refused to face the question of the centrality of the eucharist as the source of the gospel and of Christian experience.[79]

Meanwhile, several experiments with eucharistic liturgies exercised a large influence ecumenically. *An Experimental Liturgy* (1958), developed by a group of Church of England priests and laity, and *Liturgy Coming to Life* (1960), containing the rite celebrated in Clare College, Cambridge, made only moderate changes in the text of the 1662 English Prayer Book. But the title of the Clare College experiment tells the story. It was the manner and spirit in which these liturgies were celebrated that excited a revitalized experience of eucharistic worship.[80] Booklets like these, which had the text of the rite and an explanation of it on facing pages, were common in English churches, particularly cathedrals, at this time. They could be found, for example, at Coventry Cathedral, a new cathedral which attracted widespread interest, and at Southwark Cathedral, where John A.T. Robinson presided over a diocese with many forward-looking initiatives.

The eucharistic liturgy of the ecumenical monastic community of Taizé in France, published in French in 1959 and in English in 1962, succeeded in the same way, shifting attention from categories of text to categories of experience. To only read the text misses the power and appeal of the Taizé liturgy, in its simplicity, full involvement of the people in prayer and song, and atmosphere of concentrated prayerfulness.[81]

In the United States, new services came into use among Lutherans in 1958, and among Presbyterians, the United Church of Christ, and Methodists in 1964. In the Anglican Communion, Prayer Book revision was at various stages of preparation or completion. The Anglican Church of Canada issued a new Prayer Book in 1959. The Church of India, Pakistan, Burma, and Ceylon followed in 1960. The churches of Japan and of the West Indies issued revised eucharistic liturgies with other parts of the Prayer Book in 1959. Liturgical commissions were at work on revisions of the eucharist in the churches of England, Ireland, Wales, Australia, and New Zealand. New Zealand's 1966 eucharistic rite was the first Anglican liturgy to be phrased in modern contemporary English. In the Wider Episcopal Fellowship, new eucharistic rites came into use in the Philippine Independent Church in 1961, and in the Lusitanian Church in Portugal in 1963.[82] So fast did liturgical developments move, however, that within twenty years liturgies developed in the 1950s and 1960s were out of date and began to be recast.

Among Roman Catholics, the papal encyclicals *Mystici Corporis* in 1943 and *Mediator Dei* in 1947 made unmistakably evident the Roman church's commitment to liturgical reform. With *Mystici Corporis*, the Roman Catholic Church officially approved an exposition of the doctrine of the church which had been at the heart of liturgical movement theology. *Mediator Dei*, an interpretation of the liturgy itself, was taken by Roman Catholic proponents of the liturgical movement as the very charter and vindication of their efforts—though opponents were quick to point out that the encyclical put the brakes on certain experiments and practices.

"Were Our Own Liturgists Afoul?" asked one unsympathetic American Roman Catholic commentator in 1949, cataloguing what seemed to him suspicious practices of the time—most of which became official policy within twenty years. Practices such as offertory processions, mass facing the people, refusal to say mass at a side altar while another mass was being celebrated at the main altar "lest the alleged unity of the Sacrifice be interfered with," discouraging confessions of devotion because the Confiteor of the mass was held sufficient to forgive venial sins, deemphasis of public recitation of the rosary and of novenas, and, crowning horror of all, "even a people's sacerdotal offering of the Mass was taught by implication."[83]

A series of reforms to clarify and simplify the Roman Catholic rites began after World War II: a new critical edition of the Latin psalter in 1945, restoration of the Easter Vigil (1951) and then of all the Holy Week rites (1955), a simplification of rubrics (1955), codification of the kinds of liturgical participation by the people (1958), and a full code of simplified rubrics for the missal and breviary (1960).

More tangibly, reforms brought the people into a new experience of the liturgy. More use of the vernacular began to be allowed in certain sacraments other than the mass and in non-sacramental rites when a bilingual Ritual for the United States was approved in 1954. The dialogue mass (which restored a measure of active lay participation in the mass by having the entire congregation make the Latin responses in dialogue with the priest),[84] evening masses (1953), and a shortened fast before communion (1953, 1957) reshuffled people's perceptions of their relation to the eucharist, and, most basically, suggested to popular perception the notion of development and change in what seemed an ageless, changeless cult.

Voluntary associations in the United States such as the Liturgical Arts Society (1928–1972), the Liturgical Conference (1940–present), and the Vernacular Society (1946–1965) reminded Roman Catholics that the then-present order of things was not ideal and prompted them to think about liturgical issues, to discuss, and to plan.[85] Books like Gerald Ellard's *Mass of the Future* (1948) and *Mass in Transition* (1956) illustrated the dramatic changes that lay ahead in Roman Catholic liturgy and even provided photographs of liturgical experiments that showed what the future would look like.[86]

Advances in scholarship had put the study of liturgy on a new footing following World War II. Better access to ancient documents, a re-evaluation of ancient sources, a shift in presuppositions, and a growing ecumenical consensus in the interpretation of sources offered a new understanding of the nature and purpose of Christian worship, and therefore of the direction of future reform.

Dom Gregory Dix's great summation, *The Shape of the Liturgy,* published in 1945, outlined the liturgical and doctrinal problems that would have to be faced in any future liturgical revision—and succeeded in communicating the issues not just to scholars but to a reading public as well.[87] The first printing sold out within three months, and the book is still in print. The implications of Dix's "fat green book," as he called it, began to be seen in American cities in 1947 when Dix organized a series of celebrations of the eucharist according to ancient patterns in various Episcopal churches.

Dix's fundamental contribution was that he defined liturgy as an action, not as a text. He shifted attention from static to dynamic categories, from texts to structures of activity. His determination of the basic "shape" of eucharistic praying—taking, giving thanks, breaking, sharing—influenced the outline of virtually every eucharistic rite from the Church of South India's in 1950 to those in the 1993 Presbyterian Book of Common Worship. Dix also succeeded in focusing attention on the Jewish roots of Christian worship and on the Jewish idea that consecration was effected by prayer in a pattern of giving thanks, not by a particular verbal formula. This new approach moved eucharistic theology away from medieval questions about presence, sacrifice, and ontological change, and into biblical categories of thought. Dix contributed to a realization that no single form of words was essential to effect eucharistic consecration, and that a diversity of eucharistic prayers not only was legitimate but probably had been the case since the beginning.[88]

Dix articulated a shift to a biblical and patristic basis for theological reflection on the church's liturgy. For Anglicans, this involved the realization that touching up Cranmer would no longer do; the basis of liturgical scholarship had shifted from Cranmer to Hippolytus. Dix was among the first to see the considerable changes in many currently accepted ideas of liturgy and church polity implied by the text of Hippolytus. Burton Scott Easton's 1934 translation of *The Apostolic Tradition*, followed by Dix's critical edition and translation of the text published in 1937, opened for an English-reading audience the inner life, institutions, and prayer of a pre-Constantinian Christian community.

The summer liturgy program at the University of Notre Dame, founded in 1947 by Michael Mathis, C.S.C., brought European, and later American, scholars who created an American intellectual center for the study of liturgy.[89] Notre Dame's liturgy program has had a profound effect on American churches through the men and women it has trained who have gone on to teach, write, and assume positions of leadership in the liturgical affairs of their own churches.

Books developed from lectures in the summer liturgy courses, published in the "Liturgical Studies" series of Notre Dame Press, became staple reading during the 1950s and 1960s for Catholics and Protestants alike in seminaries and beyond. Students of liturgy continue to rely on many of them. Books like Louis Bouyer's *Liturgical Piety* (1954) and *Rite and Man* (1963); Jean Danielou's *The Bible and the Liturgy* (1956); and Josef Jungmann's *The Early Liturgy* (1959) were an index of the state of liturgical questions and disseminated an intellectual understanding of the theological, historical, and pastoral dimensions undergirding the liturgical movement. Jungmann's two-volume *The Mass of the Roman Rite* (1951) made accessible massive material on the development of the liturgy of the mass.[90]

Beginning in 1958 and continuing into the 1960s, the "Ecumenical Studies in Worship" series published by John Knox Press in Richmond, Virginia, made available liturgical studies by leading Protestant scholars such as Oscar Cullmann ("The Meaning of the

Lord's Supper in Primitive Christianity," in *Essays on the Lord's Supper*, 1958), Max Thurian of the Taizé community (*The Eucharistic Memorial*, 2 vols., 1960, 1961), Jean-Jacques von Allmen (*The Lord's Supper*, 1969), and others.

Books on liturgical theology by the Orthodox theologian Alexander Schmemann (*For the Life of the World*, which first appeared in 1963; current edition by St. Vladimir's Seminary Press, Crestwood, New York; and *Introduction to Liturgical Theology*, London, Faith Press, 1966) contributed an eastern perspective to liturgical thought.

Beginning in mid-century, a steady stream of studies in ritual, symbolism, sociology, and comparative religion influenced an understanding of liturgy as a product of a culture, and of a culture's influence on theological presuppositions—which prompted Anglicans to question the continued viability of sixteenth-century theology and its Cranmerian ritual expression.

The seminaries of the Episcopal Church played a key role in interpreting the flood of new liturgical information and preparing the church for liturgical reform.

William Palmer Ladd in the late 1930s had insisted that liturgy, "far from being a sort of extra or specialty, is at the very heart of the theological curriculum, and is an essential subject of study for parsons as for seminarians." If the church was to reach an alienated culture, the dean argued, the ideals of the liturgical movement had to permeate the church's leaders of parish worship.[91] After World War II, several seminaries began to teach liturgics. A.P. was well-represented among seminary faculty. Massey Shepherd, of course, was a founding member of A.P. and indebted to Ladd. Shepherd was prominent in shaping the liturgical perceptions of the rising postwar generation through his teaching at Episcopal Theological School, Cambridge, Massachusetts (1940–1953), and at Church Divinity School of the Pacific, Berkeley, California (1954–1981). Shepherd also gave many Episcopal priests their introduction to liturgical renewal while he was director of the summer graduate program at the University of the South in Sewanee, Tennessee (1951–1970).

Another A.P. member and seminary educator who was very much indebted to Ladd was C. Kilmer Myers. Myers graduated from Berkeley in 1940 and continued there as a fellow until 1942, then taught liturgics at General Theological Seminary from 1946 to 1952.[92] He was an A.P. member from 1966 to 1968, after his seminary career.

Howard H. Hassinger, who taught at Seabury-Western Theological Seminary, Evanston, Illinois, in the early 1950s, was an A.P. member from 1950 to about 1965. Frank S. Cellier, a layman who taught liturgics at Seabury-Western after Hassinger, served with A.P. from 1959 to 1966.

H. Boone Porter taught at Nashotah House from 1954 to 1960, when he went to General Theological Seminary, New York, where he not only taught liturgics to seminary students but also directed liturgical study at the doctoral level until 1970. Porter graduated from Berkeley Divinity School nine years after Ladd's death, but the school still cherished Ladd's ideals.[93] He received his doctorate from Oxford in 1954. Porter became an A.P. member in 1959 and still serves on A.P.'s council. He was president of the organization from 1973 to 1975.[94]

Two graduates of General's doctoral program, Thomas Talley and Marion Hatchett, became A.P. members. Talley taught liturgics at Nashotah House, Nashotah, Wisconsin, from 1963 to 1971, and succeeded Porter as professor of liturgics at General Theological Seminary from 1971 to 1989. He served with A.P. from 1966 to 1975. Hatchett went to the School of Theology at the University of the South in Sewanee, Tennessee, in 1969. He was an A.P. member from 1976 to about 1987.

Other A.P. members teaching in seminaries were David Babin (Seabury-Western), an A.P. member from 1966 to 1979; Dora P. Chaplin (General), with A.P. from 1966 to 1969; and Richard F.

Woods (Episcopal Theological Seminary of the Southwest), an A.P. member from 1966 to 1972.

Others who were important in shaping liturgical thought were Leonel L. Mitchell (Notre Dame and Seabury-Western), who was elected to A.P. in 1989, and Louis Weil (Nashotah House after Talley and then Church Divinity School of the Pacific), who was not an A.P. member. Mitchell was a graduate of General's doctoral program. Weil had studied for a year with Porter as a seminarian but his doctorate was from the Catholic Institute in Paris.

Charles Price (Virginia Theological Seminary) was an evangelical spokesman for liturgical issues. Daniel Stevick (Philadelphia Divinity School and Episcopal Divinity School, Cambridge, Massachusetts) interpreted issues of the language of worship and of initiation. Neither was an A.P. member.

Through its seminaries, the church was preparing itself to make a liturgical response to its age. Anglican bishops at the 1958 Lambeth Conference recognized that the Reformation-Elizabethan Prayer Book could no longer serve as the pattern for liturgy and bond of unity in worship and doctrine among Anglicans. "We have entered a period of liturgical change, with all the advantages and disadvantages of such a time," the bishops said. "The underlying assumption, and often the declared principle ... that the Prayer Book of 1662 should remain as the basic pattern, and, indeed, as a bond of unity in doctrine and in worship for our Communion as a whole" could no longer be insisted upon. "Now it seems clear that no Prayer Book, not even that of 1662, can be kept unchanged for ever, as a safeguard of established doctrine."[95]

Shepherd parsed the issue for Episcopalians in some lectures delivered in 1959.[96] Shepherd had been a member of the Standing Liturgical Commission since 1947. In the published version of the lectures he was careful to say that he spoke only for himself,[97] not for the commission, but his remarks reflected a shift in the perspective of one of the SLC's foremost members from 1946 when he thought further revision of the Prayer Book "would be untimely and unwise."[98]

> There is a larger problem to revision. . . . It is one that is only beginning to be understood, for it involves a whole new perspective of evaluation upon the fifty-year period of Prayer Book revision that culminated in 1928. The question now being raised in many minds is whether this era of revision does not represent the end of a cycle of liturgical reform that began at the Reformation and has been largely controlled by principles and perspectives both theological and liturgical established by Cranmer and his associates. It is certainly possible to pursue another major revision of the Prayer Book along the same guiding lines. But it must now be asked, would such a procedure be legitimate? Can we afford to develop our liturgical inheritance any longer within the framework of the first two Prayer Books of 1549 and 1552, by reference merely to enrichment and flexibility? Many believe that the liturgy can no longer stand the strain of such a procedure. Magnificent as was the achievement of the sixteenth-century reformers, it cannot speak effectively to the very much altered conditions in which the Church finds itself today.[99]

The next revision of the Prayer Book, Shepherd said, "will need a more ecumenical orientation and a greater sensitivity to fundamental sociological changes that have altered the situation of the Church in its surrounding world."[100]

Not only the cultural, but the theological context for liturgical revision had changed. New liturgical sources that had come to light in the previous fifty years had "received at the hands of technical scholars of all Christian communions an evaluation and interpretation that either bypasses or undercuts many of the issues of vital concern" to the sixteenth-century reformers.

> Biblical studies of the past two decades have set in a new frame the old problem of dominical institution of the sacraments, and given fresh insights into primitive liturgical forms of consecration. The whole question of the relation of Baptism and Confirmation has been reopened to creative inquiry and discussion. The Christian Year takes on fresh meaning in the light of theological interest in the meaning of time and of history, and of what is beyond time and

history. Such discussions, on an ecumenical plane, have all arisen since the work of the revisers of the Prayer Book in the 1920s, whose task was necessarily finished before the new materials and insights could have possibly come to their attention.[101]

"There are signs," Shepherd said, "among Anglican scholars of liturgical matters pointing to a whole new approach to Prayer Book revision that must at least be faced."[102]

To guide Anglican churches and provinces revising their eucharistic rites, the 1958 Lambeth Conference had called for creation of a set of recommendations on the structure of the eucharistic service "which would both conserve the doctrinal balance of the Anglican tradition and take account of present liturgical knowledge."[103]

The resulting document, "The Structure and Contents of the Eucharistic Liturgy," was published in 1965. The guidelines resulted from an unprecedented meeting of representatives of almost all the Anglican churches for exchange of information on urgent problems of Prayer Book revision and for development of channels of communication among the liturgical commissions of the various churches. The Consultation on the Liturgy which met in Toronto for two days following the Anglican Congress of August 1963 was arranged by Stephen F. Bayne, then Executive Officer of the Anglican Communion, who as noted earlier had spoken at A.P.'s 1959 liturgical conference in San Antonio.[104]

In both the structure and the content of the eucharistic rite it envisioned, the document showed Anglicanism's endorsement of the insights and emphases of a new generation of liturgical scholarship. A full service of the Word, expression of obligations to the world, and eucharistic consecration by giving thanks were its keynotes.

The document said celebration of the eucharist had five phases: 1) preparation; 2) service of the Word of God; 3) the great intercession; 4) service of the Lord's Supper; and 5) dismissal. The service of the Word should include readings from the Old Testament and psalmody; the great intercession should include prayer for the world as well as the church; the Lord's Supper should include placing of the gifts on the Lord's table, and the prayer of consecration should be in the form of "a thanksgiving for creation and for God's mighty acts in Christ and in sending the Holy Spirit," as well as a recital of the words and acts of Jesus at the Last Supper and a prayer for the communicants. Rites of preparation and dismissal should be brief and to the point.[105]

For Episcopalians on the eve of their own revision of the Prayer Book, it was the shape of things to come.

Chapter Four

The Turning Point

The need for a new Prayer Book had been apparent to the Standing Liturgical Commission since 1943. But for any new Prayer Book to win acceptance, the SLC realized, the church would have to "try on" the proposed rites.

As soon as the proposed eucharistic rite of *Prayer Book Studies IV* was published in 1953, the House of Bishops went on record advocating its experimental use at the discretion of individual bishops. The SLC, while sympathetic, interpreted the church's constitution as ruling out experimental use. So the SLC proposed to the 1955 General Convention an amendment to the constitution to make trial use unquestionably lawful.[1] The SLC's proposal never made it to the convention floor.

> In 1958 the same amendment was proposed. It got to the floor, was drastically changed after being referred to the Committees on the Constitution, and on the Prayer Book, and then was defeated.[2]

The SLC was "disturbed," it said, that its proposals had not been "properly interpreted" to General Convention. Part of the problem, the SLC said, was that parliamentary procedure prevented the SLC from presenting its proposals to the convention except through "mediate persons and groups." The SLC's amendments were referred to committees of the Houses of convention; the committees disposed of them as they wished.[3]

So just before the 1961 General Convention, the SLC made its case publicly, devoting an entire *Prayer Book Study* to explaining the reasons for trial use, the precedents for it among other Anglican churches, the mechanics of how it might work, and the advantages it had over any other method of Prayer Book revision. The SLC argued in *Prayer Book Studies XV: The Problem and Method of Prayer Book Revision* that the method of trial use was

> the best we can devise to ensure that the whole Church—that is to say, all its members—may have an opportunity to participate and express themselves in the development of our common liturgical life.[4]

A.P. wholeheartedly supported the SLC's attempt to have trial use authorized by the 1961 General Convention. Through its members, A.P. circulated a model resolution which local diocesan conventions could adopt to support the SLC's proposal for trial use. The resolution said that the diocesan convention "heartily commends" trial use "as a wholly practicable, desirable, and conservative method ... for testing the actual value of a liturgical text or form in advance of its final approval."[5] It is not clear if A.P. was the author of this resolution or only one of its propagators, nor how many dioceses adopted it, though a letter to Massey Shepherd in A.P.'s files mentions that the dioceses of California and West Texas had done so.[6]

The SLC had no member in the House of Deputies at the 1961 General Convention, so Shepherd was given the courtesy of the floor to present the SLC's report on trial use—and still nothing happened.[7] The convention's inertia arose from a combination of caution, complacency, and fear, in the estimation of Urban T. Holmes. The imperative for liturgical renewal simply had failed to touch the church as a whole.

> Most people really did not believe that there was a problem—church attendance was up—or, if they sensed a problem, they were fearful of doing too much too fast. The 1950s was a time of having orthodox theology, and the evidence of church loyalty was contributing to a building fund. Trial use was seen correctly by some as a challenge to classical theology.[8]

A.P. Opens Its Membership

At the same time, A.P. was tapping a rising curiosity in the church about the liturgical movement and an eagerness to get involved after the national exposure of A.P.'s three major liturgical conferences of 1958, 1959, and 1962. A.P. was at a threshold. Should it expand its membership and attempt to direct the accumulating pressure for liturgical reform, or should it remain a leaven in the church?

The issue for A.P., Massey Shepherd suggested in a 1959 *Sharers* article, was how to balance an extension of A.P.'s constituency with the productivity engendered by a closely knit, private group.[9] Immediately after the hugely successful 1959 San Antonio conference, A.P. received several requests to hold diocesan or regional liturgical conferences around the country. The only justification for such expansion of A.P.'s activity, Shepherd said, was if A.P. had something concrete to offer.

"How essential is commitment to our Corporate Program?" if A.P. decided to expand, the members asked themselves. Frank Cellier suggested A.P. could take on "affiliates." But this raised the question of the manageability of large numbers at A.P.'s semiannual meetings. And there was a larger question, too, of the effect on the wider liturgical movement of any expansion of A.P. "What group, regional or otherwise, is going to do what within the Liturgical Movement?" A.P. asked itself.

Growing public interest was evidence of a demand for what A.P. had to offer. "It is fully realized," said the minutes of the A.P. meeting that followed the 1959 liturgical conference, that the "impact of A.P. is being felt in many areas. Dare we remain just as we have been?" A.P. understood the issue as larger than mere self-promotion. It was a matter of A.P.'s responsibility to serve the church by furthering the liturgical movement, William Spicer said. At the same time, Shepherd warned, the nature of A.P. created its own "particular dilemma relative to wholesale expansion," namely, the ethos of a handpicked group versus a public organization. A three-member panel was assigned in 1959 to study the issue and work out specific recommendations for expansion of A.P.[10]

The turning point for A.P. came in 1963. In a crucial decision for A.P.'s future and its involvement in Prayer Book revision, A.P. in 1963 opened its membership to anyone—parish or individual, clergy or laity, Episcopal or not—who wanted to further the work of the liturgical movement in the Episcopal Church. On what turned out to be the eve of the 1964 General Convention's call for Prayer Book revision, A.P. had positioned itself to be a rallying point for liturgical reform and renewal, publicly in the swing of things, the nucleus for a critical mass of people supporting liturgical renewal. A.P.'s decision to open its membership had enormous consequences. It meant new personnel in A.P., new sources of ideas and even pressures on A.P., and a new direction in A.P.'s work. Most importantly, it created a new constituency in the politics of liturgical reform.

The minutes for A.P.'s meetings during this vitally important change in direction are missing. The minutes of the Spring 1962 meeting, as well as of the Spring and Fall meetings of 1963, 1964, and 1965, are not to be found in A.P.'s archives or in the Archives of the Episcopal Church in Austin, Texas. Correspondence with several A.P. members failed to locate the missing records. Paul Z. Hoornstra recalled, however, that he offered the enabling motion to open A.P.'s membership at the April 22–26, 1963, meeting at A.P.'s "mother church," Grace Church, Madison, Wisconsin, and that it was unanimously adopted.[11]

There was a groundswell change going on in A.P. at the time, according to Henry Breul, who became an A.P. member in 1962. New, younger members felt the time had come to alter course. The fight within A.P. to back desegregation in November 1962 was one sign of a more aggressive temperament within A.P. Some members, like Hoornstra, mark this period as the start of a shift in A.P.'s commitment from strictly liturgical change to concern with the political and social context of liturgy, which culminated during the years of urban riots, campus protests, and the Vietnam war.

Some members became increasingly frustrated with A.P.'s approach of trying to effect liturgical renewal by revivifying Cranmer. A rising exasperation with futile attempts to fashion a parish education curriculum based on the 1928 Prayer Book's eucharistic propers was one symptom. H. Boone Porter wrote in 1962 to secretary James Joseph that he wondered whether he even wanted to come to meetings as long as "that everlasting filibuster" on "this hopeless project ... still drags on." And he added, "Perhaps I am not the only one who feels this way."[12] Evidently he was not; in 1966 A.P. dropped the parish education program.

Certainly, the new attitudes and ideas in A.P. were barometric. In a conversation with the author, however, Breul reconsidered an earlier account he had given Urban T. Holmes which suggested that A.P.'s new direction was the upshot of a power struggle between the old guard and young turks, which came to a head in one climactic meeting in 1962 at which A.P. decided to push for a new approach in liturgical reform.[13] Two separate events are at issue, A.P.'s opening its membership in 1963, and the advent of trial use and Prayer Book reform, behind which A.P. mobilized in 1968 as will be discussed below. Others who were A.P. members during the early and mid-1960s recall that A.P. developed consensually and organically, particularly in its advocacy of Prayer Book revision.

A.P. co-founder Samuel E. West, who was president of A.P. in 1966 and 1967, said he was "most confident" that A.P. made "No specific decision" to agitate for a new Prayer Book. It didn't have to.

> Out of the careful study A.P. did from 1946 on, in using and studying in depth the 1928 revision in preparation for our first series of published teaching brochures in the light of the insights of the Liturgical Revival, the need for revision became more clear to us. Unlike so many in the Church, especially clergy, we were aware of the decision of the General Convention that produced the '28 book to begin to prepare for [the] next eventual revision. At that convention, explicitly or implicitly, it was recognized that the '28 book was incomplete. In response to that, General Convention, through the Standing Liturgical Commission, began to prepare a series of *Prayer Book Studies* for the entire Laos, mostly clergy, to give substance in preparing for the next revision whenever GC order the Church to proceed. Too few people, especially clergy, paid attention to the *Prayer Book Studies* publications or did not take them too seriously. A.P. did.[14]

Paul Hoornstra, who was A.P. president in 1968 and 1969, concurs. To the suggestion that A.P. began to lobby the church for a new Prayer Book in the mid-1960s, Hoornstra said, "No, I don't recall it to be that way."

> When the Standing Liturgical Commission recognized that very good work was being done by the A.P., our experience and talents were made part of the SLC's work. That brought A.P. into the "legitimate" and "institutional" phase of what was happening in the Episcopal Church.[15]

Bonnell Spencer, O.H.C., who was A.P. president in 1971 and 1972, said, "I do not recall any agitation by A.P. officially to prompt the undertaking of revision. But once the General Convention began the process, A.P. worked hard to forward it."[16]

Once A.P. opened its membership in 1963, the closed, self-perpetuating corporation of about thirty men and women which had been A.P. now became the council of the new and larger A.P. The council, however, continued to be a self-perpetuating corporation, not elected by the membership, which controlled the policies, publications, meetings, and conferences of A.P., and served as a kind of steering committee for the larger A.P. organization. The old closed membership policy, said Hoornstra,

> had been in effect so that the earliest efforts of the A.P. could be kept on the course initially taken by the founding fathers. There was the feeling of protecting the efforts invested by the first "visionaries," the first venturers, in this work.
>
> When we felt that our sense of direction and the goals had been clearly enough established, and also that a large number of serious minded people were interested in being part of the work and being supportive with dollars as well as influence in their local situations, we made the membership "open."[17]

In June 1963 A.P. publicly announced its reorganization and invited new members to join A.P. in a newsletter written by A.P. President Frederick W. Putnam. (Putnam, incidentally, had just become the first A.P. member elected to the episcopacy. He was consecrated suffragan bishop of Oklahoma on May 20, 1963. The diocesan bishop, W.R. Chilton Powell, told Putnam he did not want his work as bishop to interfere with his work for A.P.)[18] A.P.'s expanded constituency was not to be the occasion for a bid for political power in the church, Putnam said. "An abiding principle of the Associated Parishes, Inc., since its founding, has been that A.P. must always exist to further the Liturgical Movement and must never become a 'party' with the Episcopal Church," Putnam said, speaking for A.P. "We intend to continue this important principle with our enlarged organization."[19]

A.P. also resisted the temptation to over-organize. "We do not contemplate, in fact we will not allow[,] the formation of Diocesan or Local 'chapters' of A.P. We want to keep the organizational part just as simple as possible," the group pledged.[20] The new members would be kept abreast of liturgical issues and A.P.'s work through a newsletter and through copies of every A.P. brochure or pamphlet as they were published. By participating in A.P.'s conferences, they would directly contribute to spreading the liturgical movement.[21] And they also were eligible for election to the council.[22]

A new document published in 1964, *A Parish Program for Liturgy and Mission*, spelled out for new members what they were signing on to. Like A.P.'s Accepted Corporate Program, on which it was based, the parish program covered liturgical worship, parish organization, Christian education, social action, lay apostolate, liturgical arts and architecture, pastoral ministrations, church extension, and ecumenism.[23] New parish or individual members did not have to fulfill the whole parish program before they could become A.P. members; they only had to agree to work toward its goals, either as a parish or within their parishes.[24] By 1968, however, when A.P. mobilized to support trial use of a new eucharistic liturgy, the first step toward Prayer Book revision, the Parish Program as well as its predecessor Accepted Corporate Program simply faded away.

A new identity seemed to call for a new name. Shortly after A.P. expanded its membership, it expanded its name—to the Associated Parishes for Liturgy and Mission. Though the records are missing, Hoornstra recalled that the change occurred at a 1965 meeting in St. Louis. "Otis Charles was the spark plug for that change, though all of us agreed that an expansion of the name would more clearly define our function and goal."[25] The name change reflected A.P.'s lifelong insistence on the connection between liturgy and society, of course. But against the background of the social turmoil of the 1960s, the new name also hinted at A.P.'s sensitivity to a society in flux and a desire to minister to that change and to incorporate change within the church as well. Concerned about servicing its new members, the council decided in 1966 that one of A.P.'s semiannual meetings would be open to all A.P. members, with the other for council members only, a pattern that served until 1970 when A.P. began to meet only once a year in a spring session for council members alone.

Trial Use Begins: The Liturgy of the Lord's Supper

A new era in liturgical renewal dawned on December 4, 1963, when the Second Vatican Council (1962–1965) promulgated the Constitution on the Sacred Liturgy. Its implementation in the Roman Catholic Church was decisive. To the person in the pew, change seemed sudden, though it was not instantaneous. By 1970, the centuries-old Latin Mass was abandoned and the active participation by the people in the vernacular put in its place. Rome's example made other churches bold to press ahead with liturgical reforms that had been gestating for a generation.

Meeting just ten months later, the October 12–23, 1964, General Convention in St. Louis took the first step toward a new Prayer Book. "The time seems ripe," the convention declared, for a revision of the Prayer Book "so that the language may be more easily understood of the people, and the forms of services more suitable to the present age."[26] To pave the way, the convention, after two decades of resisting arguments for liturgical reform, passed the first reading of an amendment to Article X of the constitution to allow trial use. Since trial use involved a constitutional change, it would have to pass two successive General Conventions before it could come into effect—that is, not before 1967. Looking ahead, the 1964 convention called for the Presiding Bishop and the President of the House of Deputies to appoint a joint commission to propose to the next General Convention in 1967 a plan for revision of the Prayer Book "with a special view to making the language and the form of the services more relevant to the circumstances of the Church's present ministry and life."[27]

The SLC's plan for Prayer Book revision which the 1967 General Convention approved consisted of six points.[28] Its salient features were:

Role of the SLC: The SLC, rather than some specially appointed body, was designated as the instrument for Prayer Book revision. The SLC itself would initiate, coordinate, and produce a draft revision of the Book of Common Prayer. To do that, the SLC requested a temporary increase in its membership to sixteen, by the addition of four new members.

Consultants: The SLC estimated it would need about two hundred consultants—bishops, clergy, lay men and women—to serve as readers and evaluators of proposed services. Some of them served as well on drafting committees for the various Prayer Book rites. The numbers of consultants and of drafting committees grew during the period of trial use. By the end of the process, nearly three hundred consultants and twenty-seven drafting committees were operating.[29]

Coordinator: The complex task of coordinating the work of the drafting committees, communicating their work to the SLC, and acting as liaison between the whole revision effort and other agencies of the church would be best handled by hiring a coordinator, the SLC said, who would be accountable to the SLC. With the help of a small clerical staff, the coordinator would ensure that drafting committees met deadlines, coordinate the publishing of draft liturgies and circulate them for comment, and in general keep open the flow of communication among the drafting committees, and between them and the SLC. Leo Malania was selected to be the Coordinator for Prayer Book Revision. He and his staff directed the paper flow from drafting committees to consultants and back again, to the SLC, and to other church agencies.[30]

Trial Use: Individual draft services would be authorized by General Convention for trial use for three-year periods at a time. Each subsequent General Convention would authorize revisions of the texts as well as texts of new services written by the drafting committees and proposed by the SLC. Meanwhile, the liturgical commission of each diocese would gather and send to the SLC reports and comments from parishes and individuals on the rites in trial use. In guidelines to diocesan bishops, the SLC had urged dioceses and missionary districts that did not already have them to appoint a Diocesan Liturgical Commission. By 1969 the SLC could report that "almost all" jurisdictions had functioning liturgical commissions.[31] As this process was going on, the SLC would begin unifying the separate rites in a single volume constituting the *Draft Proposed Book of Common Prayer*. This phase of the revision process lasted over three trienniums extending from 1967 to 1976.

The vehicle for launching Prayer Book revision was a new eucharistic rite published by the SLC in 1966, *Prayer Book Studies XVII: The Liturgy of the Lord's Supper*. That the 1967 General Convention would approve trial use of the new eucharistic liturgy, and so take the first step toward a new Prayer Book, did not look inevitable on the eve of the convention. The Episcopal Evangelical Fellowship, for example, had sent a circular to its members urging them to write to Charles M. Guilbert, Custodian of the Standard Book of Common Prayer, to ask for changes in the text of the proposed rite. Some clergy in the diocese of Los Angeles, for another example, told their bishop of "their total dissatisfaction with the new liturgy, with what they call the 'optional' Penitential Order, and with the Commission's total disregard of man's sin in the liturgy."[32]

A.P. President Samuel E. West tried to keep the focus on the issue of approval of trial use. Textual criticism could come later. A.P. members needed to urge clerical and lay deputies to General Convention to approve trial use, West told A.P.'s membership, and see to it that deputies clearly understood that a vote for trial use was not a vote for approval of the trial liturgy as it stood. "The EEF has every right to have criticisms of the proposal," West wrote. "Probably we all will have some. BUT TO CRITICIZE THE TEXT AT THIS STAGE MISSES THE POINT." When trial use is approved, "the Church will then be free to TRY, USE, CRITICIZE and REPORT on the proposed revision. . . . [D]eputies should be clear about this."[33] There appeared to be a very real chance that deputies would turn down trial use by voting "either in ignorance or on hearsay," according to A.P. newsletter editor Larry Rouillard.[34] At stake was not just the fate of a proposed rite, but the future of liturgical renewal.

In its report to the 1967 General Convention in Seattle, the SLC was able to add another argument to the impetus for liturgical reform. Not only other parts of the Anglican Communion, but other major Christian bodies, Protestant and Catholic, were revising their liturgies and being drawn closer together in the process. Could the Episcopal Church afford to be left out?

> Churches which have been separated for centuries are finding that revisions and improvements of worship are, in fact, bringing them closer together. Especially in the celebration of the Eucharist, the Holy Communion, there is increasing ecumenical agreement about the pattern and form of the service, and such agreement has been consistent with the doctrines and tradition that this Church has always maintained.
>
> In such an age, Episcopalians, naturally, do not wish to fall into the background.[35]

From "incomparable liturgy" to "falling into the background" is a long way.

The SLC emphasized to the 1967 convention that it was "strongly committed" to trial use of rites "before they are adopted and imposed upon the Church through legislation." The SLC envisioned a democratic process by which "the clergy and the laity of the Church can play a direct part in the development and revision of new liturgical material."[36] The SLC estimated it would take at least nine years from 1967 before a finished revision of the Prayer Book was ready. "Therefore, in the opinion of many, it is now high time for the process to begin, lest the end-product be even further delayed," the SLC said.[37]

The 1967 General Convention got a taste of the new eucharistic liturgy when it was used September 20 at the Ingathering of the United Thank Offering. The next day, General Convention over-whelmingly authorized trial use of the new rite for the next three years.[38] Response to the published text of the rite had been "enthu-siastic," the SLC said.[39] When it began trial use of the new rite, the church was trying on more than a new order of service. It was trying on a new identity.[40]

Analysis of The Liturgy of the Lord's Supper

The Liturgy of the Lord's Supper summarized the theological and liturgical aspirations that had grown up since World War II. The new rite also announced the thinking and spirit which would ani-mate revision of the coming new Prayer Book.

The project of drafting *The Liturgy of the Lord's Supper* began in 1960.[41] The rite passed through eleven editions in the course of its development. Each version was scrutinized by SLC members and other liturgists and was put to "the acid test of employment in actual celebrations under varying conditions, and both said and sung."[42] Response to the SLC's previous essay at revision of the eucharistic rite, the 1953 *Prayer Book Studies IV*, convinced the SLC that it was "unwise to engage in a mere revision of its revision in *Study IV*" and that a "fresh start on the subject" was needed.[43]

The ecumenical revolution in liturgical renewal and reform that had begun in the late 1950s, and the dramatic reforms that had begun in the Roman Catholic Church, helped convince the SLC that "the time is ripe for a more radical searching after the goal of an 'ideal' liturgy." But no one church's example dominated the SLC's thinking. The commission was conversant with all the factors which were creating new perspectives in liturgical renewal, and with "the inter-confessional and ecumenical spirit of exchange that informs this concern."[44]

Of the members of the SLC at the time of *PBS IV*, only Massey

Shepherd still was a member in 1966. *The Liturgy of the Lord's Supper* bore the stamp of the theological perspectives and liturgical concerns exemplified by Shepherd's scholarship and by the liturgical movement. The chairman of the SLC, Bishop W.R. Chilton Powell of Oklahoma (who had A.P. member Frederick W. Putnam for his suffragan bishop), had high praise for a draft copy of *The Liturgy of the Lord's Supper* which Shepherd had sent him, and for Shepherd's contribution.

> Frankly I hate to part with it. Send me another copy when you can for my own amazement.
> The text just does not seem to wear out. It is simple, direct, modern, yet beautiful. All the major emphases and actions of the old Rite are included without redundancy or lugubriousness. I tell you now that the Church owes you an unlimited debt for your scholarship, flexibility, and patience. I am proud to be associated with you and with this work. . . . I pray that this, or something very much like it, will be our way of speaking to God, in eucharist.[45]

The Liturgy of the Lord's Supper, said the SLC, "follows the basic recommendations" of the inter-Anglican Consultation on the Liturgy which in 1965 published nonbinding guidelines for Anglican churches revising their eucharistic rites.[46]

The new liturgy still was identifiably Cranmerian in its ethos. "You" and "your" was used in speech between people, while God still was addressed as "thee," "thy," and "thou" with their antique verb forms, the same usage as the Revised Standard Version of the Bible which had become familiar to many people. But the SLC acknowledged that liturgical revisions in other churches "are pressing us in the Episcopal Church to a more critical examination of our inheritance [of Cranmerian English]."

> Our Prayer Book is no longer "copied" by the Protestant Churches in their recovery of liturgical worship. The English vernacular now introduced in the Roman Catholic Church has been a shock—perhaps a providential stimulus. There is no good reason to suppose that there is a single, proper "style" of liturgical expression,

much less any particular value in every Church's exhibiting the same "style" in its liturgical vernacular.[47]

The Sanctus and Our Father of *The Liturgy of the Lord's Supper* were in their familiar Prayer Book forms; other texts, like the Gloria, creed, and thanksgiving after communion were lightly revised in Cranmerian diction. The Prayer of Humble Access was gone. The consecration prayer still was the familiar Prayer Book version but with repetitive phrases excised and with a fuller recital of the theologically significant themes of creation, thanksgiving, anamnesis, and epiclesis.[48] Significantly, this was the first eucharistic rite authorized in the American church which treated the eucharistic prayer as one prayer, rather than as a preface, Sanctus, and then a prayer of consecration. In place of the Prayer for the Whole State of Christ's Church was a litany which preserved some familiar phrases from Cranmer's prayer but which included wider and more modern concerns.[49]

It was a liturgy of compromise, a bridge between the old and the new, and as such it reflected where the church was at the moment, said Alfred R. Shands, who was a member of the Drafting Committee on the Eucharist until February 1970. Most fatally, though, the rite exhibited "a basic inconsistency and odd dichotomy between its spirit and intent and its form."[50]

For all its lingering Tudor atmosphere, *The Liturgy of the Lord's Supper* clearly was moving out of the medieval-Reformation orbit and coming under the influence of the modern liturgical movement. In several ways it demonstrated the spirit that was animating Prayer Book revision.

Shape: The rite provided captions in block capital letters for main divisions of the eucharist: The Ministry of the Word, The Offertory, The Consecration, and The Breaking of the Bread. The rite accepted Dix's idea that the basic shape of the liturgy was the taking (Offertory), blessing (Consecration), breaking, and giving of the eucharistic gifts (Breaking of the Bread, which included the act of communion). The SLC deliberately chose not to highlight other portions of the service, like the Preparation, or the Thanksgiving after communion, or the Dismissal.[51]

PBS XVII also accepted the liturgical movement's insistence on the co-equality of a full service of the Word as well as of Sacrament—not only by captioning the Ministry of the Word as a distinct part of the service, but also by including an Old Testament lesson and psalm. That lesson and psalm were to be selected from the 1928 Prayer Book's table of "Psalms and Lessons for the Christian Year." Though that lectionary was designed for Morning and Evening Prayer, one of the Old Testament lessons assigned for each Sunday morning had since 1940 been marked with an asterisk as being "particularly appropriate for use when Morning Prayer with one Lesson precedes the Holy Communion." Evidently, that was to be the preferred lesson for use in *The Liturgy of the Lord's Supper.*

Ministry: In its directions to "The Ministers of the Liturgy"— which it defined as bishops, priests, deacons, and laypersons—the rite left behind a medieval ecclesiology based on ordination and moved toward an understanding of the church based on baptism. It laid down the rule that the officiating minister at the eucharist, whether bishop or priest, should be "assisted by other clergymen" (endorsing a collegial view of ordained ministry and opening the way for concelebration) as well as "laymen," and gave "laypersons" specific functions in the liturgy.[52] The SLC said it wanted to use "more imaginatively, and in accordance with ancient tradition, a wider ministry of both clergy and laity in the Eucharist."

> In particular, we have sought to restore the time-honored ministry of the Diaconate—especially so, now that so many of our parishes have a regular service of one or more Deacons. We believe also that laymen should have responsibilities as lectors, bearers of the oblations, and, where effective, leaders in prayer. Above all, the Bishop should be acknowledged as the liturgical president and primary teacher of his flock, whenever it is possible for him to be present in the Eucharistic assembly.[53]

The primacy of the bishop (that is, the bishop as president at the eucharist, not as one having precedence of rank and power), the collegial nature of ordained ministry, and the liturgical priesthood of the laity were explicitly recognized in the new rite.

Rubrics: The nature of the rubrics indicated that the rite was shifting out of clerically centered assumptions about the liturgy. Most rubrics in previous Prayer Books concerned the officiant, not the people. *PBS XVII* left in the text of the rite only those directions concerning the whole body of worshipers. Details of order, alternatives, and regulation that were the responsibility of the officiant or of a master of ceremonies were gathered in one place at the end of the rite.[54] *The Liturgy of the Lord's Supper* deliberately left behind the clerical mindset of earlier Prayer Books and of what lay behind them, the medieval presupposition that worship was primarily the concern of a professional class.

Format: In its very typography and layout, *PBS XVII* told the church that here was something new. Generous use of white space, a modern typeface, arrangement of texts in sense-line format, unfussy use of titles and subtitles, balanced spacing of texts on a single page, and printing of rubrics in red to distinguish them from recited texts—all demonstrated a new spirit animating Prayer Book revision.

Reaction to Trial Use

The trial liturgy went off like a bombshell in the Sunday mornings of most Episcopalians. They simply had no idea that anyone in their church wanted to change their Prayer Book or the religion they associated with it. "What is happening to our beautiful church?" cried one Florida parishioner.[55]

A Massachusetts rector replied, "I would say that we're finding a new concept of beauty which is as meaningful to us as apparently sixteenth-century Prayer Book verbiage is" to some, and he added that the real significance of the liturgical change was the evidence it gave of "a new and open attitude in the hearts of churchmen."[56]

The SLC solicited reactions to *The Liturgy of the Lord's Supper*. It distributed more than 1.5 million questionnaires for the laity and 10,000 for the clergy. Twenty-seven dioceses sent in results. Reactions to the new liturgy in the questionnaires and in the church press showed that considerable anxiety and suspicion surrounded Prayer Book revision, the SLC reported in 1970. The very credibility of the trial use process and of the SLC was at stake. Bluntly put,

> a sizeable body of Churchmen simply did not believe that the Commission meant it when it said that trial use was precisely what it claimed to be, namely, the testing and evaluation of a new rite in situations of actual worship. Many people seemed to think that trial use was a public relations device designed to sell "the new service". Many were not convinced that their views would be taken into account if they ran counter to what were assumed to be the views of the Standing Liturgical Commission.[57]

The SLC needed to demonstrate that the "considerable amount of suspicion" expressed and "the vehemence of the language used by some correspondents" was being heard and acknowledged by the people in charge of liturgical change.[58]

The trial liturgy acted as a lightning rod for popular grievances and anxiety, attracting all manner of discontents. As Francis Bowman told a 1968 A.P. meeting, "Trial Use carried burdens of resentment against civil rights, the National Council of Churches—all these frustrations."[59] "So many of the people who are reacting against the Trial Liturgy are really saying: 'I don't like change,'" was A.P. President Henry Breul's blunt assessment.[60]

A lifelong Michigan churchman reportedly took one look at the new *Liturgy of the Lord's Supper,* tore up the book, and walked out of the church vowing never to return.[61] Some people scorned the "newspaper language" quality of the trial liturgy,[62] its "clumsy and verbose" sentences which "offend my ears and eyes," and its "ungraceful, tortured 'English.'"[63] "In my estimation the idea to institute this change is the result of insecure negative faith," a Wisconsin parishioner said.[64] A nineteen-year-old college student pronounced the new liturgy "awful ... I've been a faithful communicant, but when I'm away at school, the new liturgy makes it just that much easier for me to be 'too busy' to go to communion on Sundays. And I'm not alone."[65]

But others liked it. An eighty-year-old Michigan parishioner exclaimed, "Why, it's a very *good* Liturgy."[66] "I find it rhythmic, spiritually satisfying, and stimulating," a Providence, Rhode Island, churchwoman wrote. "I find phrases from it coming into my mind at odd moments, bringing pleasure and comfort." When her parish went back to the 1928 Prayer Book rite after a three-month experiment with the trial liturgy she felt "a definite sense of loss."[67] "The more we've used the New Liturgy, the more it has grown on us," reported a churchwoman in Costa Rica.[68] Among the advantages that a California priest saw in the new liturgy were its "logical and clear structure," more modern language, a more complete ministry of the Word, and the litany of intercession.[69]

The trial use liturgy brought home to the pews some of the recategorization in theological thought that had been going on since the end of World War II. Some people objected that the new liturgy changed the meaning of words in the creed. "Are we to believe that modern man is too sophisticated to accept primitive Christian tenets?" a Fort Wayne, Indiana, churchman wanted to know.[70] Changes like the omission of the Holy Spirit proceeding from the Son, and changing "by whom all things were made" to "through whom" aroused suspicions.[71] Others, unaffected by developments in eucharistic theology since Odo Casel, feared that the words, "Take them in remembrance that Christ *gives* himself for you ... " seemed to revive what Article of Religion XXXI condemned as "blasphemous fables."[72]

A churchwoman from Wisconsin argued that since modern society had no precise theoretical understanding of the function of language nor certainty of religious belief, this century, this day, was not an appropriate time for liturgical revision.[73] The subjective, individualistic presuppositions of many worshipers were challenged by the new rite. The "we believe" of the creed "allows evasion of individual commitment," said a California priest.[74] Use of the plural posed a "real shock" to one North Carolina woman who realized the rite supposed that "you are not in separate communion with your God, you are speaking for all in the Church. But do they all believe? You only know about yourself."[75]

Some were bothered by the communal kiss of peace: "I am glad to greet my neighbor, but I'll be darned if I shall hold hands with him," said a Pennsylvania woman.[76] An Ohio priest snapped back, "How would you feel about washing your neighbor's feet?"[77] On the other hand, a Philadelphia woman reported, "After the service was over, the woman next to me actually introduced herself! I suppose because we had touched hands she realized someone was sharing the pew." It was only the second time someone she did not know had spoken to her in ten years at that church.[78]

At the same time, the trial liturgy had to contend with rumors and fears that "the people who drew up the new liturgy were responding to an outside force to phase the Episcopal Church out of existence," and after that, Christianity.[79] Leo Malania, the coordinator for Prayer Book revision, was "presiding over the evaporation of the church," a rector in Denver said.[80] When Malania was asked in 1971 what he would do "after this difficult task of revision is completed," he smiled and answered, "If I survive, I intend to write a book entitled *Elegant Insults I Have Received.*"[81]

Many believed that the Standing Liturgical Commission already had made up its mind and simply would not hear negative assessments of the trial liturgy. One Missouri churchwoman described her reaction to the trial use questionnaire as "BETRAYAL." The questionnaire "is slanted to a YES reply, and if you are in the upper age bracket and admit to being a communicant for a long period of time, well you are 'over the hill,' . . . so that your reply need not be taken seriously."[82]

Opponents of the new liturgy were taxed with their age, conservatism, stupidity, and even idolatry, one Iowa parishioner complained. But "[t]here are many laymen who possess a fairly adequate knowledge of the history of the Book of Common Prayer, who are aware of its former revisions, and who will gladly agree that it is always open to further revision." Their point was, this revision did not look better to them than the 1928 Prayer Book.[83] "So many times people who love the Prayer Book and are reluctant to have it changed are accused of being themselves resistant to change of any kind," a Wisconsin woman wrote. "This is not true at all, for often these are the very people arguing constantly for change in other directions." What these people feared losing, she said, was that sense of stability and continuity that the Prayer Book conveyed.[84]

On other people, the very point of liturgical renewal was lost. The whole idea of a new liturgy seemed "completely irrelevant and inappropriate. When there is so much to be done in the world in the area of human welfare it seems absolutely inconceivable that astute men of the church could spend their time and energy . . . fooling around with the format of a church service."[85]

Whatever words the church chooses for its worship, said a New York parishioner, they should suggest "that God is both among us and beyond us, and that this will continue to be the case whenever and wherever men gather together" before God.[86] In fact, with the "flexibility and variety for which Anglicanism is famous . . . why not a variety and catholicity of rites—the best of the ancient and the best of the modern?" one Schenectady, New York, rector asked.[87] Variety wasn't exactly a new phenomenon, another priest pointed out. "[A]s there was room . . . in the church for both traditional Jewish and new Greek ways, so there is now for both Prayer Book and modern experimental services."[88]

The Liturgy of the Lord's Supper slowly made headway in the church. By 1970, the SLC reported, 53,537 copies of *PBS XVII* had been sold, as well as 711,184 copies of the pew edition of the eucharistic rite alone, and 5,455 copies of the large altar edition of the rite alone.[89]

A.P. Backs The Liturgy of the Lord's Supper

As soon as *PBS XVII* was published in 1966, A.P. mobilized to insure that the new liturgy would get an informed and thorough hearing in Episcopal parishes. A committee of David Babin, chairman, Paul Hoornstra, and Frank Cellier was appointed in 1966 to write a study guide for the new liturgy.[90] The guide appeared in 1967, the same year that trial use of the new rite was approved. *The Liturgy of the Lord's Supper; Leader's Guide and Workbook* was designed to lead a parish study group through a five-session course on liturgical renewal and the proposed new eucharistic rite, climaxing in a celebration of *The Liturgy of the Lord's Supper.*[91]

Whether a parish adopted the trial liturgy for regular use or not, A.P.'s guide urged follow-up meetings in the parish. A.P.'s intent was to keep the issue of liturgical reform "on the front burner," and to stimulate within the parish "a nucleus concerned with, committed to, and informed about Liturgical Renewal." Not only could this group form the core of a parish liturgy committee, but it also could serve as the link between the parish and the Diocesan Liturgical Commission, reporting to the commission on their community's experience with trial use.[92]

A.P.'s strategy was to promote trial use by educating the parishes of the church in the premises of the new eucharistic rite; by making possible informed, quality celebrations of the new liturgy; and by causing parishes to have a stake in the process of Prayer Book revision by making them realize that their experience and reactions would be heard and would matter at the national level when their Diocesan Liturgical Commission reported to the SLC.

Chilton Powell, the SLC chairman, called A.P.'s study guide "excellent" and recommended it to all the church's bishops and chairmen of Diocesan Liturgical Commissions for "programs of training in preparation for a further period of trial use starting later in 1968 or early 1969."[93] Charles M. Guilbert, who as Prayer Book custodian was also an SLC member, told A.P. that the SLC had tried and failed to come up with just such a study guide. Guilbert told A.P. that its publication "was just the thing they had been working for and were very grateful that A.P. had gotten the study guide out."[94]

The SLC had no money to launch an extensive educational program, Massey Shepherd recalled years later, other than the Prayer Book Studies themselves.[95] A.P.'s study guide was not just one alternative among several. It was a unique and important means of educating parishes not only in how to celebrate the new liturgy, but also in why the church was engaging in the monumental task of liturgical renewal and what it hoped to achieve. "We came out at just the right moment" with the trial liturgy study guide, A.P. President Henry Breul said. "It sold like hot cakes and obviously served a tremendous need."[96]

Soon after the new rite came into use, A.P. issued a brochure to help musicians and clergy select appropriate music for the trial liturgy. Music was either a help or a hindrance to the liturgy, A.P. recognized. It was rarely neutral, and lack of good music was one factor holding up acceptance of the new rite.[97]

There was an immediate need for fresh information on the new liturgy if trial use was to succeed. A.P.'s *Parish Eucharist* brochure had been a reliable guide since 1950. A.P. hastily added new pages, two at the beginning and two at the end of the brochure, and reissued it. The new material explained the intent of trial use, the structure of the new eucharistic rite, and suggested appropriate ceremonial to bring out the new rite's meaning.[98] If the old brochure sounded dated by now, there was no mistaking the tenor of the new material wrapped around the front and back of the brochure. A stunning cover of bright orange, red, and yellow abstract design with the title in script running vertically up the right side of the front cover announced newness and change before one had even read a word. A new bibliography suggested books not only on liturgy but on the phenomenon of cultural change itself.

A.P. had a feistier sense of itself and its task since the cautious days of the 1950s. In the midst of "striking and pervasive change" in society, "how is the Church to respond?" A.P. asked in the re-issued brochure.

> It is the purpose of Associated Parishes to assist local worshipping communities in making as fully creative a response to their changing environment as possible; to remain open to new possibilities; to direct rather than be directed by change. ... As a member [of A.P.] ... [y]ou will be part of a growing network of individuals and worshipping communities who are shaping questions and developing answers which affect the capacity of the Church to survive in a secular culture.[99]

Engagement with society, creative openness, directing change, defining crucial questions and answers, being part of the very survival of the church in the midst of dramatic cultural shift—that was how A.P. understood the liturgical task now and what it offered to prospective members. Trial use and the atmosphere of cultural change which attended it gave A.P.'s message of liturgical renewal a context which had not existed before. Privately, A.P. spoke of being "a continuing irritant to the Church so it may be faithful to God's mission in the world."[100] The advent of trial use and the ecumenical ferment in liturgical renewal that began in the mid-1960s changed A.P.'s "whole manner of functioning and thinking ... [about] renewal," Otis Charles said. Now it was apparent that A.P. had "to ask some more basic questions."

> Maybe the kind of renewal that came out of Vatican II and has been very much in the wind was kind of the end of the beginning.

For this reason it seems that what A.P. has to do now is not just pass down the word: "This is it!", but keep people opening up.[101]

By 1966, A.P. was rethinking the nature of liturgical reform, where it thought the Episcopal Church needed to go, and A.P.'s role in getting it there. The April 1966 council meeting formed a committee on liturgy and mission to review A.P.'s liturgical efforts. The areas the committee was assigned to investigate show the direction of A.P.'s thinking: that "current theological thought be evaluated critically;" that the "language problem" that exists in the Prayer Book be studied by A.P.; that the "whole question of ministries of the church be studied;" that there "is a need for better understanding of celebrating in the Holy Eucharist;" and, significantly, that A.P. "consider how we can have some influence in General Convention regarding liturgical improvements needed in the church."[102]

The Crisis:
A.P. Mobilizes for a New Prayer Book

Despite the popularity of its study guide for *The Liturgy of the Lord's Supper*, A.P. was frustrated with what it characterized as the inept trial use that the new eucharistic rite was receiving. At the council's April 1968 meeting in Los Angeles,

> Bill Wendt observed that in many quarters of the Church there is a rather strong negative reaction to the trial Liturgy. This "backlash" is fed by the botched-up usage practised in so many places.[103]

The SLC had offered no effective guidelines for celebrating the trial liturgy, Wendt said, and there was no guarantee that evaluations of the rite, if any, would reflect anything more than discontent with performances of the new liturgy that gutted its intent. If *PBS XVII* sank, so would prospects for a new Prayer Book.

What A.P. should do, Wendt said, is get official recognition from the church "in order to assure ... [the] best possible trial use and an adequate understanding of liturgical reform and practice." For example, he said, A.P. could work with Diocesan Liturgical Commissions to set up conferences or workshops before trial use of the new liturgy in dioceses or parishes.

That, responded Henry Breul, would require a full-time staff person for A.P., an executive secretary. The whole council began debating the idea. With a full-time staffer, A.P. could take the lead in liturgical reform. An executive secretary, for example, could expand A.P.'s membership to represent a broad base of support for liturgical reform, plan conferences, offer the services of A.P. in promoting liturgical renewal, and identify people around the country who could form a network educating parishes and dioceses during the years of trial use that lay ahead. Breul urged the council to "gamble now. At least we will have entered the fray. It's an announcement to the world that we are serious."[104]

Within hours, a committee had come up with a job description for an executive secretary, decided to seek official endorsement and funding for the project from the church's Executive Council, unanimously nominated A.P.'s Secretary E. Otis Charles for the new position of executive secretary, and unanimously approved him.[105] Between 10:50 a.m. and 2:15 p.m. on April 25, 1968, A.P. had redefined its mission: it decided to drop everything and focus itself on one issue, the successful promotion of trial use, the first step toward a new Prayer Book.

A.P. wanted to position itself "to assume an active role in the process of shaping liturgical practice in the Episcopal Church." It was offering "to supply the expertise to make liturgical reform operative at the local level."[106] More than just a pedagogue or adjunct, A.P. now wanted to be a shaper and director of liturgical renewal for the whole church. The beginning of Prayer Book revision just seven months earlier in September 1967 brought to a crisis A.P.'s two decades of debate about whether it should be a leaven or leader.

At that same April 1968 meeting, the council streamlined its internal operations by simplifying the process for selecting new members which had been in place since the beginning in 1946. The old method had been to have nominees for membership attend two successive A.P. meetings as guests. The council unanimously decided at its April 1968 meeting to amend the bylaws to eliminate that process and have nominees attend only one meeting at which they would be voted on. Instead of a unanimous vote being necessary for election, a vote of two-thirds of the members present would suffice. As the tempo of liturgical reform began to pick up, A.P. was positioning itself to bring new talent aboard quickly and to handle its internal matters expeditiously so that its energy could be spent on Prayer Book revision. Meanwhile, A.P.'s new executive secretary was directed to gather a conference to develop a plan to present to the SLC that would make A.P. an official player in the biggest liturgical event in the history of the Episcopal Church. Otis Charles also was to contact the Executive Council of the church to see if it would finance A.P.'s proposal to be an official agent for liturgical change.

Some time after its April 1968 meeting, A.P. gathered a "think tank" of eight people, six of whom were not on the A.P. council, and asked them, "This is what A.P. has been. How do you think we could use these resources to the best advantage of the Church?"[107] One of the think tank's suggestions, made by Jack Miller, was to develop a "communication network for liturgical reform around the country," which was envisioned as "a network of parishes which are trying new programs, offering new architectural possibilities, and in general attempting to update the celebration of the Eucharist."[108] In other words, a nationwide system of A.P.-sponsored people who could be on the spot to help parishes and dioceses do liturgical renewal.

In September 1968, Otis Charles, Boone Porter, and Henry Breul met with Charles M. Guilbert, who also was Secretary of the Executive Council. Guilbert was enthusiastic about A.P.'s plan. He told A.P. of a $1 million gift to the church which produced some $40,000 a year specifically for "education in experimentation in the life of the Church." Guilbert told A.P. he "would be glad to hand into the priority committee ... our proposal as the kind of program the national church ought to support."[109]

A.P. recast its request for funds, from support for an executive secretary to support for an educational system of field consultants. The church endorsed A.P.'s plan. In March 1969 the Executive Council gave A.P. a $30,000 grant for the project. A.P. immediately announced plans to set up twelve "field consultants" across the country who would be "resource persons for local congregations involved in the process of liturgical development."[110]

A.P. said publicly it was concerned that trial use of the new eucharistic liturgy was being

> introduced and used so poorly in many places (and scarcely given any trial at all in some places) that the result might well be a rejection of all proposals for any revision or renewal at all. Bad initial experience and poor understanding about the purpose of liturgical change might easily and quickly become a hard barrier to any progress at all.[111]

The parishes of the twelve men and women, clergy and laity, whom A.P. named as field consultants were to be "places where people can 'go and see'" what is being done in renewal of worship, Charles said. Looking ahead to the other experimental rites that would begin coming from the SLC in the next three years, Charles said an urgent part of the consultants' task was to communicate to parishes the reasons for liturgical renewal.[112]

Though the SLC was directing the official process of Prayer Book revision, Charles said, "it is apparent from response [from chairmen of Diocesan Liturgical Commissions] ... that strong A.P. leadership, increased grassroots communication through expanding A.P. membership and A.P. stimulation of conferences, liturgical commissions and resource developers is very much desired."[113] A.P. was "at the heart of what the Church's life is at this point," president Henry Breul told a membership meeting in Milwaukee in 1969. "And we are desperately needed. I don't see anyone else on the horizon who will do the task."[114] John O. Patterson, the catalyst for A.P. nearly a quarter-century earlier, looked on from his post at St. Stephen's School in Rome and approved. "Patterson excited about the future of A.P.," reads a lone sentence in the A.P. records for 1969.[115]

A lack of money threatened to cut short A.P.'s activities, though. The grant from the Executive Council was solely for the liturgical consultants network. Funding for the executive secretary and the rest of A.P.'s work depended on the financial support of A.P. members and others. An unspecified "substantial gift" from Chester Byrns of St. Joseph, Michigan, in November 1970 not only helped keep A.P.'s work afloat but also was a vote of confidence in A.P.'s role in liturgical reform.[116]

By the following summer of 1971, however, A.P. faced a crisis. Otis Charles had just been elected Bishop of Utah and A.P. was looking for someone to replace him. Two council members were opposed to hiring a new executive secretary. Boone Porter urged that no successor be chosen. He wanted the council to return to its earlier model for organization and work, namely, its more direct, hands-on style of direct involvement in decision making by the whole council.[117] But the majority of the council wanted a new executive secretary. In July 1971, A.P.'s executive committee unanimously elected the Rev. Jeffrey Cave with a salary of $12,800.[118] His election was rendered moot, however, by the continuing financial crunch. Within two months, A.P. had decided that "we cannot ... now undertake the employment of a new executive secretary," and the executive committee took over the duties of the executive secretary.[119]

A.P.'s experiment with a salaried executive officer had lasted just three years. The transformation in A.P.'s sense of its mission and in its operations had been so dramatic, however, that some members wondered how A.P. could sustain its pace in Prayer Book revision without a full-time administrator. "How do we operate without an Executive Secretary?" the council asked itself at its April 1972 meeting. Founding member Samuel West reminded them of how A.P. had gotten this far. "We are a working not just an advisory council," he said.[120]

A.P. Members on the SLC and Drafting Committees

Within the official apparatus of Prayer Book revision, the SLC and the drafting committees were the places where the most direct influence could be exerted on the direction, the shape, the very words themselves, of the Prayer Book to be. A.P. permeated the structure of Prayer Book revision. It was part of the machinery of the reform process and had direct access to the unfolding thinking and progress of Prayer Book reform through its members who served on the SLC and on various drafting committees.

Throughout the years of trial use, the minutes of A.P. meetings show a two-way flow of information, reactions, and opinions from drafting committee members to the A.P. council, and back again. A.P. members reported on their drafting committees' activities and solicited the council's responses, and the council served as a sounding board for thinking about the issues and implications raised by the drafting committees' work. At its April 1969 meeting, for example, the A.P. council had an extensive discussion on the prospects of the reform process itself, and on revision of the eucharist, baptism, ordinal, daily offices, visitation of the sick, and the catechism.[121]

The SLC: When trial use began in 1967, A.P. had three members on the SLC—Massey Shepherd, the SLC's vice chairman; H. Boone Porter, Jr.; and Bonnell Spencer, O.H.C. (A.P. member Frank S. Cellier's term on the SLC expired in 1967.)[122]

By the last triennium of Prayer Book revision and trial use, 1974 to 1976, A.P.'s presence on the SLC had doubled. In addition to Shepherd, Porter, and Spencer, two A.P. bishops were on the commission—Otis Charles (Utah) and William A. Dimmick (Northern Michigan)—as well as Vivian Kingsley, who became A.P.'s first woman president in 1975.[123]

The Drafting Committees: A.P. was represented on the two key committees on the eucharist and on baptism and confirmation, as well as on various other drafting committees. A.P.'s Bonnell Spencer chaired the baptism-confirmation committee.

During the 1968–1970 triennium, A.P. had nine members serving on eight drafting committees.[124] A.P.'s SLC members chaired three of the drafting committees: Shepherd on the calendar, eucharistic lectionary, and collects; Spencer on baptism-confirmation; and Porter on the ordinal.

Among other A.P. members on drafting committees from 1968 to 1970, A.P.'s first lay member, Francis F. Bowman, served on the drafting committee on the eucharist, along with David E. Babin. Otis Charles served on the drafting committee on the ordinal. Thomas J. Talley was on the committee dealing with rites for the sick.

By the final stage of Prayer Book revision, the 1974–1976 triennium, nineteen A.P. members were serving on eighteen drafting committees. Among them was Marion J. Hatchett, who served on four drafting committees and was a corresponding member of two more. In addition, A.P. members were chairing five of the drafting committees: Shepherd on calendar, eucharistic lectionary, and collects; Dimmick on daily offices; Porter on church year and on episcopal services; and Hatchett on the ad hoc committee on a common eucharistic prayer.[125]

After the 1979 Prayer Book was adopted, several members of drafting committees were elected to the council of A.P. Leo Malania, coordinator for Prayer Book revision, became an A.P. member in 1981. Other drafting committee members who became A.P. council members were James H. Litton, 1980; Ormande Plater, 1981; and Leonel L. Mitchell, 1989.

As momentum for Prayer Book revision gathered, Shepherd's "practical observations based on his wide experience of clergy and laity throughout the Church became very helpful to A.P.," according to Samuel E. West. Shepherd's advice "helped channel the group's enthusiasm for revision."[126]

The increasing demands on Shepherd, however, gave him less and less time with A.P. In 1964, Shepherd was an invited Anglican observer at the third session of the Second Vatican Council, and reported his experiences to A.P. members.[127] In 1966 he was named as one of only six non-Roman Catholic observers to the Consilium for the Implementation of the Constitution on the Sacred Liturgy. The ecumenical members had no vote or voice in the consilium's sessions, but could offer written opinions and had frequent informal discussions with members of the consilium and their consultants.[128] And in 1967, Shepherd was named a member of the Anglican-Roman Catholic Joint Preparatory Commission which paved the way for ecumenical dialogue between the two communions. On the Protestant liturgical scene, Shepherd became a member of the Commission on Worship of the Consultation on Church Union in 1966. Shepherd was largely responsible for the text of its eucharistic rite, *An Order of Worship*, published in 1968.[129] And in his own church, Shepherd was fully involved in Prayer Book revision.

In 1966 Shepherd wrote to the A.P. council that his schedule of activities had so greatly increased, he wondered if he could continue serving effectively as a council member. A.P. was larger than Massey Shepherd, but clearly the group did not want to lose so prestigious a member. (In 1952, for example, A.P. elected Shepherd president for the following year even though he was going to be in Europe for eight months.)[130] The council acknowledged A.P.'s "great appreciation" for Shepherd's "great contributions from the beginning of A.P." and unanimously decided in November 1966 to let Shepherd continue as a member of the council without requiring him to fulfill specific assignments. They also suspended the rule for him that required council members who missed meetings to pay a fine.[131]

After 1966, Shepherd is recorded to have attended only one A.P. council meeting, in the fall of 1967.[132] A.P. gave Shepherd "honorary status" in 1968,[133] and in a reorganization of membership categories in 1972, he was made an "honorary member".[134] Shepherd made his final appearance at an A.P. gathering in 1988, two years before his death, in San Francisco, during which the surviving co-founders of A.P. were honored. Samuel West, who had been one of the original four co-founders forty-two years earlier, recalled the event:

> Massey made a special effort to be there even though he was in constant pain from the arthritis which had long plagued him and from the pain of [his wife] Gabriela's death. He was in good humor, however, telling jokes to those near him. He renewed friendships with former A.P. colleagues as he recalled "the old days." He was delighted to be seen and be greeted by former students and other friends.[135]

A.P.'s Regional Liturgical Conferences

As the church experimented with trial rites and took the first steps toward a new Prayer Book, A.P. sponsored a series of regional liturgical conferences around the country that helped build a positive climate of opinion for liturgical renewal within the church. Beginning in 1965, the conferences usually were co-sponsored by a parish, diocese, or diocesan liturgical commission. A.P. saw itself as contributing to the vitality of the liturgical movement and to the renewal of the church through these conferences. They were one more way in which A.P. worked to assure the success of trial use and acceptance of a new Prayer Book.

Frederick W. Putnam prepared a manual in 1968 for potential co-sponsors of regional conferences, laying out in detail the specifics of planning and mounting a conference. A.P.'s purpose was not only to disseminate information about the liturgical movement, said the *Manual For Regional Liturgical Conferences Sponsored By The Associated Parishes, Inc.*, but also to get "feedback from the grass roots, to find out where the people are in this matter of Church renewal."[136]

Regional conferences were held in New York in 1965 and Washington, D.C. in 1966. "The Total Ministry of the Church" was the theme of the Chicago gathering in 1967. Papers delivered at the 1968 Los Angeles conference were published by A.P. as "The Liturgy: A Celebration of Worldly Men." The Boston conference in 1969 focused on "Christian Initiation." Other conferences were planned for Kansas City, 1969; Washington, D.C., 1970, on baptism; and Lake Forest, Illinois, 1970, on "Liturgy and Space," but it is not clear from A.P.'s records whether these occurred. Despite its manual of suggested procedures, A.P. had to disabuse potential co-sponsors that it had "a package we are selling," Otis Charles said. A.P.'s design was to cooperate with local parishes and dioceses to help them address the liturgical issues that were on their minds, not to impose some product known as the liturgical movement.[137]

A.P. seems not to have co-sponsored any more regional liturgical conferences after 1970. Its focus shifted that year to helping the Diocesan Liturgical Commissions start their annual meetings, and A.P. remained involved in that work for the next several years. Also, Otis Charles' election to the episcopate left A.P. without a full-time administrator to plan and coordinate more regional conferences.

Open

A.P. realized that it was crucial to the success of Prayer Book revision that people know not only what was going on but why. People needed to be brought into the insights and experiences that were animating liturgical reform. Since A.P. stopped publishing *Sharers* in 1962, the church had not had a forum dealing exclusively with liturgical renewal and the parish. Otis Charles outlined ideas for a new publishing venture at the A.P. council's November 1968 meeting. Perhaps a big poster—one side being something of some lasting value and the other being newsletter-type material. Or perhaps sometimes it could be a box "and we could include in the box a variety of things you couldn't get into the newsletter," Charles said. As for what to call it, Charles and council member Jon Olson came up with the name *Open*. "It gives a job description as well as a request," they said.[138] *Open* it was and still is more than twenty-five years later.

By 1974, A.P. had settled on a standard printed format for *Open* of about sixteen pages per issue, but from 1968 to 1974, the format of *Open* was flexible. Some issues were printed, in varying sizes and number of pages; some were single sheets of legal-size paper. But what subscribers remember vividly are those extraordinary boxes that arrived at irregular intervals. Posters, buttons, 45 r.p.m. recordings of music, cleverly designed foldouts and who-knows-what might turn up in them. "The name of the game was 'blow your mind,'" one recipient recalled with a smile.[139] Unfortunately, none of the boxes survive in A.P.'s archives. They were evanescent artifacts, reflecting the liturgical spirit of the time. But they were meant to speak to and encourage a "continuously innovative and self-renewing Church" to grapple with where it was and where it ought to be as it did liturgical renewal in the midst of cultural flux.[140]

One issue of *Open* in 1969, for example, carried articles on activist clergy and what it meant to be the church; a report on an Episcopal "floating" parish; the future of church architecture; the future of the local congregation; reports on the recently concluded Special General Convention in South Bend; and an attempt to go behind talk about the "shape of the liturgy" to get at the primary role of the people, who shape the liturgy.[141] About this time, A.P. also published a broadsheet titled "House Church," giving theological and scriptural bases for such a community and some practical suggestions for running one.[142] In 1975, just before the *Draft Proposed Book of Common Prayer* was to come before General Convention for a vote, *Open* was carrying articles on theological understandings of the new rites and trying to convey to readers a sense of why cultural shift necessitated a renewed appropriation of liturgy.

Since passage of the 1979 Prayer Book, *Open* has prodded the church's thinking on direct ordination to the presbyterate and episcopate without passing through another order; debated the issue of delegating confirmation to presbyters; and advocated reform of the calendar of saints and provision of a daily eucharistic lectionary. A.P. has published musicians' insights on use of *The Hymnal 1982*; reported on A.P.'s work at General Convention for inclusive-language liturgical texts; and critiqued convention's implementation of the 1979 Prayer Book as exemplified in the liturgies at General Convention. *Open* has reported on the annual meetings of the Association of Diocesan Liturgy and Music Commissions; on the progress of Lutheran-Episcopal dialogue; on inculturation of the liturgy; on architectural implications of the 1979 Prayer Book; and has carried articles on social justice, theological reflection on liturgy, and specific suggestions for celebrating the rites of the Prayer Book. All this was in addition to regular reports on A.P. council meetings, book reviews, a music column, and commentary. No other publication in the church has fostered the conversation about those kinds of issues from a liturgical perspective. No other publication has been dedicated to reflecting on the specific what, why, and how of the renewal of the church which is at the heart of the liturgical movement.

A.P. Considers Merging With the Liturgical Conference

As A.P. stepped into the forefront of the trial use process, it considered merging with the mostly Roman Catholic Liturgical Conference as a way of extending its influence. A.P. council member William A. Wendt, who was on the planning committee for the Liturgical Conference's 1969 Liturgical Week in Milwaukee, reported that the conference would welcome an A.P. member on their board of directors. "We couldn't begin to do what they do," Wendt said. If A.P. joined forces with them, the conference's Liturgical Weeks in effect could give liturgical renewal in the Episcopal Church an annual showcase.[143]

Otis Charles invited the Liturgical Conference's executive director, James Colaianni, also a member of A.P., to make a presentation at the council's April 1969 meeting. Colaianni proposed a joint membership in the Liturgical Conference for A.P.'s members. A.P. would receive space in the conference's publication *Liturgy*, office space, administrative services, representation on all the conference's standing committees, and official status at the annual Liturgical Week with the opportunity of presenting special programs for A.P.'s own constituency. A formula for dividing membership dues also was proposed.[144]

After Colaianni left the A.P. meeting, council reaction was full, frank, and detailed. The advantage of cooperating with the Liturgical Conference, as members like Thomas Talley and Henry Breul saw it, was that A.P. would acquire an ecumenical dimension. A.P. should be prepared to "allow ourselves to die in this larger organization," Breul said. Set against this, however, as Talley pointed out, A.P. had a $30,000 commitment to the Episcopal Church "that we can't back out of" to develop field consultants for promoting trial use. Besides, Episcopalians were coming into A.P. because of what they perceived A.P. to offer and what they needed, Otis Charles said. A.P. would be "shifting horses midstream" by changing its image. A.P. also questioned whether, with its seven-hundred members, it could be an effective voice in the trial use process that had just begun if it merged with the nine-thousand-member Liturgical Conference. "[I]f our peculiar task is to alert Episcopalians in the U.S. to the winds of change that are going on, we must somehow maintain our stature as Episcopalians," John Sweeney said. And members had reservations about A.P.'s voting rights in the Liturgical Conference, "the election of a genuine board of directors," and the absence of non-Roman Catholics in any of the Conference's editorial positions.[145]

A.P. got a closer look at what the Liturgical Conference had to offer when it held its fall meeting in conjunction with the conference's Liturgical Week in August 1969 in Milwaukee. "On the whole," the A.P. council felt, the convention "had been poorly thought out but was useful." A.P.'s executive committee reported to the council that "[t]here have been some disappointments in our discussions" with the Liturgical Conference but that "we want to keep our contacts open."[146] A.P. planned to take part in the 1970 Liturgical Week in Boston, but the conference canceled it, apparently for financial reasons. Affiliation with the Liturgical Conference was not pursued, though A.P. occasionally did cooperate in issuing statements, for example. A.P. held discussions with Liturgical Conference representatives again in 1983, but nothing came of it.[147]

A.P. cooperated and exchanged information with other liturgical organizations but not with an eye toward merger. With liturgical renewal breaking out in its own back yard, A.P. felt its proper sphere of activity lay closer to home. David Babin reported to the council in 1966 on his contact with the Order of St. Luke, the Methodist liturgical renewal group, but A.P. had no formal contact. In 1968, a proposal that the council subscribe to the publications of Parish and People in England and of Liturgy and Laity in Australia failed to find any support. But A.P. did agree to circulate news of an upcoming conference for Friends of the English Liturgy, a Roman Catholic group, in 1968. In later years, A.P. participated in "Worship '75" sponsored by the Canadian Liturgical Society in 1975. A.P.'s Canadian council members Joseph Fricker and Borden Purcell helped plan the conference on "Celebrating the Word," and A.P. council members Boone Porter and Thomas Babbit led workshops. With some misgiving, A.P. joined Pewsaction, a confederation of various renewal groups in the Episcopal Church, for a one-year trial membership in 1975, but decided not to renew the connection the next year.[148]

Special General Convention 1969

For some Episcopalians, revision of the familiar 1928 Prayer Book during a period of social turmoil was the last straw. It seemed to them that the same liberals who had led the church into social activism were now forcing their views on its worship life.[149] The 1969 Special General Convention epitomized the social and political struggles and controversies that gripped the nation and the church from roughly 1965 to 1975.

The 1969 Special General Convention which met from August 31 to September 5 in South Bend, Indiana, was an emergency session called to deal primarily with issues of social ethics in the crisis atmosphere of urban race riots that began in 1965 in Los Angeles, the black civil rights movement, campus unrest, and the escalating war in Vietnam.[150]

Though liturgical issues were not the focus of this session, the convention did agree to eight changes in *The Liturgy of the Lord's Supper* recommended by the SLC "to allay anxieties" about the direction and intent of Prayer Book reform.[151] The changes did not touch the substance of the rite but involved matters such as making the penitential order a normal part of the service while allowing for its occasional omission, providing a briefer litany form of the prayer of intercession, and other rubrical clarifications.

The A.P. council got a preview of those changes at its April 14-17, 1969, meeting, four months before they were submitted to the convention. Bonnell Spencer told A.P. the SLC had decided not to push for major revisions to *The Liturgy of the Lord's Supper* at this point, but to wait until 1970 to do a major revision, asking only for some rubrical changes now. "Particularly ... we felt some loosening and further experimentation could be done," Spencer said. The A.P. council discussed the SLC's proposals and also some possibilities for more substantial changes, such as providing several alternative forms for the prayer of intercession instead of only one.[152]

At the center of heated and emotional debate at the 1969 convention was the $9 million General Convention Special Program, which was a fund to combat racism and social inequities in ways that were not being reached through existing church channels. Presiding Bishop John E. Hines had conceived it; the 1967 General Convention had approved it. The fund was highly controversial because its administrators made grants to black and Hispanic organizations which were perceived to be "radical," sometimes over the explicit objections of local bishops. Many church members were shocked that their church seemed to be subsidizing anarchy and violence. In reaction, some conservative church members began to withhold financial support from their dioceses, which in turn withheld it from the national church. By 1970 diocesan support for the national church had fallen $3.5 million short of its needs. At the same time, church membership declined steadily from a peak of

3.4 million in 1966 before rebounding and stabilizing in the 1980s at under three million members. Though the 1969 convention continued the special fund, General Convention discontinued it in 1973.[153]

In addition to 144 bishops and 698 lay and clerical deputies at South Bend, 311 "additional representatives" attended to give voice to groups usually not heard in the church's ordinary ways of governing. Present were Black Panthers, anti-war activists, youth representatives, liberation theologian Robert McAfee Brown, anti-war activist Dr. Benjamin Spock, Andrew Young of the Southern Christian Leadership Conference, representatives of "alternative" churches and "floating" parishes, and many more, all reflecting a country and a church convulsed and struggling. Two AWOL American military men protesting the Vietnam war requested sanctuary at the convention. About 400 of the 1,000 members of the House of Deputies came forward to support them.[154]

A.P. had been asked to conduct special liturgies at the convention.[155] A.P.'s midnight eucharists following the convention evening sessions were an attempt "to react eucharistically to the events of the day" and "were seen as a reconciling agency in a most difficult convention and were praised as such in both houses."[156]

A.P. was the instrument for a transforming moment at that difficult convention. Delegates had spent an exhausting day in highly emotional and heated debate about the Black Manifesto, which accused the Episcopal Church of racism. At one point, Mohammed Kenyatta of the Black Economic Development Conference had grabbed the microphone from a lay deputy to demand $200,000 in reparations from the Episcopal Church for past offenses against black Americans. The convention ultimately approved a grant to the Black Economic Development Conference.[157] But that night the House adjourned late, having postponed action until the next morning. That Tuesday night was a moment of despair for the convention, Henry Breul reported.

The debate in the lower house had been bitter and terrifying and a feeling that the Church was through pervaded the Convention. After a discussion on the grass in front of Stepan Center, Bishop [C. Kilmer] Myers [of California] stood up and pointed to the loaf and the chalice and said, "Here are Bread and Wine ... tell me about them." The congregation one by one added the Prayer of Consecration beautifully and movingly and when all the elements for consecration were present, the Bishop lifted up the loaf, broke it and we ate and drank. At the end he asked that instead of the blessing, we greet each other with the peace. There were tears and weeping for joy, for what had started as a Mass of Penitence and Despair had emerged through the operation of the Spirit into a Mass of Hope.[158]

On the final night of the convention, Otis Charles "led a huge group with many bishops in an exciting Eucharist of thanks which really wrapped up and resolved many of the tensions that had been shattering the convention," Breul reported.[159]

Breul's assessment was that "A.P. has surfaced in the eyes of the Church at a time when its insights and creativity are desperately needed."[160] A.P.'s liturgical expertise, social sensitivity, and political acumen made it not just an adjunct to this Special General Convention but a part of its essence. Other liturgies which A.P. sponsored at the convention provided a liturgical venue for the inclusion of blacks, students, and experimental churches.[161]

A.P.'s sense of humor, too, leavened the atmosphere at the Special General Convention. The centerpiece for A.P.'s presence this time was not a tasteful seventeenth-century altar, as in 1961—it was something called the "Joy Box." The distance between the two measures signaled a revolution in liturgical tastes and ideology that occupied A.P., and the ecumenical liturgical scene, during the sixties. The Joy Box "will take a bit of explaining."[162]

The Joy Box was brainstormed by A.P. members Thomas Babbit, an architect; Vienna Anderson, an artist; and Otis Charles. It made its first appearance at the Liturgical Conference in Milwaukee the week before Special General Convention.[163] The box was a big contraption that people were invited to step into. Standing outside the box were "a couple of bermuda-shorted, knobby-kneed clerics who were in place as the front men for the Associated Parishes exhibit" and Vienna Anderson, a "sylph-like ... perfectly stunning creature to look at."[164]

The exterior of the box was "[s]plashed with red paint and flower-power slogans. ... Billowing forth from the top of the box were streams of soap bubbles, apparently engineered by the A.P. staff on duty. ... Part of the side of the box was reserved for impromptu graffiti by the passers-by." Passing through a beaded curtain, people found themselves in utter darkness. As they groped around they encountered one another, and sooner or later realized that the clue to the box was the buttons covering the walls which they were meant to explore. Touching the buttons set off "[s]trobe lights. Pleasant gurgley noises. Sirens, bells, horns. The master light switch illuminates the whole interior of the box, but once you know where it's all at, you want the master switch off, so that you can feel by yourself."[165]

Of course, there was a deeper meaning to this *chambre de plaisir.*

> The box gives a group of people an experience in sharing, for the lights and sounds operate only when people cooperate and touch and press the module. Those pressing have difficulty in seeing the results of their own work, but actually provide the goodies for others in a different area of the box; thus they not only have to cooperate, but actually give their cooperation to someone else to enjoy. One woman in Milwaukee was heard to say, "Gee, this is better than my husband!"[166]

Emerging from the Joy Box, each person was offered a button saying "BE" and bread and wine. Seven or eight hundred bishops, deputies, and visitors went through the box in one night in South Bend, A.P. reported.[167]

To criticize the phenomenon would be churlish. The Joy Box was an emblem of another time and attitude. Between us and it a great gulf is fixed, and none may pass from hence to us. But in

1969, A.P. was pulling it off, putting it on, and inviting people in. It was a toy, an absurdity, a liturgy by surprise, and people loved it.

Most people, at least. "People really get hostile with it sometimes," A.P. reported to its members.[168] And it was possible to miss the point entirely, "to walk through the space and emerge saying (as one woman did), 'Your exhibit isn't working.'"[169] Some people were "upset," in those days when debate about women's ordination caused anxiety, that it was women who offered bread and wine after the Joy Box experience.[170] And for some people, the Joy Box produced "apprehension," A.P. reported. "Some people didn't like it at all; I don't just mean they didn't get it: I mean they *did not like it*. Some people flinch even from hearing it described!"[171]

The box took a lot of maintenance, was not too hardy, and required the presence of a staff to keep it functioning. It was used again after South Bend at the New Idea Festival in Detroit, November 30 to December 4, 1969; at the Eighth General Assembly of the National Council of Churches; and finally at the 1970 General Convention in Houston, outside the House of Bishops.[172] From thence it passes from history.

A.P.'s engagement with the liturgical temper of the times was not without reflection and discussion. It was inevitable, perhaps even salutary, that a group which saw itself on the "cutting edge" of liturgical awareness should have experimented using the cultural *lingua franca* of the day. But behind the ephemera lay some serious discussion by the A.P. council of issues like the future of the church and A.P.'s role in "alerting Episcopalians ... to the winds of change that are going on."[173]

"If we can reconcile those who have been forgotten and those who are breaking out with liturgical worship, we can make a genuine contribution to the church of today and of the future that will be of immeasurable value," the council said in a discussion in 1968. Council member Jon Olson said that the issue for A.P. was how to communicate the essence of the gospel.

The issue that has been on my mind is how it is possible to be the Church by doing, by saying, by being the good news that things as they are are desirable, that things as they are are grace-filled and open-ended and not a cul de sac. Particularly liturgically and in terms of structures. How to be the Church? How to express the fact that there is good news?[174]

Or as council member Arthur Walmsley said, "We are facing questions which affect the capacity of the Church to survive."[175] Beneath the high spirits and pop liturgies of the moment lay some thinking about substance.

One issue A.P. seems not to have examined, though, was how its identification with things like the Joy Box and political activism may have shaped people's perception of what Prayer Book revision was all about. A.P. did not issue the kind of cautionary footnotes about the Joy Box that it did about a Jacobean altar eight years earlier. Episcopalians whose ideas about liturgical renewal were embryonic and whose capacity for flowered chasubles and appeals to primal emotions was limited, might be forgiven for equating Prayer Book revision with liturgical "prancing before a psychedelic calf," as one correspondent to *The Living Church* put it.[176]

Romantic, superficial, and sentimental the "pop" liturgies of the period may have been. Yet these liturgies said clearly that the grip of the past was dead, the future open-ended, and all things could be made new. Liturgical tastes had changed in the sixties and A.P. reflected the change. What remained constant was A.P.'s vision of the renewal of the church, rooted in the liturgy.

A.P.'s Liturgical Experiments

A.P.'s liturgical experiments from 1965 to 1967 consisted of the kind of textual rearrangements of the 1928 Prayer Book that had begun to appear in the experimental rites published in the late 1950s and early 1960s. After 1967, A.P. began experimenting with a more radical, free-wheeling liturgical style, which lasted roughly until sometime in the early 1970s.

What descriptions of textual and ceremonial rearrangements do not convey is the exciting sense of engaging fresh ideas that anticipated the future. Thanks to Larry Rouillard, who edited the *A.P. Newsletter* in the mid-1960s, we have several descriptions of eucharistic liturgies at A.P. council meetings and conferences.

At the liturgy in St. Timothy's Church, St. Louis, during the November 1965 council meeting, all the sacred ministers wore their street clothes—and the "subdeacon" was a woman! Mrs. Keith Durrall took her place at the altar with presider Nicholas Kouletsis and concelebrants Massey Shepherd and Samuel West. Pete Woodward was deacon, Carl Sayers preached, David Babin was "officiant" (master of ceremonies, perhaps?), and Robert Iles was crucifer.

The liturgy began with shortened Morning Prayer. A plainsong Te Deum (vv. 1–12) led into the eucharist. Morning Prayer and the Ante-Communion were read from the front pew on the epistle side of the holy table. Gelineau psalms were sung by the choir with the congregation joining in the antiphons for the gradual and communion. The gospel procession took deacon and preacher to the pulpit behind the table. In the sermon, Sayers related the gospel to the recent Selma-to-Montgomery, Alabama, civil rights march in which he took part. After the creed, the deacon received the *ex tempore* intercessions of the people, saying after each one, "Lord, hear our prayer," and the people answering, "And let our cry come unto Thee." The Liturgy of the Eucharist began with the Kiss of Peace. Deacon and subdeacon prepared the table. The three concelebrants stood together behind the table facing the people. Deacon and subdeacon stood at each end. At communion, the congregation moved to two stations at each side of the table to receive.

From today's perspective none of this causes one to sit up with a start. It sounds like many a standard liturgy on any Sunday in any of hundreds of parishes. But that is the point. Its involvement of the people in popular psalmody, spontaneous prayer, and procession at communion, the climaxing of the liturgy of the Word with a gospel procession, the topicality of the sermon, the egalitarianism expressed by the ministers' clothing, the collegiality in presbyteral ministry expressed by concelebration as well as the diversity in the church's ministry represented by the deacon and the ministry of a woman at the altar—all contributed to an experience of the essence of what liturgy was about and to its connection with contemporary life which, in the context of 1965, was revolutionary. And that despite the fact that the text used must have been that of the 1928 Book of Common Prayer.[177]

A.P. experimented with an informal living room setting for the liturgy at the council's April 1966 meeting at Orleton Farms, a conference center in Ohio. "Knowing something of the structure of the proposed revision of the Eucharist, we designed the Prayer Book Eucharist along its order," Rouillard reported.

People sat in a circle around the table and the president preached from his chair. Communion, using bread baked by the conference center's cook, was administered to people where they stood. Susan Calvin's newly composed "Orleton Mass," dedicated to A.P., was the music for the Kyrie, Sanctus, and Agnus Dei. The liturgy at this meeting probably was the utter limit to which Cranmer could be taken in informality and modernity.

> With a real sense of the fullness of the Liturgy of the Word and Sacrament, enriched by the music carefully selected, and the sense of our community in Christ and with one another, the Eucharist was indeed the confrontation by God in Christ and of His people gathered there. One might add, too,—in 40 minutes![178]

What worked in a small, prepared group did not translate to a larger scale, though. The first of two eucharists at an A.P.-sponsored regional liturgical conference in Chicago in April 1967 featured the *Experimental Liturgy* of Cope, Davies, and Tytler published in 1958, and included a play by high school students as the gradual.

The major weakness of the entire service was its unfamiliarity. Not only was the rite not known and understood but the addition of the play and for many, the novelty of Susan Calvin's music made the whole service lack a sense of joy, spontaneity, and movement. There was the dichotomy between a quite avant-garde dramatic form, an only slightly changed language, and the difficulty of music including the Hymnal Suppliment's [sic] *Magnificat*, Susan Calvin's Mass, and one hymn at the Offertory with something of a let-down at the end with a simple said-ending using the prayer of Thanksgiving and a Dismissal. Also, with the Bishop [Hallock of Milwaukee] present, and without either an Absolution or a Benediction, one could justly ask, "Why was he present since he did not preside?"[179]

A second eucharist at the Chicago conference, held at dining tables immediately before an evening banquet, seemed to work better. Bread and wine were set on each table for the priests present to concelebrate with the presider, who wore a "psychedelic" chasuble "with big brightly colored flowers on an orange background." This time the text was the 1928 Prayer Book eucharistic rite, omitting the penitential order, inserting an Old Testament lesson, and following the general structure of *The Liturgy of the Lord's Supper,* which did not receive approval for trial use until the following September.

The corporate concelebration and communion at each table was powerfully and dramatically effective in the liturgy. Even those who were at first hesitant about it found themselves caught up in the total action and involved completely. Here was to be found a sense of community in Christ, a joy and spontaneity within the basic prayer book language and structure.[180]

All the correct liturgical virtues of the 1960s seem to have been present at that 1967 celebration—the overcoming of fear of new things, involvement, community, joy, spontaneity.

Not the eucharist, but the daily office was the issue that polarized the A.P. council and marked a shift to more radical liturgical experimentation after 1967. A.P.'s bylaws required daily Morning and Evening Prayer at council meetings. Cranmer's quasi-monastic offices were beginning to chafe, however. Rouillard wrote in 1967:

I do feel that A.P. should become as experimental as possible in any daily forms of prayer and praise that it may use at its meetings. There is much that is being done in conferences of ecumenical dimensions regarding corporate prayer services—Bible vigils, thematic services, the celebration of penance, contemporary litanies, etc. The time has come for us to break out of the Prayer Book structure and find ways to create new forms that grow out of our life and experience today.[181]

The April 1968 council meeting began one day with "informal prayers and reflection on a nonverbal exercise" instead of Morning Prayer.[182] At the following November's meeting the group had "considerable discussion" on whether even to have Morning and Evening Prayer.[183] By the following April the subject was so touchy that the council tried an end run around it. "After our blow-up last year I thought those who wanted to say the offices could gather together," A.P. president Paul Hoornstra said. "The Executive Council believed we should have the offices and anyone who has serious hang-ups could stay away."[184] The April 1969 meeting also decided to use the Consultation on Church Union's new eucharistic rite, just published the year before, for its only eucharistic celebration.

A.P. achieved the last word in liturgical romanticism with a bucolic eucharist celebrated at its 1970 spring meeting in St. Louis.

We had a memorial for Jack Sweeney and Thaddeus Clapp, former Council members who had died within the last few months. We had it alfresco in the beautiful Spring atmosphere. Taking with us blankets, bottles of wine, and assorted breads, we went to the pond for our Eucharist—consisting of listening to readings from St. Luke, "The Road to Emmaus" Easter Monday Gospel; Antoine de St. Exupery's *The Little Prince,* and Sam Keen's *Apology for Wonder.* Then each of us, wearing vestments and stoles, went alone to meditate on a piece of bread and cup of wine—drinking and eating and feeling—bringing back enough to feed each other. The Eucharistic Prayer was put in constellation fashion with a contribution from each one of us and a gathering by Bill Wendt, the central celebrant. At the great moment of communion Bill simply said, "Feed each other." We had our lunch of wine and bread and cheese and fruit in the sun.[185]

Beyond The Liturgy of the Lord's Supper

Even as the 1966 *Liturgy of the Lord's Supper* was in use and being evaluated, the SLC was receiving criticisms, comments, and suggestions from its two hundred and sixty consultants and from the chairmen and members of the Diocesan Liturgical Commissions. The SLC decided to press ahead simultaneously with a further revision of the eucharistic liturgy.[186]

A.P. council members got a look at the latest revised rite at their November 1968 meeting. Francis Bowman, who also was on the SLC Drafting Committee on the Eucharist, distributed copies of his committee's suggestions at the A.P. meeting. The council decided not to try to celebrate the proposed rite at its meeting; members were to study it and write their responses to Bowman.[187]

The SLC reported in 1970 that the reordering of the basic shape of the eucharist in *Liturgy of the Lord's Supper* had won "almost unanimous" acceptance, but there was "a good deal of disagreement" about whether to keep Cranmerian English or to adopt a modern idiom.[188] For example, as early as December 1968, the Drafting Committee on the Psalter, at its second meeting, had said it "rejects the compromise" of producing two versions of the psalms, and proposed to submit a version in which only modern English was used "even for direct address to God."[189]

The SLC's revision of *The Liturgy of the Lord's Supper,* published in 1970 as *Prayer Book Studies 21: The Holy Eucharist,* offered both a First Service in "1928 Prayer Book" language but following the revised structure, and a Second Service in modern English that also used the ecumenical translations of common liturgical texts prepared by the International Consultation on English Texts, which were in contemporary English. Henry N. Hancock, a member of the Drafting Committee on the Eucharist, was the person most responsible for the option of a eucharistic liturgy combining a new structure with traditional language.[190] *PBS 21* also included a third service,

An Order for Celebrating the Holy Eucharist, which was not a complete rite but an outline for celebrations at times other than the main Sunday or weekly eucharist.

The SLC's decision to include a traditional language option was the result, said Massey Shepherd, of the questionnaires responding to *The Liturgy of the Lord's Supper,* which showed a fifty-fifty split over the language issue. "About fifty percent felt that we had gone too far, and the other half that we had not gone far enough. The responses had no relation to age. Many young people were negative in their reaction, and many of the elderly were enthusiastic." Still, anxieties multiplied because many people in the church believed that they had to choose between the traditional language rite and the modern language one. The SLC "was never able to allay these fears and misapprehensions," Shepherd said, in large part because it had no money to launch an extensive educational program.[191]

At one level, the SLC was pragmatically responding to pastoral and political realities in providing a traditional language option. But at another level, the SLC was recognizing officially that pluralism without partisanship,[192] even at the heart of the liturgy, was allowable, even desirable. More than any specific revision of a text or structure, the admittance of pluralism between the covers of the Prayer Book was a most significant aspect of Prayer Book revision.

To many church people, Prayer Book revision reduced itself to the single issue of modernizing its language, a loss of Cranmerian English which alarmed some and saddened others. A.P., however, felt no need to address this issue during the crucial years of trial use from 1967 to 1976; minutes and transcripts of A.P. council meetings for the period reflect no concern with the matter. A.P., through its members who were on the SLC and on various drafting committees, was aware of the direction that language for the new rites was taking. In 1968 and 1969, for example, the council heard reports from SLC and drafting committee members that rites were being produced in modern English. It was not an issue that originated with A.P., nor one it had to organize, argue for, or spell out the liturgical implications of. The official process of Prayer Book revision had produced the decision, it accorded with the temperament of A.P.'s work, and A.P. assumed it as part of the context of liturgical renewal.[193]

But the use of modern English for common prayer disturbed some people's profoundest religious perceptions. After a lifetime of calling God "Thou," which implied a reverence one cannot feel for the people about us, said a California woman, why "should it suddenly become necessary for me to call him 'You'?"[194]

But use of "thou" and "thee" for God and "you" for human beings had nothing to do with theology, others argued, and everything to do with mundane rules of grammar governing singular and plural pronouns. "The notion of 'thou' and 'thee' for the deity and 'you' for human beings has nothing to do with Prayer Book usage, and I can't imagine how it got started, for if one ever reads the Prayer Book one can't help but see otherwise," said a Tennessee organist.[195] And a Connecticut rector added, "Whom, after all, is the Priest addressing when he says, 'Thou shalt love the Lord thy God' or 'The Body ... given for thee'; or to whom do the people say, 'And with thy spirit'?"[196]

The most violent antagonisms began to surface as Prayer Book revision continued. This "wretched Prayer Book revision" was being "jammed down our throats by a small group of cynical New York sharpies," a California priest fulminated.[197] The whole thing was "liturgical coercion,"[198] a Pennsylvania rector said; a chance, fumed an Oregon vicar, for "people who made a lifetime study of liturgics ... to lay their trip on a whole church."[199] Advocates of changes in the liturgy "are asking us to toss out the window all that we have been taught by the entire Book of Common Prayer ... and it now appears that this has been their purpose all the time," one North Carolina parishioner said.[200]

Who asked for Prayer Book revision anyway? outraged church people wanted to know. Everyone, a Georgia priest suggested, who ever did not use the 1928 book as it stood.

> In my lifetime in the Episcopal Church there never has been a time without a call for revision. On the one hand, I have lived through *The People's Anglican Missal,* non-communicating Masses, the importation of "Wee Bookies," and innumerable additions being made to the ordinary of the Eucharist. On the other hand, I have seen the norm of Sunday eucharistic worship flouted by the establishment of non-canonical Sunday services of Morning Prayer and Sermon and Offering and more prayers.
>
> The call to Prayer Book revision has been loud and clear and the Liturgical Commission should be commended for their efforts to meet this call.[201]

Opposition to Prayer Book revision focused in the Society for the Preservation of the Book of Common Prayer (later shortened to the Prayer Book Society), formed in 1971 at the University of the South, Sewanee, Tennessee. The SPBCP lobbied the 1973 and 1976 General Conventions in an attempt to stop Prayer Book revision. The society represented conservatives' and traditionalists' horror at the loss of the incomparable English of the 1928 Prayer Book. It also represented their awakening to the paradigm shift that had been driving the liturgical movement since the 1830s and which took its modern shape after the Second World War.

Behind the new rites lay not just a question of literary taste, but a theological response to an age in which sixteenth-century theology was no longer viable. "The shift, then, in liturgical renewal in the Episcopal Church coming at this time away from Cranmer and the Tudor deity should not then be at all surprising," said Urban T. Holmes.[202] The theological criticisms of the SPBCP proceeded from a classical, pre-critical, sixteenth-century theology, said Holmes,[203] couched in what Massey Shepherd characterized as "negative and misguided propaganda."[204]

The SPBCP said that changes in the language and structure of the eucharistic rite had changed the meaning of the rite. "Theology is at stake," said Harold L. Weatherby, a spokesman for the society. If anyone was guilty of sectarianism or schism, it was those who wanted to substitute a modern liturgy for the traditional Anglican pattern. As far as the SPBCP was concerned, loyalty to the 1928 Prayer Book "really means a defense of the church against heresy and schism," Weatherby said.[205]

But such allegiance sounded to some church people "too much like the sort of statement that binds some people to the King James version of the Bible as the only true word of God."[206] They were wary of making the Prayer Book "into what it is not: an unerring record of what has been the faith and practice of the catholic church."[207]

Faculty at the School of Theology at the University of the South, where the SPBCP had been founded, publicly dissociated themselves from the society. The spirit within the church that produced the Prayer Book in the first place "is precisely the spirit of renewal and revision which the society for its preservation seems to oppose," they said.[208]

Besides, said a Brooklyn churchwoman, the fact that three General Conventions (1964, 1967, and 1970) had agreed on the principle of major revision—one more convention than necessary to adopt a new Prayer Book—"seems to me to cast considerable doubt on the status of the 1928 Prayer Book as an object for loyalty."[209] The Son of the Living God, said a New York priest, "I am sure, can make the transition to the second half of the 20th century as readily as he did to the first."[210]

Prayer Book revision was launched, but it was not at all clear at this point that the process would move forward. The initial stage of Prayer Book revision had met with a mixed reception in the church. Associated Parishes had shifted to an experimental direction that the church was not ready to accept. The forces of reaction seemed to stand a good chance of bringing Prayer Book revision to a halt. But the Standing Liturgical Commission steadily proceeded with its work and, as the next chapter shows, the shape of the new Prayer Book began to emerge.

Chapter Five

The Creation of the 1979 Prayer Book

An Overview of Developments From 1970 to 1976

The eucharist had been the knotty issue that launched Prayer Book revision. After 1970, the center of gravity in liturgical reform shifted to initiation, reflecting a church asking itself basic questions about discipleship, ministry, and the nature of the church. A new trial liturgy for baptism, as well as further revision of the eucharist and other Prayer Book material would come up for approval for trial use at the 1970 General Convention in Houston. As early as 1968 A.P. began mapping its strategy for the crucial 1970 General Convention. A.P. saw its task as "building opinions and responses to change within the church," as executive secretary Otis Charles told the A.P. council at its November 1968 meeting. "We don't know what the situation will be after [1970]. All we can do is keep that convention open and responsive to change."[1]

A.P. met with deputies to the 1970 General Convention, which met from October 11 to 22, and contributed to *Issues*, an "alternative" daily news sheet by A.P. and several other unofficial church organizations. A.P. sponsored 11 P.M. eucharists outdoors in front of the convention hall—all of them "fairly free and experimental."[2] The new button A.P. handed out at this convention said either "ON" or "NO," depending on how you turned it. "Wear it the way you feel," was A.P.'s advice.[3]

Without doubt, the reformed rite of baptism proposed to the 1970 convention by the SLC in *Prayer Book Studies 18: Holy Baptism With the Laying-On-of-Hands* marked the high tide of liturgical reform. The rite combined baptism with confirmation and first communion; presented baptism as giving the full gifts of the Holy Spirit and membership in Christ's Body, the church; and set forth the bishop as the chief minister of the rite, though a priest could act for the bishop in the bishop's absence. The rite presented the church with profound questions about sacramentology, ecclesiology, and ministry—questions which, as we shall see, the church was not ready to resolve.

Seven new *Prayer Book Studies* by the SLC were presented to the General Convention for approval in 1970. They included, in addition to the revised initiatory rites, revised rites for ordination, marriage, and burial, part of a revised psalter, a restructuring of the church year, and other material.[4] The 1970 convention approved them all for trial use during the 1971–1973 triennium. Some significant restrictions on the baptismal rite proposed in *PBS 18*, however, essentially gutted the proposed revision, as we shall see.

For convenience' sake, the new rites without their accompanying studies were collected and published in 1971 as *Services for Trial Use,* known as the "Green Book" from the color of its cover.[5] "Something very much like a new Book of Common Prayer was now appearing in the pews of many Episcopal churches," Urban Holmes said.[6] But some people had the notion that the Green Book was a complete Prayer Book, which from now on would be a poorly bound paperback.[7] They found its composition confusing and its provisions for options within various services bewildering and possibly compromising Anglican unity.[8]

Loss of the 1928 Prayer Book was blamed for "the damage we see everywhere in terms of attendance, finances, and devotional fervor."[9] The Green Book was one more indication that "there seems to be a concentrated and organized effort to abolish the Episcopal Church," a Wisconsin priest said. "One quick and certain way of achieving that goal is to destroy the book which contains the catholic faith as it was handed down from our blessed Lord to the apostles and which has been practised for nearly 2,000 years."[10] A Kansas woman voiced the depth of some people's antipathy to liturgical renewal. "Isaac too was laid on the altar of sacrifice as our Book of Common Prayer is now, and God intervened. I pray that God will intervene again in history and place the abominable Green Book in its place."[11]

One of the hundreds of consultants to the SLC assured all the authors of letters to the SLC that "we spend a great deal of time considering the feedback from the parishes and striving to find a viable way to express the Gospel in our day and time."[12] At the same time, other church people were getting tired of three years of hysteria. They pointed out that the new services of eucharist and Morning Prayer were enlivening parishes from South Carolina to Oregon, and that people taking active part in the services were discovering that "it's not really too bad."[13] People found that the second eucharistic service in the Green Book, for example, was "much more suited to *doing*" than the 1928 rite, a Colorado rector said. "They like the strength and the vitality of the contemporary English, they like being able to participate in the intercessions and the variety that the different forms offer, they like the affirmation in the prayer of consecration, they like ending the service with a final 'Thanks be to God.'"[14] For every parish that had experienced problems with the Green Book, said a Wisconsin priest, he could name half a dozen where it has been very well received. "I should think the proposed services would be the foundation of a Prayer Book around which Episcopalians of almost every stripe could rally."[15]

A.P. was taking nothing for granted. At the 1973 General Convention in Louisville, A.P. member Frank Cohoon of Topeka, a convention delegate, "was active on the floor in the House of Deputies," and "steady quiet explanation by A.P. members helped" in the convention's "overwhelming endorsement" of continuing Prayer Book revision.[16] A.P.'s booth at the 1973 convention was staffed "with persons who can discuss the issues of liturgical change. Lobbying for the proposals ... [was] in the [A.P. hospitality] suite where daily strategy meetings involving any Council members ... [were] held," A.P. reported.[17] A.P.'s voice on liturgical matters also reached the delegates through its contributions to *Issues*. A.P. was asked to organize the evening services after the convention sessions and was commended by the church's Executive Council for its work. Bishop Lyman Ogilby presided at the first service and was presented with a stole and chasuble from A.P. designed by Vienna Anderson in recognition of his support for the extemporaneous order for celebrating the eucharist that eventually was included in the 1979 Prayer Book.

The 1973 General Convention approved trial use of the remaining *Prayer Book Studies* rites which would comprise the new Prayer Book, as well as changes and variations in the trial rites already published. The controversial rite of baptism was revised as *Prayer Book Studies 26: Holy Baptism, together with A Form for Confirmation or the Laying-On of Hands by the Bishop with the Affirmation of Baptismal Vows*. A further revision of the daily office was issued and new rites for the dedication of churches and for celebration of new ministries appeared.[18] Now all the materials and rites that would be included in a future Book of Common Prayer were available for study, experiment, and use. The SLC assured the church in its report to the 1973 General Convention that it still urgently sought responses to the proposed rites and that "no part of its work has as yet reached the stage at which it may no longer be revised."[19]

All of the new rites that congregations normally would need for public worship were published in 1973 as *Authorized Services*, known colloquially as the "Zebra Book" from its striped cover. The pew edition contained the calendar and the services of baptism, confirmation with reaffirmation of baptismal vows, the three orders for the eucharist, daily morning and evening prayer in its first and second service forms as well as services for noonday, close of day, and for individuals and families, and the psalter. An expanded edition included, in addition, the lectionaries for the daily office and the eucharist, and the collects.[20]

The 1973 convention also accepted the SLC's proposal for a timetable to bring the process of Prayer Book revision to completion. The convention called for the presentation of a *Draft Proposed Book of Common Prayer* to the 1976 General Convention.

Before the 1976 General Convention in Minneapolis, A.P. mailed to all bishops and deputies a pamphlet explaining *The Advantages of Revision*. Boone Porter briefed the council in 1975 on the revisions of rites which the *Draft Proposed Book* would embody and gave a preview of the theological commentary on the new rites being prepared by the SLC's theological committee, published in 1976 as *Prayer Book Studies 29, Introducing the Proposed Book*, by Charles P. Price. At the 1976 convention, A.P. concentrated on lobbying delegates, contributing to *Issues*, and distributing on three successive days three A.P. pamphlets explaining and supporting the *Draft Proposed Book*.[21]

The *Draft Proposed Book of Common Prayer* which the SLC presented to the 1976 convention embodied the final consensus on the trial rites in use since 1967. The "Blue Book" or the "Blue Whale" as it was called from its sky-blue cover and 1,001-page size represented a typographical shift away from the bold, new look of *Prayer Book Studies XVII-24* produced through 1970. The individual Prayer Book Studies had used a variety of type faces; *Services for Trial Use* had simply reprinted the services (without their commentaries)—resulting in a book with no consistency in typefaces. The *Draft Proposed Book of Common Prayer* was printed in a typeface reminiscent of the 1928 Prayer Book, but kept the new style of format with generous use of headings and subheadings. Rubrics not needed by the congregation in the course of any service were gathered at the beginning and end of each rite ("Concerning the Service" and "Additional Directions"). It "looked like" the Prayer Book, in that respect, but layout, use of white space, and use of headings and subheadings gave it an uncluttered, new appearance.

Opposition focused in the Society for the Preservation of the Book of Common Prayer, now claiming 100,000 members, which lobbied the 1973 as well as the 1976 conventions. Samuel West recalled that at some public hearings, probably at the 1976 convention,

> when that society claimed it had not been given a fair hearing, even though A.P. and the society had been given equal time, A.P. stepped aside. After discussion with other council members present, then president Vivian Kingsley made a very brief report during the hearing on Prayer Book, [sic] and turned over the remaining (most of the) time to the society.

A.P. had invited the society's officers "to attend ... several meetings of [the] A.P. council to hear our discussions and to witness our liturgical celebrations," West said, but the offer never was taken up.[22]

The *Draft Proposed Book* won overwhelming approval from the 1976 convention: in the House of Deputies by more than ninety-five percent in the clerical order and eighty percent in the lay order, and in the House of Bishops by near unanimity.[23] It thus became the

Proposed Book of Common Prayer, and no further revisions were permitted. The vote at the 1979 General Convention was to be a straight yes or no to the entire *Proposed Book* as it stood.

The years from 1970 to 1976 were crucial in the development of the Book of Common Prayer 1979. With this quick sketch as background we turn now to look at the events of this period in more detail. First, we examine the most critical issue of this stage of Prayer Book revision—the controversial revision of the rites of initiation. The last two sections of this chapter examine developments within Associated Parishes during this critical period, and A.P.'s work in interpreting the new Prayer Book to the church once the book passed its first reading in 1976.

The Controversy About the Rites of Initiation

The Problem of Initiation: Background to PBS 18

Before the late 1950s, liturgical scholars had paid less attention to the history of the rites of initiation than to the evolution of the eucharist. One of the principal reasons for this, as Paul F. Bradshaw has pointed out, was that baptism had been relegated to the status of a private "pastoral office" in the practice of most churches rather than being seen as part of the mainstream of the liturgical life of the church. Until the later phase of the liturgical movement began to have an effect on initiation rites, there was not the same sensitivity to their shortcomings nor the same pressure for their revision as was felt in the case of the eucharist.[24]

Part of that pressure arose from an abiding unease among some churches with their practice of infant baptism, particularly in the face of a societal change in which it no longer made sense to expect that those baptized as infants would persevere as Christians, or that by baptizing children on demand, the church was having some kind of leavening effect on society. Who is a proper candidate for baptism?

What is a sacrament and how does it work? What is the church, or what ought it to be, and how should it engage an indifferent if not actively hostile culture as it goes about its work of making disciples? Initiation is where the church creates itself, and it was there that tensions surfaced about the church's self-identity vis-a-vis its surrounding culture.

Anxiety among Episcopalians manifested itself in debate over such issues as these: Should baptized children be admitted to communion before confirmation? If they are admitted before confirmation, should they receive prior instruction at a suitable age as English-speaking Roman Catholics customarily did? Is it important to provide a rite for mature personal profession of faith? How can the church prevent the lapse of church members after confirmation? In addition, new scholarly debate about the historical and theo-logical relation of confirmation to baptism had been gestating since the late 1940s.

The poles of the historical and theological debate were defined by Gregory Dix and G.W.H. Lampe. Dix argued in his 1946 book *The Theology of Confirmation in Relation to Baptism*[25] that in the New Testament and early church, water baptism into the death and resurrection of Christ and anointing with the Holy Spirit were two distinct actions which together constituted a single rite of Christian initiation. In the course of time, the two elements had been separated and the theological content of confirmation shifted to water baptism, with confirmation coming to be understood as an increase of grace. Dix argued for a return to the "primitive" understanding of confirmation as the bestowal of the Spirit which completed initiation. Baptism and confirmation should remain separated in time so that a conscious affirmation of faith could be made at confirmation.[26] Dix's perspective underlay the SLC's proposal for reform of baptism in 1950 in *Prayer Book Studies I*.

Lampe's reply to Dix, *The Seal of the Spirit,* published in 1951, argued that to associate the gift of the Spirit exclusively with confirmation contradicted scripture and Anglican tradition.[27] Lampe found no evidence for Dix's distinction between water baptism and Spirit baptism. When in the course of Western history the rite of initiation began to split into two parts, a doctrine of confirmation was developed to rationalize the division: the initial gift of the Spirit was assigned to baptism while confirmation was said to be a new gift of the Spirit for strengthening. The Spirit is conferred on infants at baptism, Lampe argued, though the realization of its effects may come either gradually during a lifetime or suddenly in a moment of conversion. Confirmation is an important moment, providing what Lampe called a fuller realization and actualization of what already had happened proleptically in baptism. In the case of adults, confirmation still is valuable but loses its force when separated from their baptism.[28]

Between these poles the theological and pastoral debate oscillated in books, theological journals, the popular church press, specially commissioned studies, and liturgical committees. A certain ambiguity surrounded Anglican understanding of confirmation, as Louis Weil, professor of liturgics at Nashotah House and member of the drafting committee on initiation from 1974 to 1976, pointed out. Because the Prayer Book withheld communion until after confirmation, some people saw confirmation as carrying some initiatory meaning. And because of nineteenth-century Roman Catholic influence, some people understood confirmation as "gift of the Spirit," an understanding which permitted a sacramental theology that saw baptism as incomplete.[29]

By the late 1960s, Episcopalians were questioning in earnest the Anglican initiatory pattern of baptism, catechesis, confirmation, communion. As Ruth A. Meyers' study demonstrates, there was a growing understanding of Christian initiation as a complex of rites, but there was no consensus on the meaning of confirmation or the action of the Holy Spirit in initiation. Confirmation was understood variously as a bestowal of the Holy Spirit or its gifts and as a public affirmation of faith.[30] A growing desire to restore the unity of the rite as in the early church led to proposals to restore an anointing with oil to baptism, emphasizing the objective conferral of the Spirit as integral to Christian initiation.[31] Some proposals linked conferral of the Spirit to a postbaptismal anointing, thus maintaining a distinction between water baptism and Spirit baptism, while others stressed that the Spirit is active throughout the initiatory process.

Adult baptism increasingly came to be understood as the normative pattern for initiation, but there were no serious proposals in the Episcopal Church or in the Church of England to eliminate infant baptism. A shift away from a theology of original sin which encouraged baptism of infants as soon as possible continued, however. A personal profession of faith was thought to be important, but there was no agreement on how this was to be done for those baptized as infants. In the Episcopal Church there was increasing frustration with confirmation as an "admission ticket" to communion and a graduation from Sunday school. This led to proposals to admit children to communion before confirmation, but most of these required some kind of instruction beforehand, a requirement which copied Roman Catholic practice and also reflected pastoral uneasiness as well as theological uncertainty over basic questions of ecclesiology and sacramentology.[32]

Already in 1964 in lectures at General Theological Seminary (published in 1965 as *Liturgy and Education*) Massey Shepherd argued there was "no good reason why we should not reintegrate in one single rite Baptism, Confirmation, and admission to the Eucharist," administered to either infants, adolescents, or adults depending on pastoral needs in the respective cases. Christians should be fully initiated once and for all, Shepherd said, and it is "spiritually healthy" for initiated children to enjoy the full privileges of the family, eating and drinking at the family table. The first step in reconstruction of the initiation liturgy, Shepherd said, would be to restore the presidency of the bishop in the total rite of initiation, not just confirmation.

"There is more meaning in the episcopal office, succeeding from that of the apostles, when it is viewed as a mission to preach and baptize than when it is restricted to a duty to visit and confirm," he said.[33]

In 1968 A.P. began to urge bishops to recognize baptism as the primary sacrament of conversion and initiation, and it argued for baptism as the only requirement for admitting children to communion. A.P. presented the issue as a pastoral question, urging all the church's active bishops "to create a climate which will support clergy who wish to communicate Baptized children. ... We believe our children should not be able to remember when they had not received communion." A.P.'s theological rationale for communicating children rested on an ecclesiological argument: when children were baptized, A.P. said, "they were admitted to the church or koinonia and the koinonia expresses its commonness in the Eucharistic meal." It also pointed to the ecclesiological anomaly of the 1967 General Convention's allowing baptized members of other churches to receive at Episcopal altars while "our own children are not given this opportunity."[34]

A.P. urged the church to take up either of the paths recommended by the 1968 Lambeth Conference for study and experiment: admission of children to communion after baptism and adequate instruction, with confirmation deferred to a later age; or infant baptism and confirmation together followed by admission to communion.

The Reform of Baptism: From PBS 18 to 1979 Prayer Book

A.P. made history when for the first time in the Episcopal Church a unified rite of baptism-confirmation-communion was administered to an infant in 1969. Four-month-old Sean R. Lampert was initiated by Anson Phelps Stokes, Bishop of Massachusetts, and his Coadjutor Bishop John Burgess on October 3, 1969, in Cambridge, Massachusetts, at a liturgical conference on Christian Initiation co-sponsored by A.P. and the Diocese of Massachusetts Liturgical Commission.

The rite used was that proposed by the Standing Liturgical Commission in *Prayer Book Studies 18: Holy Baptism with the Laying-On-of-Hands*, scheduled to come up for approval for experimental use at the 1970 General Convention in Houston. A.P.'s purpose in celebrating the rite was "to demonstrate what will become common practice if passed by the convention," according to a news report.[35]

PBS 18 not only recognized baptism as full initiation into the church, it included confirmation as part of initiation and eliminated it as a separate rite, allowed communion of initiated infants, and permitted priests to replace bishops in administering the whole rite. A.P.'s Bonnell Spencer, O.H.C., who chaired the drafting committee that drew up the rite, had been appointed to the SLC in 1964 and assigned to work on baptism and confirmation. Spencer, who had no expertise in the area, enlisted Leonel L. Mitchell, who in 1967 also served on the drafting committee. In 1964 Mitchell had just completed his doctoral dissertation on baptismal anointing in the liturgies of the early church to the tenth century, published in 1966 as *Baptismal Anointing*.[36] From 1964 to 1967, when the process of official Prayer Book revision began, Spencer, in consultation with Mitchell, presented to the SLC a series of reports which stressed that any revision should treat baptism, confirmation, and eucharist as one continuous act. On the knotty question of how and when the Holy Spirit is bestowed in baptism and confirmation, the reports argued that the Spirit was not *initially* bestowed either in water baptism or in confirmation; that baptism was the personal surrender by faith that permitted the already-present Spirit to take possession of the individual soul in an objective and sacramental way, while confirmation following at a later time after infant baptism allowed a deepening of commitment and receptivity to the influence of the Spirit. The laying-on-of-hands, with or without an anointing with oil, "somehow" completes the work of baptism and is associated with the gift of the Spirit, as Spencer put it in a progress report to the SLC in 1966.[37]

Revolutionary as *PBS 18* was, its drafters had not taken long to compose it once they sat down to write the new service. Spencer briefed the A.P. council at its spring 1969 meeting on *PBS 18* on the eve of its publication.

> The first thing Margaret Mead [the distinguished anthropologist who served on the drafting committee] said was: "You know we can't put this together the first time we try." And I said, "Of course we can't." And to our astonishment we started at 2:00 and this liturgy emerged by 9:30 that evening.[38]

Behind that draft, however, lay extensive discussions and position papers on theological and pastoral issues by Spencer, Mitchell, Mead, William S. Spilman, and other members of the drafting committee.[39] The A.P. council's discussion of the proposed text which Spencer presented centered around such issues as the use of sponsors, the communal dimension of initiation, the use of oil, and some details of text. Which is to say, A.P. supported the unification of the rite and its administration to infants. Only one A.P. councilman, Canadian member Borden Purcell, asked whether the drafting committee had considered administering initiation sometime in the candidate's teen years and admitting infants to the catechumenate. Spencer replied that "our feeling was very strong that a child should never be able to remember when he was not fed at the family table."[40] Spilman had been one advocate on the drafting committee for restricting initiation to adults, but the weight of opinion on the drafting committee was against his idea.[41]

When *PBS 18* got into the hands of Episcopal bishops, they perceived the rite as threatening their identity by removing one of their defining functions, confirming; and they perceived the rite as undermining their one time of contact with ordinary parish life, their visitations. In fact, the proposed rite strengthened the role of bishop as chief pastor who was to preach, baptize and celebrate the eucharist—not a chief executive officer who drops in and confirms.

"Its recommendations were more than the bishops of the

Episcopal Church could fathom," wrote Urban T. Holmes, who served on the rite's drafting committee from 1974 to 1976. "They had been out of seminary too long and were too threatened."[42]

The SLC had taken the stand that the theological and pastoral integrity of baptism should not be broken or overshadowed by a separate rite of confirmation. It had suggested to the church a new practice in which personal commitment to one's baptism should be made not once and for all at confirmation, but many times over, preferably within the context of a service of Baptism with the Laying-on-of-Hands which, the SLC hoped, would become a principal service of the congregation three or four times a year, one of these being the Great Vigil of Easter. But the SLC recognized that in addition to this congregational reaffirmation of baptismal vows, there was a need for a form of individual commitment at critical points in a person's life—such as a graduation, a change of vocation, the beginning of military service, the undertaking of a course of training, and so on. To fill some of the former functions of confirmation, the SLC in 1970 proposed "A Form of Commitment to Christian Service" in *Prayer Book Studies 24: Pastoral Offices*. Its intent was to enable a baptized person to affirm and renew his or her personal commitment to the service of Christ in the world. Such a public commitment, the SLC said, would in fact be a reaffirmation of baptismal promises in a specific context of Christian service.[43] The form was included in *Services for Trial Use* in 1971 and ultimately passed into the 1979 Prayer Book, but not as a replacement for confirmation, as the SLC had envisioned.

Holy Baptism With the Laying-On-of-Hands was printed unaltered in *Services for Trial Use*, but with a statement of the 1970 General Convention's specific guidelines regulating its experimental use. The most germane of the restrictions were: 1) the rite in its entirety could be used by bishops only; 2) only the baptismal section of the rite could be used by priests and other ministers, omitting the "confirmation" elements of laying-on-of-hands and its preceding prayer invoking the gifts of the Spirit; 3) children could be admitted to holy communion before confirmation, subject to the direction and guidance of the bishop—thereby accepting the principle that baptism, not confirmation, was the basis for admission to the eucharist.

Meanwhile, the Drafting Committee on Christian Initiation had begun to receive comments and suggestions on the basis of trial use of *PBS 18* and prepared "several major amendments" of the rite which were scrutinized by the SLC and its consultants. At a meeting in 1971 in Pocono Manor, Pennsylvania, the House of Bishops made emphatically clear that the bishops wanted a separate rite of confirmation presided over by a bishop.[44] Their insistence determined the direction that further revision of initiation would take. The House of Bishops considered the whole question of initiation at its Special Meeting in New Orleans, October 29 to November 3, 1972. The House of Bishops asked its theological and its Prayer Book committees to meet with the SLC to study the proposals on initiation and come up with a report. That joint meeting took place in Dallas December 2 to 9, 1972, and an ad hoc committee issued its report. Their "Statement of Agreed Positions" recognized that Christian initiation is an unrepeatable act of "baptism by water and the Spirit," administered in a rite that included hand-laying, consignation (with or without chrism), prayer for the gift of the Spirit, and eucharist, presided over by a bishop when one is present. But the statement went on to say that nonetheless a mature affirmation of faith before a bishop was strongly encouraged as a normal component of Christian nurture—though it was not completion of baptism, was not necessary before admission to communion, and could be repeated at significant times in a person's life. Still, the occasion when we affirm the baptismal vows made on our behalf in infancy "is a significant and unrepeatable event. It is one's 'Confirmation Day.'" The statement, prudently, did not attempt to disentangle the theology involved in recognizing the once-for-allness of baptism but still demanding a confirmation which is said to have an unrepeatable nature.[45]

After that, the disintegration of an integrated rite of baptism-confirmation-eucharist is reflected in the evolution of the rite's title, with confirmation reemerging as a full-fledged rite by the time of the 1979 Prayer Book. The 1972 "Statement of Agreed Positions" was the basis for further revision of initiation. Confirmation reappeared in 1973 and was separated from baptism in *Prayer Book Studies 26: Holy Baptism, together with A Form for Confirmation or the Laying-On of Hands by the Bishop with the Affirmation of Baptismal Vows.* But the SLC carefully tried to avoid assigning any initiatory quality to confirmation: the laying-on-of-hands in the confirmation rite in *PBS 26* is headed "Dedication to Mission." Simultaneously with the publication of *PBS 26,* the SLC published under its auspices a commentary on *PBS 26* (by Daniel B. Stevick with the aid of Leonel Mitchell and Thomas J. Talley) which downplayed the word "confirmation" in favor of the word "affirmation:" *Supplement to Prayer Book Studies 26: Holy Baptism, together with A Form for the Affirmation of Baptismal Vows with the Laying-On of Hands by the Bishop also called Confirmation.*[46] The pew edition of various rites authorized for trial use, however, was uncompromising: in *Authorized Services,* 1973, the titles of the initiation rites appeared as they were in *PBS 26.*[47] The SLC revised *PBS 26* in 1975, and confirmation was made even more emphatic in the title: *Holy Baptism; A Form for Confirmation, for Reception, and for the Reaffirmation of Baptismal Vows.*[48] In the 1976 *Draft Proposed Book of Common Prayer,* and in its successor, the *Proposed Book of Common Prayer* of 1976, the distinction is unambiguous; there are two separate rites: one for "Holy Baptism" (with provisions for incorporating confirmation, reception into the Episcopal Church, or reaffirmation of baptismal vows) and a rite for "Confirmation, with forms for Reception and for the Reaffirmation of Baptismal Vows"—a distinction which carried into the final 1979 Book of Common Prayer.

By way of tracing a path through these documents, we may note that after the bold proposal of 1970 in *PBS 18,* the Episcopal Church by 1973 had reasserted the necessity of confirmation for all those baptized at an early age; and in the Proposed Book of 1976, a new rubric, inserted in the confirmation rite by the 1976 General Convention,[49] said explicitly that even those baptized as adults were "expected to make a public affirmation of their faith and commitment to the responsibilities of their Baptism in the presence of a bishop and to receive the laying on of hands"—unless they had been baptized with laying on of hands by a bishop.[50]

Clearly, what the framers of the 1976 rubric were aiming to preserve was their understanding of the role and identity of bishops, not any theological position on the status of confirmation. Confirmation, the rubrics said, was but a "mature public affirmation of ... faith and commitment to the responsibilities of ... Baptism."[51] If that were the case, what reason was there to "expect" an adult, who already had made a mature public affirmation of faith and commitment to the responsibilities of baptism when he or she was baptized with water by a priest, to again make another mature public affirmation and commitment before a bishop? Evidently, the reason was not that he or she needed to receive something else, such as the Holy Spirit, but only to allow "a bishop" to be involved.

Even the difference in the confirmation rubrics of the 1976 Proposed Book and the 1979 Prayer Book between the words "the" and "a" is ecclesiologically significant. In the rite's first rubric (the substance of which first appeared in 1973 in *PBS 26*), confirmands are expected to make a mature profession of faith before "the bishop"—as if to say, the bishop of their diocese, the bishop they are in pastoral relationship with. In the confirmation rite's second rubric, inserted by General Convention into the 1976 Proposed Book, those baptized as adults are instructed to make a public affirmation of faith before "a bishop"—as if to say, any bishop, so long as it's a bishop. The ecclesiology implicit in the first rubric is that of pastoral relationship; that of the second is of the power and status of bishops.

Theologically, the 1979 baptismal rite affirmed that "Holy Baptism is full initiation by water and the Holy Spirit into Christ's Body the Church."[52] Baptism consisted of: 1) immersion in, or pouring of, water in the name of the Trinity; 2) a prayer over the candidate(s) thanking God that "by water and the Holy Spirit" they have received forgiveness of sin and new life, and asking God to "sustain *them* ... in your Holy Spirit," and alluding to the traditional seven gifts of the Holy Spirit (this prayer was moved to this spot in *PBS 18* from its place in the 1928 confirmation rite); 3) a signing of the forehead with a cross (using, if desired, chrism consecrated by the bishop) while saying, "*N.*, you are sealed by the Holy Spirit in Baptism and marked as Christ's own for ever. Amen."[53]

The 1979 confirmation rite presents itself as a reaffirmation or renewal of the baptismal covenant, a claim which seems not to compromise the statement that baptism is full initiation by water and the Spirit. But on the other hand, confirmands are described as now "committing themselves to Christ," they are described as now being sent forth in the power of the Spirit to serve God, and in the first of two alternative formulas for hand-laying, the bishop prays for a strengthening with the Holy Spirit so that the confirmand may be empowered for service.[54] These statements could be interpreted as not contradicting the baptismal rite since the confirmation rite does not explicitly say that a fresh outpouring of the Holy Spirit is now taking place, nor does it say that baptism is now somehow being completed. On the other hand, the tenor of these examples suggests that something new is happening in confirmation, that the Holy Spirit is now being invoked for strengthening, and that the point of this new strengthening is to empower the confirmands now for service. The textual evidence is ambiguous and the rubrical evidence—the fact that a rite of confirmation is required at all—does nothing to dispel the ambiguity. Nor does it help that the 1979 Catechism assigns confirmation the status of a "sacramental rite."

Liturgically, theologically, pastorally, and politically, the result reflected uncertainty on basic issues of sacramental theology, ecclesiology, and ministry.

But the church's struggle with the question of Christian initiation did accomplish a fundamental, significant reform. Holy Baptism in the 1979 Prayer Book is designed for use with adults, with appropriate modifications for use with infants. The structure of the rite is significant: adults and older children are presented for baptism first; the interrogations, renunciations, and wording of the baptismal covenant presume that the candidates can speak for themselves. The rite implies an adult or mature commitment. Adult baptism is taken as the pattern and infant baptism is made sense of in the context of an adult believing community.

The 1979 Prayer Book also elevates baptism to a proper dignity as a gospel sacrament in the mainstream of the church's life. Baptism is to be publicly celebrated at the principal Sunday service, according to the rubrics. The congregation has an active role, participating as the representatives of the household of God, welcoming the newly baptized, and recommitting themselves to living a baptismal life. The bishop, when present, is the chief minister of the sacrament, preaching the Word and presiding at baptism and eucharist. In addition to an episcopal visitation, baptism is most appropriately administered on four baptismal feasts in the course of the year: the Easter Vigil, with its focus on dying and rising with Christ through baptism; Pentecost, which celebrates the Spirit's work of enlightenment and empowerment; All Saints' Day, or the Sunday after, when the function of baptism as incorporation into the community of the church, Christ's Body, receives emphasis; and the feast of the Baptism of our Lord, with its emphasis on baptismal vocation and mission. Taken together, these provisions amount to a reassignment of the place of baptism in the modern church and a reassessment of its significance. Baptism had long been classed as a pastoral office and often was administered privately, corrupting the intent of Cranmer and of Anglican tradition as reflected in English editions of the Prayer Book. Now baptism has taken its place in the mainstream of the life of the church as the church defines itself as separate from society and intentional about making disciples. The pastoral and theological vistas that baptism opens up invite new thoughts about what it means to be a Christian in the late twentieth century.

Popular Reaction to PBS 18

Although the baptismal rite of *PBS 18* generated a considerable amount of controversy, it did not stir the kind of popular anxieties and passions that revision of the eucharist did. Baptism lay on the margins of most people's experience of religion. Confirmation was the issue people recognized. They did not reject a united rite of initiation, said Louis Weil, so much as they felt that eliminating confirmation as an occasion for personal profession of faith and pastoral contact with the bishop entailed a loss of profound pastoral importance to Anglicanism. And hesitancy about giving communion to children reflected an abiding uneasiness about infant baptism itself.[55]

A proposal by Bishop Frederick J. Warnecke of Bethlehem, Pennsylvania, for example, to administer confirmation as a rite of adult commitment at age eighteen or thereabouts, with no suggestion that the Holy Spirit was received in confirmation (since it had already been received in water baptism) articulated one understanding of the sacrament among Episcopalians and appealed to many as a pragmatic reform. Confirmation had become a "grab-bag" of "ill-assorted" matters packaged together, Warnecke said in a March 1969 article in *The Episcopalian*: fulfillment of the commitment of baptism; reception of the sevenfold gifts of the Spirit; admission to communion; and the occasion of an episcopal visitation. He called for the church to experiment with a new initiation policy: water baptism of infants, admission to communion after preparation somewhere around ages eight to ten, and confirmation when one was ready for mature commitment.[56]

The idea delighted many readers, mostly because it seemed a sensible answer to problems they recognized: the issue of the right age for admission to communion; the need for a conscious commitment to the faith; the right age to allow for a thoughtful weighing of options before making a mature commitment; and a reform which would assist the church in holding on to church members after confirmation.[57] One Massachusetts churchman did warn that changes in the practice of confirmation would be only superficial without "an adequate theology of the laity which will point the people of God into the world through the apostolic mission of the Church."[58] But for the most part, people's perceptions seemed to bypass the theological perspectives being raised by *PBS 18*. Yet one woman, baptized and chrismated as an infant in the Russian Orthodox Church, suggested that if the Episcopal Church adopted "the use of holy oil at the Baptism of babies, Confirmation may not be necessary."[59]

A.P. President Henry Breul argued in a 1970 letter to *The Living Church* that the present practice of confirmation really amounted to a corruption of the office of bishop. The bishop "comes in full panoply to a parish to administer a *minor* sacrament that is not even mentioned in the catechism"—a situation which has forced the church "into the anomaly of suffragan bishops, that is, bishops without authority." *PBS 18* had the virtue of putting the bishop "in a clear position as the chief sacramental person in the church, and thus restores his apostolic role," Breul said. Some moment of adult reaffirmation is needed—maybe after a person has left home—but tying that moment to entrance into the eucharistic community "is a denial of the meaning of baptism."[60]

A 1970 editorial in *The Living Church* feared that the church would lose two great values, pre-confirmation instruction and a sacramental high point which a person could remember forever. It urged the 1970 General Convention to vote no on *PBS 18*. Trial use of the proposed rite would cause confusion as to who was confirmed and who was not if the experiment were abandoned after a few years, would set Episcopalians moving in the opposite direction on confirmation from Roman Catholics and Lutherans, and would offend those already confirmed by suggesting there was something amiss about the way they were confirmed. The editorial saw in *PBS 18* nothing but "another convulsive change" which would do nothing but "alienate a large number of faithful churchpeople who are already having to endure grievous tensions."[61]

A North Carolina priest in reply demythologized the experience of confirmation. Most people can't remember what they learned in confirmation classes, and the sacramental high point often amounted to nothing more than release from Christian education. The church would gain more than it lost by adopting *PBS 18*, with its provision for renewed allegiance throughout a person's life accompanied by continuous Christian education.[62]

PBS 18 was attempting to face up to two important issues in the life of the church, said the Rev. Henry I. Louttit, Jr., of Valdosta, Georgia. Theologically, he pointed out, it makes little sense to rationalize confirmation by saying that a baptized person has got the Spirit but hasn't got the Spirit's gifts. Psychologically, the practice of confirmation actually works as a graduation from Christian education and "from any deep commitment to the Lord."[63]

After the baptismal portion of *PBS 18* was approved for trial use, a 1971 editorial in *The Living Church* wondered if the proposed baptismal rite didn't express a "Bowdlerized Christianity," a substitution of optimistic Americanism for scriptural Christianity. Instead of promising to war against the unholy trinity of the world, the flesh, and the devil until their life's end, baptismal candidates were required only to renounce "evil in all its forms"—"which is about as drastic and heroic as coming out fearlessly for motherhood."[64]

"Take the devil seriously, if you like," a priest and scholar replied, "but please do not draw the conclusion that it is essential to Christianity that one must believe that the devil exists, that he has an ontology."[65] But a Los Angeles churchman agreed that *PBS 18* was a "modernist replacement for the Gospel" and "a reduction and an alteration amounting to a repudiation" of the faith.[66] In any event, when the baptismal rite was revised in 1973 as *PBS 26*, the triumvirate of Satan, the world, and sinful desires that draw one from the love of God made their reappearance in the renunciations, where they remain in the 1979 Prayer Book.

Associated Parishes consistently gave strong support to the initiatory reforms being proposed by the SLC. The rediscovery of baptism was, A.P. declared, the most important element in the renewal of the church. And the recovery of the rites of initiation in the midst of the church's life was the most important event in the process of church renewal that was going on.[67] Throughout the debates surrounding initiation, A.P. worked to make explicit what it saw implicit in the new rites.

While the 1970 General Convention had placed restrictions on the use of *PBS 18*, it did permit baptized but unconfirmed children to receive communion. Convention left it to local bishops to establish guidelines and procedures. A.P. moved in to fill the educational need created by that situation with the publication in 1971 of a course on Holy Communion for children who had already been admitted to the sacrament but not formally taught about it. The course, titled *Celebration: Community and Communion*, was designed, not to teach conceptual knowledge of the eucharist, but to let children grow in understanding of the sacrament through participation in various exercises, experiences, and discussions.[68]

1970 to 1976:
A Time of Transition in A.P.

The late 1960s and early 1970s represented a transition period for Associated Parishes. When Prayer Book revision began, A.P. emerged as an organization that was especially well-equipped to guide the church through the process. A.P. prepared for its new role by employing an executive secretary and organizing field consultants. Later, a part-time national liturgical consultant replaced the executive secretary. At the beginning of this period, A.P. adopted an experimental approach to liturgical revision—evidenced in its "Joy Box" at the 1969 Special General Convention and in A.P.'s publication of *Create and Celebrate*, a loose-leaf "cookbook" for liturgical experimentation for which A.P. issued new materials from time to time. While A.P. was moving in an experimental direction, another group for which A.P. had served as a midwife emerged to offer leadership in preparing the church for liturgical revision—the diocesan liturgical commissions. By the mid-1970s A.P.'s membership, which had grown enormously in the late 1960s and early 1970s, began to decline precipitously. By the end of the period A.P. had reassessed its experimental orientation and refocused its energies on helping the church understand and implement the new Book of Common Prayer which passed its first reading in the General Convention of 1976 and was adopted by the General Convention of 1979.

A.P. Membership

Building its membership was one way A.P. sought to be a rallying point within the church during the make-or-break years of trial use of new rites of eucharist and baptism. A.P. succeeded in building its membership to a peak by 1970, which was early in the trial use process, but by 1973 numbers began falling off. A.P. had opened its membership to all comers in 1963, yet on the eve of trial use in 1966 it could count only 115 members, and by June 1968 it had just 94 dues-paying members. A.P. felt that "a broad based membership" was one of its most urgent needs, and in 1967 and 1968 the council grappled with the nuts and bolts of how to get it. The problem had been that A.P. had neither the expertise, time, nor resources to promote itself and recruit members. With a full-time administrator now handling A.P.'s business, Executive Secretary Otis Charles was handed the job of membership development.[69]

A mailing sent out after A.P.'s Los Angeles regional liturgical conference in April 1968 doubled A.P.'s membership to roughly 188 by November 1968. The initial mailing was followed up with the mailing of a poster depicting a trumpeting angel, with the text, "Due to the shortage of trained trumpeters the end of the world will be postponed for three months"—and on the reverse, "There is still time for renewal. Send your membership in today." A little imagination, a little humor, the image of being in the swing of things, was how A.P. "packaged" its recruitment campaign, which did not neglect the sound business technique of follow-ups to successful solicitations.[70]

"We want to increase the membership," Charles told the A.P. council in November 1968, "not only from the point of view of influence but to establish contact and receive financial support." What we want, the council feistily contended, was "[s]omething to make people want to join us, to make our enemies hate us a little bit more and which will make our friends love us a great deal more."[71] Five months later in April 1969 Charles reported that membership had quadrupled to 739 as a result of mailings to clergy. Response had been so dramatic that mail solicitation would continue, he said.[72]

Trial use was awakening more and more people in the church to liturgical reform and renewal, and A.P. was perceived as its prophet. A larger membership, with more immediate and urgent needs, meant that "[w]e can't play the old comfortable game of being quietly A.P. every six months," A.P. President Henry Breul said.[73]

"Our membership in the past have been told politely that they can give us $10.00 and isn't that nice," Breul told A.P. members in August 1969. Now the stakes were higher, and Breul asked for "a broad base of support—in communication and in financing" from the members as the council tried to maneuver A.P. into "a central position where people can rally within the life of the Church."[74]

By April 1970 Charles reported that A.P.'s membership had exploded to about 1,550, representing every state, Puerto Rico, the Philippines, and "about 30 in Africa."[75] Seven months later, membership was at 1,800. A.P. was riding the crest of a wave. As treasurer Frank Bowman reported in November 1970, "What had started as a candy store on the corner was now a $40,000 a year operation."[76]

Create and Celebrate

One of the resources which A.P. prepared during this period was *Create and Celebrate*, a kind of cookbook for experimental liturgies. Published in 1970, it was in one respect a manifestation of the liturgical mood of the times. But at another level, it was a practical attempt to answer the question of how the church should communicate and inculcate its faith. The idea for the book came from the Drafting Committee on the Catechism, Offices of Instruction, and the Thirty-Nine Articles, on which A.P. council member William A. Wendt was serving.

The drafting committee agreed at its first meeting in 1968 that a new Prayer Book should not have a Catechism or Offices of Instruction.[77] (In fact, the 1979 Prayer Book does have a Catechism and the Thirty-Nine Articles, but no Offices of Instruction.) The drafting committee was "convinced that the Church communicates its faith by *celebrating* it, not by the didactic teaching of it," and asked A.P. to collect and publish texts of experimental services for the Christian year which would fulfill the function of the Catechism and Offices of Instruction. Such a collection would be a kind of 1970s counterpart to A.P.'s 1958 *Holy Week Offices*, which the drafting committee called an example of experimental services which had found wide acceptance and enriched the church's worship.[78]

Create and Celebrate was a loose-leaf notebook containing texts of services, songs, sermons, commentary, and photographs. Dividers in the book marked sections on initiation, scripture, music, marriage, death, eucharist, renewal, ordination, and resources. From time to time A.P. mailed additional material for the book to members. A.P. originated some of the material, but most of it was collected from other sources or sent in by A.P. members. The life of *Create and Celebrate* was brief. By 1972, A.P. decided not to reorder the binders to replenish stocks which were running low. The liturgical experimentation this book encouraged had nothing to do with the official rites approved for trial use in the 1970–1973 triennium by the 1970 General Convention. For some people, that may have confused the issue of liturgical reform—was it about the orderly production of a new Prayer Book, or did it mean a future of ad hoc, loose-leaf liturgies with their emotional and political atmosphere? A.P., of course, was deeply involved with the official revision of the Prayer Book, but at the same time it was experimenting with questions like "What is liturgy for?" and "How does liturgy do what it does?"— questions which defined a context for reform and pushed thought about the limits of the possible.

A.P.'s National Liturgical Consultant

A.P. had seized the moment in 1968, when Prayer Book revision got underway, to promote liturgical renewal by hiring a full-time executive secretary and organizing a network of field consultants. For three crucial years when Episcopalians were getting their first taste of new liturgies, 1968 to 1971, A.P. had the money, the manpower, and the vision for the job. But funding from the church's Executive Council for the experiment with field consultants ran out in 1971 and Otis Charles resigned as executive secretary that same year to become Bishop of Utah. Within a year of Charles's resignation A.P. revived plans to offer itself as a national agent for teaching dioceses and parishes what the new rites were about and how to do them—a task the Standing Liturgical Commission had no money or resources for.

The SLC, which had three A.P. members on it at the time (Massey Shepherd, Boone Porter, and Bonnell Spencer), supported A.P.'s request to the Trinity Grants Program of Trinity Church, New York, for a $50,000 grant to enable A.P. to hire a national liturgical consultant for three years to make A.P.'s resources available to the church.[79] A.P. told the Trinity Grants Board that it "wishes to be a responsible agent for change and is ... interested in doing all it can to help move the Church through this period in a way that could be beneficial to all involved."[80]

Trinity was enthusiastic about A.P.'s proposal and in March 1973 it granted A.P. $25,000 to develop a national liturgical consultant program. Trinity's Rector, Robert R. Parks, explained that Trinity did not grant the entire $50,000 A.P. requested because it wanted to get a "multiplier effect" from its own grant funds by calling for matching funds wherever possible. Parks wrote to A.P. President William Gray:

> I want you and your A.P. colleagues to know that the Board joins me in sincere appreciation for this proposal. We view Associated Parishes as the right instrument to help in the whole process of enlivening and updating the liturgy of the Episcopal Church.[81]

The main difference between the new liturgical consultant and A.P.'s former executive secretary was that the consultant was not expected to manage A.P.'s affairs, though he would be accountable to the executive committee of A.P.'s council. The consultant's full-time work was to promote trial use of the new rites that would prepare the church for a new Book of Common Prayer. He was to work with Diocesan Liturgical Commissions, parishes, the Standing Liturgical Commission, the A.P. council, and seminaries, as well as train other leaders to direct conferences, seminars, and parish workshops. In short, he was to be available to anyone and in any place that might provide an opening for liturgical education.[82]

A.P.'s executive committee selected Michael Merriman, rector of St. Barnabas Church, Garland, Texas, as A.P.'s national liturgical consultant in May 1974.[83] The experiment was short-lived, however. A.P. had written to all Episcopal bishops and to all Diocesan Liturgical Commission chairmen about Merriman's availability for their use in liturgical education.[84] Merriman also had organized several local and regional liturgical conferences.[85] But in his 1975 report to the council Merriman warned that all was not well. His consulting work had not raised money and was confined largely to the Washington, D.C., area, except for a little work at Trinity Church, New York City, and in the Diocese of New Hampshire. Prospects for continued funding were not bright. In the end, Merriman said there was "not enough demand to warrant continuing the work." The A.P. council voted to close the program at the end of 1975, a decision Merriman agreed with.[86] But A.P. still had an "indispensable role" in helping the church to use the coming new Prayer Book well, Merriman said. "I don't think that liturgical renewal is understood by most people in the Church as the renewal of all aspects of the Church's life as many of us have found it to be," he said. "A.P. can spend many years just communicating that fact and giving parishes some of the resources to use in their renewal."[87]

By 1973 it was evident that A.P. needed to reassess the direction in which it was moving. It could not find funding for a permanent staff. *Create and Celebrate* had not proved an appropriate organ for the task at hand. And membership was continuing to drop. A.P. began to be "concerned" about a drop in membership that began in 1973. Some 200 people had not paid their dues since 1972, coordinator-treasurer Arthur Jenkins reported in November 1973. "Some angry responses [were] generated by dues' notices," Jenkins said, though A.P.'s records offer no elucidation.[88] By 1974, membership renewals had dropped 15 percent, Jenkins reported, though 54 new members had joined A.P. since June 1973. A.P. had a total of 1,452 members, he said, including 44 Canadians.[89] Some 600 people dropped out of A.P. in 1975, leaving membership at 810. A.P. still was realizing about $9,000 from membership dues, Jenkins reported.[90] A.P.'s membership since has hovered around 900.

A.P.'s records offer no analysis of the reasons for the decline in membership. But several factors probably came into play. Many of those who joined A.P. in this period undoubtedly expected that A.P. would continue to produce materials similar to its older brochures as resources for introducing the revised liturgical texts being issued by the Standing Liturgical Commission. In other words, they anticipated that A.P. would follow its traditional approach in addressing the issues of liturgical revision. Instead they discovered that A.P. was moving in an experimental direction characterized by "pop liturgies" and identification with social activism. While this appealed to some, it failed to address the needs of the majority who were searching for materials designed to commend a revised Prayer Book to a perplexed and sometimes angry church.

After 1973 a new direction began to emerge in the work of Associated Parishes. A.P. abandoned its experimental orientation and focused its energies on commending to the church the Book of Common Prayer now being set forth by the Standing Liturgical Commission. The commitment to focus on the adoption of the new Book of Common Prayer entailed some difficult decisions for A.P. Perhaps the most difficult of these was the decision to take no stand as an organization on the ordination of women.

A.P. and Women's Ordination

A.P. was accused of what Samuel West called "guilt by association" in women's ordination, but in fact it had not associated itself with the cause up to this time. Within the A.P. council, said West, some "conspicuously and vocally" supported ordination of women, some may have agreed to it, and "certainly there were those who then opposed these ordinations."[91] On the eve of the September 1976 General Convention, at its May meeting, the A.P. council had two days of "heated discussions, resolutions, and counter-resolutions" on whether A.P. should join in supporting the National Coalition for the Ordination of Women to the Priesthood and Episcopacy.[92]

Considerable sentiment on the council was against confusing the issue of Prayer Book revision, with which A.P. was identified, with any other issue, especially one as polarizing as women's ordination. The issue of the Prayer Book and its approval must be kept distinct in the minds of General Convention delegates and in the opinion of church people, some council members argued. A.P.'s proper sphere was the liturgy. Discussion became "hotter and hotter." Someone proposed a resolution against A.P.'s entering into a coalition—but not necessarily opposing ordination of women. Debate continued during the council's business session and "spilled over even more heatedly" during a recess before dinner. On the second day of the debate, Frederick Putnam offered a substitute resolution that A.P. make no statement for or against ordination of women. With Otis Charles and Lawrence Rouillard dissenting, the council passed the resolution.[93]

A.P. fully accepted General Convention's action in 1976 and has had clergywomen on its council, but advocacy of women's ordination has not been central to its mission or message. A.P.'s decision not to publicly support women's ordination in the 1970s was based not on theological objection to women in holy orders but on tactical considerations. Even some council members who supported women's ordination nonetheless opposed linking A.P. to that volatile issue because they thought it would compromise chances for passage of a new Prayer Book, which they believed was A.P.'s proper task.

Ecumenism and Lay Leadership for A.P.

The new rites that gradually were coalescing into a new Prayer Book reflected one of the most significant facts of modern church life, the two-way street of mutual ecumenical influences. A.P. deliberately set about adding an ecumenical dimension to its meetings beginning in 1967 by looking for members from the Roman Catholic and Reformed traditions.[94] It took a while to find a suitable candidate, but in 1971 the council elected its first ecumenical member, Horace Allen, who was the Liturgical Officer of the Presbyterian Church U.S.A. and the United Presbyterian Church.[95] From 1971 until his resignation in 1981, during years of trial use, Allen was a full voting member of the council.

The council expanded its membership ecumenically among sister Anglican churches as well when it extended full council participation to two priests of the Anglican Church of Canada in 1971. Borden Purcell and Joseph C. Fricker were elected to full voting membership on the council as Canadian Associates. After the Canadian church issued its revised liturgical texts in 1985 as *The Book of Alternative Services*, A.P. began to include cross references to the Canadian rites in its brochures.

Baptismal ministry, lay leadership, and the role of women in the church all converged for A.P. in 1975 when the council elected the first lay president of A.P.—Vivian Kingsley of Holland, Michigan. Kingsley served for an unprecedented three terms as A.P. president, "not because she was a woman but because she was the most qualified," as Samuel West said.[96] Kingsley's concern as A.P. president for full representation and participation by all the baptized, clergy and laity, in the church's life reflected a conviction which was becoming more prominent as the church wrestled with revision of its baptismal rites. Neither Kingsley nor A.P. questioned the specific sacramental and canonical responsibility of clergy, but out of her wide experience in church work Kingsley had some advice for bishops as well as priests: "Let go of some of the strings so that others can learn how to do it. Don't be afraid."[97]

A.P. and the Diocesan Liturgical Commissions

The Diocesan Liturgical Commissions, which began to form in the late 1960s, "became valuable forums, depending on the commitment of the bishop, for reflection, education, and agitation" during the years of trial use.[98] The Standing Liturgical Commission's 1967 plan for Prayer Book revision had envisioned that the DLCs would play a mediating role in the process, funnelling responses from parishes to the SLC and from the SLC back down. A.P. recognized that how Prayer Book revision was experienced and perceived in the dioceses depended to a large extent on the DLCs. But many of them were unprepared for the job of leading liturgical renewal.

A.P. stepped in to sponsor the first annual meetings of chairmen of the DLCs. At the first meeting in January 1970 near Cincinnati, sponsored by A.P., fifty-five dioceses were represented by the sixty-five people who participated. The meeting, A.P. found, "suddenly gave us a lot of friends—people who had not been involved with A.P. before and saw A.P. as being very useful to them." A.P. began to develop this contact—getting names of DLC members who were deputies to General Convention, soliciting the chairmen's views on new rites, and so on. There even was some thought given to having the DLC chairmen as A.P.'s regional liturgical consultants in the program it was developing at the time. A.P. was eager to exploit this network to build support for trial use of the new rites coming up for approval at the 1970 General Convention.[99]

Ten months later the A.P. council spent two days with representatives of fifty-four DLCs before the council's November 1970 meeting. A.P. said it wanted "to listen." What it heard was that the DLC chairmen were not up to A.P. speed; they needed the kind of guidelines for organizing liturgical renewal in parishes that A.P. had been developing for twenty-four years. "They need the ABCs."[100]

By 1973, A.P.'s relations with the DLC chairmen had become "cordial" but "cool." A.P. had written to the chairman for the DLC's annual meeting in November 1973 in Oklahoma City, saying the A.P. council wanted to remain a "very interested participant." But, pleading lack of space at the conference center, the DLC told A.P. it wanted only chairmen at its meeting—"thereby," according to A.P., "excluding lay participation to which we are committed"—and any A.P. members who chose to attend would have to put up at a nearby motel. All of which caused A.P. to wonder "where did we really stand in relation to the commission chairmen and any other members of liturgical commissions?"[101]

In the end, some A.P. council members did attend, "with A.P. making significant contributions and receiving praise and recognition" from Bishop Chilton Powell, chairman of the SLC who addressed the DLC meeting. A.P.'s assessment was that the chairmen primarily were seeking information about the liturgical changes in the works, so they hardly were in a position to be agents of change themselves. In A.P.'s view, the DLC chairmen needed to develop a strategy for 1974 proposing changes they wanted to see in the rites before the SLC drafted a proposed Prayer Book; and they need to have "much greater lay involvement ... as approved last year by DLC Chairmen but not carried through this year."[102]

The period from 1970, when A.P. midwived the first national meeting of DLC chairmen and suddenly gained a lot of friends, to 1973, when relationships between the two groups cooled off, matches the bulge in A.P.'s membership. The DLC chairmen were seeking nuts and bolts information about the rites being prepared for trial use. They were being expected to put liturgical change into effect in their dioceses, but they were getting no help from the national Standing Liturgical Commission about how to do it. They wanted help in understanding the new rites and in telling parishes how to use them. A.P., on the other hand, was talking about being an agent of change; it was asking questions about the connections between liturgy and cultural change—questions which manifested themselves in experimental liturgies that seemed to bear no relation to texts being prepared by the SLC and in involvement with political issues. A certain disenchantment set in.

The chairman for the 1974 DLC chairmen's meeting, James Bethell, was "very open to our support," A.P. said, and in fact was elected to A.P.'s council in 1975. A.P. council members were asked to make a special report at the DLC's September 1974 meeting in Amarillo, Texas. The DLC chairmen made a special effort to include laity and musicians; 119 representatives from sixty-five of the church's ninety-three dioceses attended. The resolutions which the meeting adopted showed the DLCs were beginning to move beyond needing to be educated. The chairmen asked the SLC to drop the word "confirmation" entirely from the new initiation rites. Reaffirmation of baptismal vows could occur repeatedly over a lifetime, the DLC chairmen said, but baptism was full initiation and the only prerequisite for receiving communion.[103] Some A.P. members attended the next DLC chairmen's meeting beginning in late September 1975 in Ocean City, New Jersey, but A.P. decided not to hold a council meeting in conjunction with it.[104]

A.P. continued to cooperate with the DLC chairmen and its successor, the Association of Diocesan Liturgy and Music Commissions. A.P. had nurtured the group in its formative years. By sponsoring the DLC's first meetings, A.P. helped broaden the informed base for liturgical renewal at a crucial time when the church was taking up the reform of baptism. The liturgical movement in the Episcopal Church now had a much broader base of leadership. Associated Parishes continued to play its own distinctive role in that movement, but ADLMC, for which A.P. had acted as midwife, also would have an important part in the renewal of the church's liturgy.

The Work of A.P. in Introducing the 1979 Prayer Book

With passage of the *Draft Proposed Book* in 1976, A.P.'s main work in Prayer Book revision was over. Its goal for the 1979 General Convention was "to support the *Proposed Book of Common Prayer* and not deviate from that role."[105] The fight was over, all passion spent. Those who had opposed Prayer Book revision had had their say and had not persuaded the majority. Convention after convention had demonstrated that overwhelming opinion within the church favored liturgical reform. As more and more parishes began to use the "green book," "zebra book" and the *Proposed Book of Common Prayer,* they found much to like. As they prayed their way into a new Prayer Book, they recognized it as the Book of Common Prayer. Liturgical matters had engaged the church's attention for a decade; now, the Prayer Book no longer was seen as an overriding issue.

The 1979 General Convention in Denver gave the Proposed Book near-unanimous approval, making it the official liturgy of the church as The Book of Common Prayer, 1979. The House of Bishops accepted the book with only one dissenting vote. In the House of Deputies, the vote in the clerical order was 107 yes, 1 no, 2 divided; in the lay order, it was 99 yes, 2 no, 6 divided.[106] "The Book sold itself," was how one observer put it.[107] Though A.P. was "delighted" with passage of the new Prayer Book, it did not give "*carte blanche* approval" to the entire book, Samuel West said.

> Most of us were disappointed that certain facets were not included, or that some were not as well stated as they might have been. For most of us, perhaps the most disappointing element was with the muddled confusion concerning Christian Initiation, especially with regard to Baptism and Confirmation—the waters muddied by the House of Bishops who seemed to be threatened by a clearer, more historic approach to Initiation.[108]

The days of "our incomparable Prayer Book"-type thinking were over, said West. The Prayer Book was but a means to an end and an instrument for good order. No revision had the last word, not even the 1979 book in which "so many A.P. members had invested much of their time and ministry, clergy and laity." With its task accomplished and its goal achieved, A.P. wondered whether it should not by mutual agreement disband and be given a decent burial with a "thanks be to God."[109]

It soon became evident, however, that the church had a continuing need for education in using the 1979 Prayer Book and that there still was a place for a group whose mission was to seek the constant renewal of the church through the liturgy. As Louis Weil remarked to Leo Malania, the coordinator for Prayer Book revision, the new Prayer Book "is so rich that it will take 50 years to learn how to live with it."[110]

Learning to Live the New Prayer Book: A.P.'s New Brochures

Until a new Prayer Book was approved and in place, A.P. saw no point to revising its line of brochures explaining "what we do" and "what we mean." But as soon as Prayer Book revision began in 1967 the A.P. council started to assess its current brochures, and in 1969 it cleared the decks for quick production of new brochures that soon would be needed by revamping its editorial process. Instead of having the whole council read and edit each brochure, a process which took six months to a year, A.P. decided that an editorial committee would edit and publish new texts.[111]

The need for new brochures was on A.P.'s mind from 1970 to 1975 while trial use was under way. Reports of experiences with the proposed rites from around the church kept demonstrating to A.P. that parishes needed informed guidance if the new rites were to have their effect. A.P. also realized that new brochures would have to speak to a different liturgical reality than their predecessors. With the pluriformity of the emerging rites, and multiple options within rites, loyalty to the Prayer Book now would mean variety and pluralism, not uniformity. A.P., for example, never made an issue of the language of the Prayer Book. Its new brochures made no theological claims about modern or traditional language, nor did they suggest that there is a kind of "Prayer Book within the Prayer Book," setting Rite Two over against Rite One. The brochures dealing with the services for which the Prayer Book provides alternative rites in modern or traditional language (the daily office, eucharist, and burial) acknowledged each rite equally and concentrated on explaining the new theological and ecclesiological perspectives embodied in the services.

With the appearance of the *Proposed Book of Common Prayer* in 1976, the time was ripe for new brochures since the rites were not subject to further revision. Between 1976 and 1979, A.P. immediately issued brochures on baptism, ordained ministry, the eucharist, and the Great Vigil of Easter, explicating the heart of the new Prayer Book: baptism as the source of the church and of ministry, the eucharist as the church's chief act of worship on the Lord's Day, and the Easter Vigil as the paradigmatic celebration of baptism and eucharist, the consummate ritual expression of what it means to be a baptized person offering the eucharist in the late twentieth century.

A.P.'s *The Holy Eucharist, Rite Two: A Commentary* (1976) illustrated by Boone Porter, told "how and why this service came to be"[112] and informed Episcopalians who may have thought of Rite Two simply as the liturgy in modern English that changing the language was not the point. A first printing of 4,000 copies sold out right away.[113] A.P. walked through the rite, unfolding the priorities and perceptions embodied in its structure, its options, its multiplicity of eucharistic prayers, as well as the rite's historical and theological background, showing how Rite Two was about a new way of doing eucharist.

A.P. was able to draw on the very people involved in drafting and editing the Rite Two eucharist, the brochure said, and sketched the revision process from the 1966 *Liturgy of the Lord's Supper*, through General Conventions, to Rite Two. A.P. pointed out how the new rite drew Episcopalians closer to the new eucharistic liturgies being adopted by other churches, Catholic and Protestant, as well as to newly composed Anglican liturgies in many parts of the world. Rite Two's structure and general features hearkened to the recommendations of Anglican bishops at the 1958 Lambeth Conference and to the outline for revised Anglican liturgies published in 1965 by the inter-Anglican Consultation on the Liturgy, A.P. noted. The rite's use of ecumenically agreed translations for parts of the service—the International Consultation on English Texts 1974 versions of the Gloria in excelsis, Kyrie, Nicene Creed, Sursum corda, Sanctus, and Lord's Prayer—put the Episcopal Church in step with the wider Christian community. In this way, A.P. sought to legitimate a new way of making eucharist by placing it in the mainstream of Anglican and ecumenical liturgical thought. The coming Prayer Book would have three different eucharistic liturgies, A.P. said, but all conformed to the same outline. From now on, flexibility and diversity would be the watchwords for liturgical expression; but if the underlying structure is grasped, "one will not feel lost in any one of the three orders."[114]

A.P. helped parishes to navigate the new world of pluralism embedded in the Prayer Book in its new *Parish Eucharist* in 1977, which replaced its very first brochure issued in 1950. The brochure concentrated on explaining the fundamental action of the eucharist underlying both Rite One and Rite Two. A.P. did not attempt to establish a single way of doing entrance and offertory processions, how to include local concerns in the Prayers of the People, whether to shake hands, embrace, or kiss at the peace, use of wafers or a loaf of bread, kneeling or standing for the eucharistic prayer and to receive communion, and so on. Options were mentioned, but these were matters that legitimately varied from parish to parish. What mattered, A.P. said, was that with all the variety and flexibility of the new Prayer Book, we were following a common order for the eucharistic celebration which made it clear that whatever the rite being used, we were doing the same liturgy.[115]

The brochure made the fundamental theological point that the eucharist is an action, not a thing; it "is what the parish *does*—in response to what God has done for all humankind."[116]

> It is the way the parish lives; thankfully, joyfully, as a participant in the resurrected life of Christ and servant to the world. That which we have just symboled in the Liturgy gets worked out in the day-to-day life of the parish and its members. That daily life, in turn, becomes the offering of our next liturgical celebration. *Eucharist is a way and a style of life.*[117]

The idea of self-offering, which the 1950 brochure tied exclusively to the offertory, now was discussed in connection with eucharistic praying as well as with the offertory. Indeed, the new Prayer Book made more of a moment of the offertory: representatives of the congregation bring the people's offerings of bread and wine, and of money or other gifts, to the deacon or celebrant, and the people stand while the offerings are "presented and placed" on the altar. At the offertory, said *Parish Eucharist* 1977, "we offer the life of the parish as well as the lives of its members. The Body of Christ offers itself to be made the Body and Blood and Work of the Lord."[118] But turning to the eucharistic prayer, the brochure goes on: "Our own meager offerings are made worthy by being joined to the perfect sacrifice of Jesus Christ and are received and transformed into instruments of His eternal life ... " And it speaks of "the offering of ourselves" as one of the basic elements of the eucharistic prayers.[119]

A.P. has issued two sets of brochures on baptism and ordained ministry since the *Proposed Book of Common Prayer* first went into use in 1976. The first set came out in 1978. Revised treatments of baptism and ordination were issued in 1987 and 1991. In 1978, with passage of the new Prayer Book at the General Convention of 1979 virtually assured, A.P. published *Ministry I: Holy Baptism* and *Ministry II: Laity, Bishops, Priests, and Deacons,* which spelled out the new vision of church and of ministry set forth in the new rites of initiation and ordination. The brochures, written by Henry Breul, defined baptism as "one complete action of: Renunciation, Affirmation, Washing, Anointing, Laying on of hands, Feeding," and argued that ordination was an articulation of Christian ministry already conferred in baptism.[120] Whatever the rite of confirmation might be, it "is certainly *not* the completion of something that is complete, nor can it be considered an 'ordination of the laity' since that is one of the accomplishments of baptism itself," *Ministry I: Holy Baptism* declared. As for the inclusion of a separate rite of confirmation, reception, and reaffirmation in the forthcoming Prayer Book, the brochure tartly remarked that they are "optional and indeed tentatively placed where they are out of a concern for the confusion in the Church as to what they represent."[121]

> Various uses of episcopal laying on of hands may continue until a resolution of the problem is arrived at, but it is to be hoped that "automatic confirmation" at a certain age or grade level will cease throughout the Church and that confirming of adults coming from other communions as a "completion" of their "incomplete baptism" will be seen as uncharitable if not blasphemous.[122]

A.P. argued for the use of plenty of water in baptizing—immersion, preferably, but "a real washing will serve"—enough water, at any rate, to suggest "death by drowning to the old life and arising from the waters of creation a new person." Chrism (which is optional in the rite) ought to be used at the hand-laying and signing with the cross, which A.P. called a "sealing with the gift of the Holy Spirit. ... In the anointing the person has been ordained to the lay ministry of the church completely; no other gifts are necessary for the person's full life in Christ." The brochure assumed that the eucharist will follow as an integral part of baptism and that the newly baptized, whatever their age, will receive communion—infants being communicated with a bit of the bread or some wine alone in a spoon.[123]

The tenor of A.P.'s ecclesiology is clear. Its brochures asserted that baptism is full, complete, and sufficient initiation into the church. No other gifts are necessary for the person's full life in Christ. Any other offices or functions in the church are but articulations of the ministry to which a Christian is sufficiently "ordained" in baptism. The first sentence of *Ministry II: Laity, Bishops, Priests, and Deacons* (which took its title from the Prayer Book Catechism's teaching that the "ministers of the Church are laypersons, bishops, priests, and deacons") proclaimed unequivocally that, "The full ministry of the Church is given in Holy Baptism, it is present in the People of God." Ordained ministry exists to enable the laity to perform their fundamental ministry, "which is to minister for Christ in a broken world."[124] The brochure gave nearly as much space to talking about the laity as it did to all three ordained ministries combined.

> The old idea that the clergy do the ministering *for* the congregation is obviously an inadequate concept if the laity are to live up to their baptismal covenant. The laity have been given special gifts of ministry according to who they are and what their circumstances are. ... The enabling of the laity to function in this way is the prime reason for the existence of the "ordained" ministry of the Church. All Christian education and spiritual formation should be directed so that the laity are equipped to perceive and perform their ministry at all times and in all places.[125]

A.P. based its argument on the vision which the liturgy itself presented of a renewed church served by a renewed ministry. A.P. argued that ordination was not a new gift of the Holy Spirit, but an activation of the Spirit for a particular function within the Body of Christ, an underlining and stressing of the baptismal covenant in particular ways for ministries. In the celebration of the liturgy, all ministries together, lay and ordained, made visible the fullness of the Body of Christ. Indeed, it "would be difficult to distinguish completely among the four ministries of the Church. Each ministry seems to flow into the others and partake of their richness." Nor was there a hierarchy of value in the ordained ministries, A.P. argued; "they are all equal in that they show to a fallen world the one total ministry of Christ."[126]

In practical terms, "there is no reason for these ministries to take any sort of particular form such as professional full-time over against the part-time unpaid," A.P. said.[127] As early as its 1977 "Wewoka Statement," and again in *Ministry II*, A.P. committed itself to restoration of the diaconate as an equal ministry in the church alongside the priesthood, and called for direct ordination of candidates to the diaconate and presbyterate, with deacons eligible for election as bishop and ordained directly to that order. The issue, A.P. made clear, was not one of political power, but of the implications of the new ordinal for the character and importance of each order and of the ministry of the laity.[128]

A.P. co-sponsored the first conference in the Episcopal Church on the diaconate with the National Center for the Diaconate (later the North American Association for the Diaconate) in 1979 at Notre Dame, Indiana. But along with the revival of the diaconate went fears that it would stifle lay ministry or conflict with the ministry of priests. In its "Waverly Statement" in 1981, A.P. argued from the liturgical evidence of the Preface to the Ordination Rites, from the liturgies of ordination for bishops and for deacons, and from the Catechism that the diaconate can enable and extend lay ministry and free priests to do their own particular ministry more effectively. Just what patterns of ministry might emerge and how the functions of deacons can best find expression on the present-day church needs continued dialogue and study, A.P. said, but the successful use of deacons in many dioceses had begun to point the way to a reimagining of ministry and therefore of church.[129] A.P. extended the theological principle involved by calling on the church, in its "Toronto Statement" of 1992, to revert to an ancient custom of ordaining baptized persons directly to the three orders without requiring them to pass through another order. "In baptism all Christians share in the eternal priesthood of Christ," the Toronto Statement said. "In ordination the Church calls a few of its members to several distinct offices, as focal points and sacraments of Christ in particular ministries of leadership. . . . The only sacramental prerequisite for ordaining a bishop, priest, or deacon is baptism."[130] The ordination rites in the *Proposed Prayer Book* and of the 1979 Prayer Book supported A.P. perspectives, but those implications were not self-evident. They required the kind of articulation which A.P. gave the liturgies. For example:

1) The ministry of the laity is explicitly recognized in the ordination rites in several ways. Laypersons, as well as clergy, formally present the candidates for bishop, priest and deacon for ordination. And laypeople, as well as bishops, priests, and deacons, assume their usual duties in the eucharist in all the ordination rites. No one's function is usurped, which suggests that all four "orders" are needed to image liturgically what the church is all about.

2) The three ordination rites are exactly alike in structure and in what we may call ritual "fullness," with complete liturgies of the Word, consecration of the ordinand by prayer and hand-laying, and eucharist. There is no sense that any of them is a miniature of the other, which suggests that all three have an equality of dignity and place in the church.

3) In none of the rites is it suggested that the candidate has previously held another ordained office in the church. Rubrics direct that candidates for bishop be vested in rochet or alb, and candidates for priest and deacon be vested in surplice or alb, without stoles, tippets, or other vesture distinctive of ecclesiastical or academic rank or order—which suggests that one may come to any of these orders without passing through another order first.

Ministry II did not address such traditional issues as apostolic succession and "validity," nor the question of who exactly ordains—the bishop? the community? Nor did the brochure deal explicitly with the ordination of women, which General Convention had sanctioned in 1976, though the brochure uses gender-neutral language and nowhere does it assume that clergy are male only.

That implementation of some of these perspectives might require changes in canon law was not A.P.'s point. What A.P. aimed at was stimulating the church to new ways of thinking about the implications of the liturgy it held in its own hands. Baptism was not just a pastoral rite, something done to individuals more or less in private, but was the font of the Christian life itself with practical implications for a church addressing a changing culture.

A.P. offered a theological commentary on the proposed rites of initiation in publishing Louis Weil's *Christian Initiation*. Weil tried to make the best out of the confused ecclesiological and sacramental situation surrounding initiation. "There can be no question," Weil wrote, "that Baptism is seen to be full incorporation into the Body of Christ, with no suggestion that something lacking in that initiation must later be supplied." Weil tried to locate confirmation in a context of repeated affirmations of faith in the course of one's life, but by way of justifying confirmation was reduced to echoing the 1972 "Statement of Agreed Positions" by the bishops and the SLC that "the first time a person does this in response expressive of a reasonable degree of Christian maturity, that first time is seen to have a particular and unique character." As for the anomaly of requiring those baptized as adults to repeat their profession of faith before a bishop, Weil could only hope "that this should be the exception rather than the rule simply because the integrity of Christian Initiation suggests, even demands, the unity of that sacramental reality in the case of an adult."[131]

But in 1982, pointing to continuing "great confusion relating to Christian initiation and the reception of Holy Communion," A.P. urged the church "to solve the ambiguities and the resulting confusion in terms of ... official teaching that Holy Baptism effects the fullness of Christian initiation."[132] Three years later, in 1985,

A.P. could commend the progress made by the Executive Council's Division of Ministry to Children in encouraging the full participation of all baptized children in the liturgical life of the church, and A.P. "strongly supported" the Executive Council's recommendation that children receive communion regularly from the time of their baptism.[133]

But the problem of confirmation had become no clearer, and by the time A.P. replaced its baptism brochure with a new *Holy Baptism: A Liturgical and Pastoral Commentary* in 1987, A.P. urged that at least the celebration of confirmation should not upstage baptism, "the one sufficient rite of Christian initiation."[134]

As the church grappled with the implications of reshaping its initiation rites to engage an alien culture, it rediscovered the catechumenate for adult candidates for baptism. The Roman Catholic Rite of Christian Initiation of Adults had restored the catechumenate in 1972. The Episcopal Church's 1979 *Book of Occasional Services*, borrowing from that example, made available rites and directions to encourage a revival of the catechumenate which were expanded in subsequent editions.

A.P. understood the catechumenate "as the catalyst for the constant renewal of the Church," and urged it on parishes and dioceses not only for adult baptismal candidates but also for those reaffirming their faith and for parents and sponsors of infant candidates for baptism.[135] A.P.'s 1991 brochure *The Catechumenate: Formation for Church Membership* offered a practical commentary on how to use the rites.[136]

After more than a decade of a new paradigm for ordained ministry in the 1979 Prayer Book, A.P. asked, "Do We Really Mean It?" in a new brochure published in 1991, *Holy Orders: The Ordination of Bishops, Priests, and Deacons* which replaced *Ministry II*. "The contrast between what the rites of ordination say and mean, and the way in which bishops, priests, and deacons exercise their ministries today in our church is conspicuous, to say the least," the brochure said. The problem, A.P. said, was "a new clericalism under the guise of professional and career management."[137]

Against models for ministry such as hierarchical order, or chief executive officers, or guru, A.P. set a Pauline model of the body with its equal but diverse functions.[138] Ordinations ought not to look like "an ecclesiastical Academy Awards ceremony;" they should be an opportunity to educate people about the ministry of the whole people of God in a particular place, a ministry given in baptism and now being articulated in a particular person.[139]

> The truth is that we are uncertain what ordained ministry is because we are in the midst of radical changes in our understanding of what the church is, what ministry is, and how church and ministry relate to the particular culture in which they find themselves. As the rapid changes in our understanding of mission, evangelism, and corporate life continue, the issue will be raised again and again.[140]

The new Prayer Book also made available for the first time a full round of Holy Week rites. A.P. reassured parishes which may never have experienced these liturgies that "any parish" could manage them. "Perhaps the most significant enrichment" of the Prayer Book was the Easter Vigil, A.P. said in its 1977 brochure *The Great Vigil of Easter*, powerfully illustrated by Allan Rohan Crite. The Great Vigil amounted to a summary of what it means to be a Christian, A.P. said. A.P. did not say it, but this liturgy also summarized and enshrined in the heart of the Book of Common Prayer certain key ideals of the liturgical movement. The Easter Vigil, A.P. taught, was about ministerial order (plurality and diversity of ministry, lay and ordained; the role of the bishop as chief teacher, baptizer, eucharistizer; deacons as proclaimers of the gospel). It was about the Old Covenant and the New (reappropriating the church's Hebrew birthright in the context of the culmination of God's mighty acts in Jesus). It was about initiation into the mystery of salvation (incorporation into a community; commitment to discipleship); as the "queen of feasts in the Christian year," it was the occasion when the faithful participate with a fullness of symbolic representation in the paschal mystery. And it was about eucharist (what Jesus was and did in his lifetime, and is and does eternally in the heavens, the community is to be and do in the world now).[141]

The liturgies of Ash Wednesday, Lent, the rest of Holy Week, and the Great Fifty Days culminating in Pentecost were about *Celebrating Redemption*, as A.P. titled its 1980 brochure—that is, not about celebrating penitence. The whole cycle from Ash Wednesday to Pentecost finds its meaning in relation to the liturgy of the Easter Vigil, A.P. proclaimed, and Lent and Good Friday are to be celebrated in the context of the paschal victory. The 1979 Prayer Book shifted the center of piety from penitence to redemption. A.P. made explicit that re-perception of Christian living by making accessible to ordinary parishes the meaning and practical mechanics of celebrating some of the primary rites in its own Prayer Book.

Starting from the new Prayer Book's assertion that the "liturgy for the dead is an Easter liturgy," A.P.'s brochure on *The Burial of the Dead*, published in 1980, discussed the death of a Christian in the sacramental context of the liturgy of the Easter Vigil and baptism. "We prepare for death by celebrating the Paschal mystery," A.P. proclaimed. Not personal immortality or cosmeticized reality, but the real human tragedy of death, the hope of victory, resurrection and eternal life were the lessons A.P. articulated from the texts and rubrics of the Prayer Book. The brochure also challenged the American approach to death with its suggestions of ways family and friends can repossess the body and the liturgies of the dead from the "Sleeping Beauty" world of the "funeral parlor."[142]

A.P.'s discussion of Christian marriage, too, started with baptism and life in Christian community as the context for the partners' commitment. Immersed in Word and Sacrament, the husband and wife continually integrate their lives and marriage into the dying and rising of Christ, A.P. said in its 1987 brochure *The Celebration and Blessing of a Marriage*. A.P. presented the Prayer Book's marriage liturgy in such a way as to show how it challenged societal assumptions about sexuality, experience and feeling, and romance and love. Against this, the brochure brought out the biblical concepts of human nature, sexuality, and marriage implicit in the rite. The changing social experience of marriage also was reflected in the brochure's brief discussion of the rite for the blessing of a civil marriage, now included in the Prayer Book for the first time rather than relegated to the *Book of Offices* (predecessor of the *Book of Occasional Services*).

A brochure on *The Daily Office* commended to individuals and to groups the Anglican tradition of regular daily prayer rooted in scripture and liturgy. Published in 1981, this brochure took readers step by step through the offices of Morning and Evening Prayer, and provided directions for the other offices new to the Prayer Book—noonday prayer, Compline, and a form of "cathedral" evening prayer.

The 1979 Prayer Book embodied many of the goals of the liturgical movement, but merely changing the furniture was not the same thing as renewal. The General Convention that gave final approval to the new Prayer Book in 1979 recognized the importance of full use of the book when it urged each parish to have a worship committee. A.P.'s 1988 brochure *The Parish Worship Committee* aimed to help parishes "become part of the mainstream of liturgical renewal."[143] Liturgical ministry is the work of the entire community, A.P. said; a parish worship committee can make it possible for all to participate in worship according to their order and gifts. A.P. prescribed no one structure or manner of operating; different parishes need to evolve appropriate designs. But the brochure did provide much practical guidance on composition of the committee, size, tenure, selecting a chairperson, duties, training, education, and evaluation—as well as some grounding in why have the committee at all, who the parish is, and what the parish celebrates.

Inclusive Language in the Prayer Book

The question of inclusive language began to define itself more clearly in the late 1970s and 1980s. The 1979 Prayer Book used inclusive language when speaking of people (apart from Rite One services, some instances in the psalter, and the opening anthems of the burial service). The question of how to address God began to affect liturgical texts during the production of *The Hymnal 1982*. In 1985, General Convention directed the SLC to prepare inclusive language liturgies for Morning and Evening Prayer and the Eucharist. In 1987 the SLC published *Liturgical Texts for Examination*, which were revised and issued as a new *Prayer Book Study* in 1989, *Supplemental Liturgical Texts*.[144] The 1991 General Convention approved a further revision of inclusive language texts by the SLC, *Supplemental Liturgical Materials*, which the 1994 General Convention reauthorized for experimental use. The main difference between the 1991 and 1994 materials and their 1989 predecessor was that they did not provide complete services, but a variety of inclusive language texts that could be incorporated into Rite Two celebrations of the daily office or eucharist.

"We should not be surprised to find that Prayer Book revision has created a need for further revision," *Open* editor Henry Breul wrote in 1989 just ten years after adoption of the 1979 Prayer Book.

> [I]n any period of real growth, there will be uncomfortable differences in emphasis arising and a tendency for things to go every which way. It is always possible for certain enthusiasts with blinders to "enthuse" themselves out of the Church by taking things too far, but while decency and order are to be maintained, conformism is not, has not, and cannot be a goal of liturgy, theology, or human behavior.[145]

Let the SLC practice some "benign neglect" and let groups with particular concerns, like women and homosexuals, design their own liturgies to spread through the church for a kind of trial use, Breul said. But if benign neglect was one way to deal with the ferment, another A.P. spokesman, Henry Louttit, warned in 1991 that tolerance "ultimately ... cannot allow any intolerant group to purge God's family of those with whom they do not agree."[146]

A.P. council members who also were on the SLC during the 1989–1991 triennium—Bishop Frank T. Griswold of Chicago, the Rev. Canon Michael Merriman, and the Rev. Sr. Jean Campbell, O.S.H.—made themselves "constantly available" during the 1991 Convention in Phoenix to explain the proposed texts. The greatest threat to acceptance of the texts, according to Joe Morris Doss, an A.P. council member who also was on the Prayer Book and Liturgy Committee of the House of Deputies at the 1991 Convention, is the "naive assertion" that the motives for inclusive language are secular and sociological, while feelings and sentiments against inclusive language are "founded in genuine and classical theology."[147]

The Next Prayer Book

A resolution submitted to the 1994 General Convention called for a new revision of the Prayer Book to be submitted to the General Convention of 2006, thirty years after the 1976 acceptance of the 1979 book. The resolution was modified and the SLC was directed instead "to prepare a rationale and a pastorally sensitive plan" for revision without stipulating a timetable.

On the tenth anniversary of the 1979 Prayer Book, the A.P. council considered what changes it would like to see in the next Prayer Book. Not surprisingly, deletion of confirmation and clarification of baptism as full initiation was high on A.P.'s list. Elimination of Rite One services also was a priority. Other suggestions reflected the new cultural and ecumenical setting of the church, such as including the catechumenate in the Prayer Book, use of fully inculturated language, inclusive language, revision of the lectionary, and the need for a rationale and explanation of the rites. Elimination of the *filioque* clause—"and the Son"—from the Nicene Creed, which

A.P. had long sought, actually was approved by the 1994 General Convention and the clause will be dropped when the Prayer Book is next revised.

Other changes A.P. said it would like to see included shorter options for the Great Litany, inclusion of a "cathedral" form of the daily office, a new outline for the "Rite Three" eucharist, reworking of the collects, amplification of the blessing of chrism in baptism, addition of more gospels to the Easter Vigil, development of other vigils, addition of seasonal blessings, and elimination of the Thirty-Nine Articles from the Prayer Book.

On A.P.'s twenty-fifth anniversary in 1971, Presiding Bishop John E. Hines said A.P. had "been responsible in the Episcopal Church for a recovery of (or a timely re-discovery) of [sic] the valid dimensions of the Liturgy, and the relationship between liturgy and mission." The group had been "called for by a great need" and had motivated "much vitality for the Church" through its education efforts and "the experimental innovations in liturgy" which A.P. sponsored. A.P. can "advance with an even more exciting quarter of a century with confidence," Hines said.[148]

The custodian of the Standard Book of Common Prayer, Charles M. Guilbert, said "it would be hard to overestimate the enlightenment and growth" which have come to the church as a result of a group like A.P.

> [A.P.] has interpreted the world-wide Ecumenical Movement to, and naturalized it in, the Episcopal Church. It has drawn into its orbit and has formed the outlook of most of those persons—clerical and lay—who are today charged with the responsibility of revision the [sic] Book of Common Prayer; indeed, the Prayer Book revision project, though initiated formally by the General Convention, can be seen as a tangible fruit of the prayers and studies and consultations of the Associated Parishes.[149]

Looking back on it all forty years after he sparked the founding of A.P., John O. Patterson offered A.P. in 1986 a reprise of its accomplishments and direction for the future.

Many of the things for which Associated Parishes worked and prayed have come to pass. There has been a substantially increased understanding of the ministry of the laity—to no small degree a product of A.P. sponsoring of parish councils. We see the beginnings of an awareness of the true meaning of Holy Baptism—to some extent, at least, because of A.P.'s insistence that the sacrament of Baptism be seen as a matter of concern to the congregation of the parish and be administered at a time and place of honor along with the Eucharist. Many existing church buildings have been remodelled and new churches designed so that they offer proper settings for Christian liturgy, settings marked by simplicity, clarity, and joyfulness. One could go on, mentioning A.P.'s concern for Christian education, for liturgical music, for meaningful ceremonial and other areas. All of this work has in some way or another contributed to a new Book of Common Prayer which begins with a bold statement that "The Holy Eucharist is the principal act of Christian worship."

A.P. can be grateful if any of its work has served the Holy Spirit over these past 40 years. It is my prayer that, when we think of our ministry as The Associated Parishes, we remember that most of the above-mentioned programs and activities were significant to the extent that they helped to restore the parish to its proper and significant place in the Church. If our goal is to proclaim an incarnational gospel, this should never be forgotten.[150]

Or as Massey Shepherd succinctly remarked, "Our cause has been taken up by the whole Church."[151]

Chapter Six

A Prayer Book for a
Post-Christendom Church

The liturgical movement in the Episcopal Church did not spring full-grown from the head of Associated Parishes. Prayer Book reform was beyond the control of any one group. When A.P. formed in 1946, it fitted itself into an ongoing history of revision of the American Prayer Book. Scholars like Charles Winfred Douglas, Burton Scott Easton, Edward Lambe Parsons, Bayard Hale Jones, and William Palmer Ladd were shaping awareness of new liturgical issues. The church already was engaged in liturgical reform with *The Hymnal 1940*, the *Book of Offices* of 1940 and 1949, and the daily office lectionary of 1943. The Episcopal liturgical movement was not an adaptation of a Roman Catholic agenda, nor was it the result of the permeation of Anglo-Catholic ideals, or the importation of the Parish Communion movement from the Church of England. The factors that determined the liturgical climate in which A.P. operated were these:

First, the church's liturgy, the 1928 Book of Common Prayer, was marked by an openness to modern critical scholarship, modern pastoral needs, and a growing historical and ecumenical consciousness. The book itself demonstrated that change was a fact of life in the Episcopal liturgical environment. The 1928 revision was carried through by moderate High and Broad Church elements who were becoming aware of the weakness of the Reformation settlement of worship and whose ideal was comprehensive diversity.

Second, it was William Palmer Ladd who was the first person to popularize the liturgical movement in the Episcopal Church and who was the catalyst for a liturgical awakening. As professor and as dean of the Berkeley Divinity School he influenced the liturgical formation of church leaders for thirty-seven years—most notably Massey Shepherd who helped found A.P. and whose name was synonymous with Prayer Book revision. Ladd's approach to liturgy was biblical, patristic, Anglican, and ecumenical with a sharp eye for pastoral needs and the social implications of worship. He had a shrewd appreciation of the need to have "the good sense to disregard precedent" sometimes; he interpreted history not as a straight line of development, but as the result of multiple choices in manifold situations. The purpose of consulting the past, according to Ladd, was to take some bearings in the present complex situation in order to challenge the status quo and to figure out how to move ahead. Adaptability, independence, and a sense of the open-endedness of the future characterized Ladd's definition of the liturgical movement which he wished to see the church take up.[1]

Third, the scholars involved in the Prayer Book Studies of the 1950s, which were the precursors of Prayer Book revision, were men like Bayard H. Jones and Massey Shepherd, whose study of patristic and Eastern liturgy convinced them of the distinctive strengths of the American Prayer Book and its potential for the recovery of past usages and the creation of a new synthesis. As Boone Porter has written, other American scholars, like B.S. Easton, Frank Gavin, Felix L. Cirlot, R.K. Yerkes, and Edward R. Hardy who studied ancient and Eastern sources found what they discovered so different from current Anglican usage as to be inapplicable for the present. They embraced use of the "Western rite," i.e., an adaptation of the Roman Catholic liturgy.[2] Thus they were led outside the orbit of Prayer Book concerns. The people who carried the liturgical movement forward located it within a specifically Anglican context of development—from the Caroline Divines, through the Non-jurors, to American pioneers like William Augustus Muhlenberg and William Reed Huntington. They saw themselves, not as importing a foreign ideology, but as responding from within the Episcopal tradition to twentieth-century western Christianity's encounter with new social and cultural issues.

Fourth, the fact that the liturgical movement in the Episcopal Church took place in the context of open, representative church government formed people's presuppositions, their perceptions of what was possible, and their expectations. The machinery of government functioned with the participation of the governed, lay and clerical. The possibility of change was built into the system. Change did not have to be apologized for or branded as disloyal. The ideals represented by A.P. could be matters of public debate and action. More particularly, liturgical change had a focus and a structure to carry it—the Prayer Book and the Standing Liturgical Commission, formed in 1928 and given canonical status as a standing commission in 1940. The climate, the object, and the machinery of liturgical change all were in place.

Fifth, during the two decades between the founding of A.P. in 1946 and the start of trial use in 1967, the influence of other churches on the Episcopal liturgical movement was a matter of what Shepherd called "an indefinable free play of ideas and personal acquaintances"—which is to say, not a matter of wholesale imitation. Scholarship did not stop at church boundaries, but what face-to-face contact there was depended on personal good will, not official contacts. In 1960, Shepherd could complain that the Roman Catholic Church's policy of non-cooperation with other churches excluded non-Catholics from participating in that church's activities in liturgical renewal.[3] The Second Vatican Council (1962–1965) not only brought the Roman Catholic Church into the ecumenical movement but also emboldened other churches to respond to the liturgical pressures that had been gestating for a generation, waiting to emerge. The influence of the Church of England, and its Parish and People movement, was minimal and indirect. That was largely because the English church's complex of circumstances and problems shaped the English expression of the liturgical movement. The product simply did not travel well into the American setting in which the church was not answerable to the state, lacked extreme church parties, and accepted the Prayer Book as the focus of unity and vehicle for liturgical reform.

Sixth, when the Episcopal Church did begin to issue revised rites, the eucharistic liturgy it proposed in 1966 was Anglican in structure and theology; its eucharistic prayer was Scottish-American in structure even as the overall rite was conversant with the ecumenical factors that were creating new syntheses in liturgical renewal. But the example of no one church dominated the rite. The premises and spirit of *The Liturgy of the Lord's Supper* at the beginning of Prayer Book revision continued to animate the subsequent trial use rites which culminated in the 1979 Prayer Book.

Seventh, the process that produced the 1979 Prayer Book was open and participatory. For the first time in the history of the American Prayer Book, the church's liturgy was the result of the work of the whole church. Trial use, with its apparatus of consultants, readers, and responses from parishes and dioceses, was an important instrument in that process. Yet the 1979 Prayer Book was not the result of a grass-roots desire for liturgical change. It was the result of a band of leaders who sensitively read the signs of the times and realized that the 1928 Prayer Book would not serve the church well in the cultural shifts which lay ahead. These leaders were steeped in the liturgical tradition of the church, so that the reforms which they proposed were soundly rooted and not just passing fads. Trial use helped the church assimilate the change.

In a liturgical climate defined by these factors, Associated Parishes was uniquely positioned to act as a catalyst for change and to take a role of leadership. A.P.'s membership for its first seventeen years was never more than about two dozen; at its height it was only 1,800. Since passage of the 1979 Prayer Book it has been about 900. In a total church population of two-and-a-half to three million, those numbers are not impressive. But A.P.'s influence spread far beyond its membership. A.P. held a unique position in the American church. Who else in the Episcopal Church was doing the kind of thing A.P. was doing? There were others who had put the theory and history of liturgical renewal in place, but A.P. showed ordinary parishes how to do it. A.P.'s teaching about the liturgical movement formed part of a total parish program; it was not abstract or theoretical.

A.P.'s program included making the eucharist the church's principal act of worship, a reappropriation of the ministry of the laity, and the centrality of baptism in understanding membership, ministry, and ecclesiology. In time, that platform became the program of the whole church. A.P. contributed by naturalizing the ecumenical liturgical movement in an Episcopal context. A.P. was loyal to the Book of Common Prayer as the standard of practice and teaching. Refusing to become a faction or party, it operated within the church's tradition and political structures. It offered itself as an unofficial group, free from official constraints, where people thinking about liturgical renewal could meet with leaders like Dom Gregory Dix and A.G. Hebert, engage in free discussion, and envision alternatives to the status quo. A.P. held together both the opinion-makers and the person in the pew.

A.P. also stood for something more than mere reform of the conduct of worship. It stood for the renewal of the church through a recovered understanding of the liturgy. In its publications and conferences it was able to articulate the connection between ritual and life. A.P. contributed negative as well as positive learning to the liturgical movement. Out of A.P.'s experience with the 1928 Prayer Book came a body of experience of that book's shortcomings which contributed to Prayer Book revision.

Anyone who considers A.P.'s representation on the Standing Liturgical Commission and on the drafting committees during the years of trial use and then looks at the 1979 Prayer Book to find the *ipsissima verba* of A.P. will be disappointed. A.P.'s achievement was not in getting this or that item into the Prayer Book. The 1979 Prayer Book changed the liturgical climate of the Episcopal Church. A.P.'s achievement was not creating the book, but serving as a catalyst for the change. From its founding, throughout the process of Prayer Book revision, and after the adoption of the new book, A.P. communicated to ordinary parishes the paradigm shift that was at work through the church in liturgical renewal and which came to be embodied in the 1979 Prayer Book. So comprehensive a change defies a definitive analysis, particularly by those riding the tide of change, both because involvement with one's own time distorts objectivity and also because the magnitude of the revolution encompasses the relationship with the world at large in all its dimensions, political, social, philosophical, technological. But it may be possible at least to characterize the liturgical response to the age.

Perhaps the most agonized question of the twentieth century is, Where is God? From the fourth century through the nineteenth, Christian generations answered the question by accenting the transcendent.[4] God was beyond, the one whom the scriptures speak of as the God who comes, the one who elicits the prayer "maranatha" and is known by revelation, and one whom the scriptures speak of as leading, going before to prepare a place for his followers. Piety reflected that emphasis by perceiving liturgy as oriented toward that other world where God was. Baptism saved individual souls for heaven, holy communion was a private meeting through the instruments of bread and wine with a God who otherwise has gone away. Clergy bridged the gap between the otherness of God and the here-and-nowness of people. An elevated language gave entrance to the throne room where Christ sat at the right hand of the Father, and in church priest and people set their faces toward the east window over the altar, beyond which God dwelt in light inaccessible. Language of hierarchy and authority flowed from this model of God.

In the nineteenth century, that model began to break down. The cause lay in what Massey Shepherd described in 1969 as a profound shift of philosophical approaches to humanity's understanding of the reality of which it is a part.

> In one sense it is the age-long tension between "Being" and "Becoming," between an ontological and existential way of looking at reality. The classic formulations of Christian doctrine were primarily stated in ontological terms, through the predominant influence of Platonism and Aristotelianism upon the patristic and scholastic theologians, respectively. . . .
>
> The mood of the newer theology today is distinctly existentialist, relativistic, and anti-dogmatic. It leans much upon the insights of physics and psychology. A chief source of inspiration has come from the recovery in Biblical scholarship of the eschatological dimension of the gospel. We live in a world of Becoming, and we do not yet know what we shall be. The transcendence of God is not a fixed entity, but the "beyond" of our experience that draws us in uncharted but by no means capricious paths. Reality is in the ever-changing event and situation of the moment, and is defined in terms of relationships.[5]

Urban T. Holmes observed that the death of "classical theology" in the twentieth century was symptomatic of "a theological awakening to what had actually happened to our religious consciousness in the nineteenth century." Modern people's religious consciousness had changed from a "mirror" (the cosmocentric view, as exemplified by the theology of Thomas Aquinas) to a "window" (the anthropocentric view, as exemplified by the theology of Karl Rahner).[6]

Religious consciousness asked the question, where is God, and began to answer it by saying that God is within the flux of human experience and of history. God relates to humanity, in this model, by calling people more deeply into the world. The here-and-now is the location of the transcendent. The scriptural image appealed to is of a God who abides and of a God who is hidden. The Jesus who says, "Those who eat my flesh and drink my blood abide in me, and I in them," (John 6:56) speaks to a continued presence, a "remaining with" throughout the vicissitudes of chance and change: "I am with you always, to the end of the age" (Matt. 28:20). But the presence described is a hidden presence. And, as the Emmaus story suggests, people are the locus of that presence. The memory of the Risen One hidden within is recognized as a real presence when disciples perform a liturgical action, interpreting the scriptures and breaking bread, because it results in changed lives. Language of community, shared responsibility, and the interior union of Christ with his members flowed from this model of God.

To speak of a God who comes and who leads (emphasizing the transcendent aspect) versus a God who abides and who hides (stressing the immanent aspect) is to name different human experiences of God. It is not a question of better or worse, right or wrong, but of the inadequacy of language to hold together experience of both "access" and "otherness." Each model is scriptural and all must be held in tension with one another. If the preferred model shifts over Christian generations, it is not a question of progress from error to truth, but of discovering the appropriate model for the times. Liturgy is a product of a culture and reflects the presuppositions of its culture. The crisis that lay behind Prayer Book revision was not just a question of literary taste or pastoral concern, but a theological crisis. "What made the 1928 Book of Common Prayer a difficult book to revise was that the culture and its theological concepts which produced the Book of Common Prayer in the sixteenth century no longer existed," Holmes said.[7]

At the heart of the 1979 Prayer Book stands a rediscovery of the paschal mystery—Christ's triumph over disintegration and despair, made accessible to believers in baptism and the eucharist, and proclaimed in its fullness in the Easter Vigil. It is a confident stance which says that the world of modernity in which twentieth-century Christians find themselves is not a deprivation, a sort of cultural wound which cuts modernity off from the past and which the absence of traditional religious concepts makes it impossible to heal. The 1979 Prayer Book stands open to the world of cultural change and frames its liturgical expression in patterns that catch the intellectual and spiritual questions of these times. Supremely in the celebration of the Easter Vigil, the Prayer Book proclaims that modern believers living in a time of dislocation and upheaval may discern that the flux of human experience is precisely where God is active, where "things which were cast down are being raised up, and things which had grown old are being made new, and that all things are being brought to their perfection by him through whom all things were made, your Son Jesus Christ our Lord."[8]

This shift in the focus of worship to the paschal mystery (from a Reformation model centered on the atonement, or Anglican models centered on Incarnation or Creation), and some cultural implications of that shift, are reflected in the 1979 Prayer Book's rites of the eucharist and of baptism. The eucharistic revival fostered by the liturgical movement culminated in the 1979 Prayer Book, which says that the eucharist is the principal act of worship on the Lord's Day (BCP, p. 13). Over the past twenty years the eucharist has become the normative worship in most Episcopal parishes on Sundays, which has put in place a eucharistic ecclesiology. The weekly immersion in scripture and participation in the breaking of bread gives disciples strength and courage to be sent into the world to do the work God has given them to do (BCP, pp. 365–366). One effect of the shift to a church centered on the celebration of the eucharist is that it has made it seem inappropriate to many people to treat baptized children as non-communicants. The church is still discovering the full implications of its new baptismal rite for discipleship, ministry, and the church's self-identity as it faces the culture. The baptismal rite makes clear that initiation into Christ's Body, the church, confers responsibilities to make Christ present to the surrounding culture—by serving all persons, striving for justice and peace, and respecting the dignity of every human being, even as one repents, returns to the Lord, and tries to live out the Good News of God in Christ (BCP, pp. 304–305).

The whole 1979 Prayer Book shows the church rethinking its relation to a culture in flux and rediscovering the tools it needs to speak about God to that culture. For example, ordained leadership is, by canon law, constituted by the election and consent of the community. As the ordination rites and the rubrics of each service in the Prayer Book make clear, however, no one ordained ministry may encroach on the others yet all are needed—not because the flock needs juridical control, but because the presence of Christ needs these three signifiers to accomplish what he is present in the world to accomplish, as one who serves, renews the world, and is its sovereign (BCP, pp. 543, 531, 517). The ordained do not function instead of the laity. Every page of the Prayer Book shows the people taking their part in proclaiming the Word, lifting up the world to God in prayer and in bread and wine, presenting and assenting to the ordination of those who minister to the community, and receiving the baptized into the household of faith, confessing and proclaiming the presence of the Risen One. Common humanity, the calendar of saints reminds them—people struggling with politics, gender roles, racial relations, intellectual inquiry, war and peace, spiritual questing, religious bigotry, hope and despair—is the stuff which is the instrument of God's activity. The language of the Prayer Book is in the idiom of the world modern people know, and in many churches they engage one another and their ordained ministers face to face around a central altar, with God in the midst, abiding, hidden under the forms of food eaten, word proclaimed, people assembled. A world of pluralism and flux is represented in the Prayer Book. There is not one right way to do things, but several ways, and even individual services offer combinations and recombinations of elements that mirror shifting experience of the divine. There is no objective, analytical way of knowing that God is the depth of human experience. Christians can celebrate the liturgy all their lives and never see anything more than people being washed, food being eaten, a reader reading, ministers presiding, an assembly that disperses into the world. The 1979 Prayer Book orients believers to just those things, though, to be drawn into them in order to discover more than them.

The church began to *remember* some things in the twentieth century. It remembered that, facing an alien culture, it could not assume that society automatically imbued people with Christian values and that the church had to be intentional in making disciples. It remembered how to take baptismal candidates, "marinate" them in the catechumenate, and initiate them into its life through the community's ritual enactment of itself in the Easter Vigil. The church remembered that baptism creates a priesthood charged with speaking of the world to God and with reassuring the world that it is in God's hands. It remembered that the church's essential nature is best communicated to modern people seeking community by people gathered to worship, not by hierarchies exercising juridical authority. It began to remember that a living liturgy arises out of and responds to the lived circumstances of life.

In the liturgical movement, we might say that the church was recovering a "survival kit" as it entered a post-Christendom world—a survival kit not for the preservation of institutional structures, but for handing on a word of hope to people standing on the threshold as one epoch of western history dies and another begins.

Notes

Introduction: *A Revolution in Episcopal Worship*

1. Charles Mortimor [*sic*] Guilbert, "From the Prayer Book's Official 'Watchdog,'" *Open* (no number or date, but 1971): 2.

2. See Kathleen Hughes, ed., *How Firm a Foundation: Voices of the Early Liturgical Movement* (Chicago: Liturgy Training Pubs., 1990); and Robert Tuzik, ed., *How Firm a Foundation: Leaders of the Liturgical Movement* (Chicago: Liturgy Training Pubs., 1990).

3. William Palmer, *Origines Liturgicae: or, Antiquities of the English Ritual; and a Dissertation on Primitive Liturgies,* 2 vols. (Oxford University Press, 1832).

4. See R. W. Franklin, "Gueranger: A View on the Centenary of His Death," *Worship* 49 (1975): 318–328; "Gueranger and Pastoral Liturgy: A Nineteenth Century Context," *Worship* 50 (1976): 146–162; "Gueranger and Variety in Unity," *Worship* 51 (1977): 378–399; "The Nineteenth Century Liturgical Movement," *Worship* 53 (1979): 12–39; and "Humanism and Transcendence in the Nineteenth Century Liturgical Movement," *Worship* 59 (1985): 342–353. See also R. W. Franklin, *Nineteenth-Century Churches: The History of a New Catholicism in Wurttemberg, England, and France* (New York and London: Garland, 1987).

5. See Marvin R. O'Connell, *The Oxford Conspirators: A History of the Oxford Movement, 1833–1845* (New York: Macmillan, 1969); and James F. White, *The Cambridge Movement: The Ecclesiologists and the Gothic Revival* (Cambridge University Press, 1962).

6. See Horton Davies, *Worship and Theology in England*, vol. IV: *From Newman to Martineau, 1850–1900* (Princeton University Press, 1962), pp. 114–138. For a critique of Davies, see Paul V. Marshall, *Prayer Book Parallels: The Public Services of the Church Arranged for Comparative Study*, vol. 1 (New York: Church Hymnal Corp., 1989), pp. 15–52. For ritualism in the United States, see George E. DeMille, *The Catholic Movement in the American Episcopal Church* (Philadelphia: Church Historical Society, 1941); Massey H. Shepherd, Jr., *The Reform of Liturgical Worship: Perspectives and Prospects* (New York: Oxford, 1961); and H. Boone Porter, "Toward an Unofficial History of Episcopal Worship," in *Worship Points the Way: A Celebration of the Life and Work of Massey Hamilton Shepherd, Jr.*, ed. Malcolm C. Burson (New York: Seabury, 1981).

7. Paul B. Marx, *Virgil Michel and the Liturgical Movement* (Collegeville, Minn.: Liturgical Press, 1957), pp. 313, 417–418. See also William J. Leonard, "The Liturgical Movement in the United States," in *The Liturgy of Vatican II: A Symposium in Two Volumes*, ed. William Barauna (Chicago: Franciscan Herald Press, 1966).

8. Henry H. Breul, "An Editorial," *Open* (October 1982): 6.

9. Alfred R. Shands, *The Liturgical Movement and the Local Church* (London: SCM Press, 1959), p. 27.

10. See Gregory Dix, *The Treatise on the Apostolic Tradition of St. Hippolytus* (London, 1937; revised ed. by Henry Chadwick, Ridgefield, Conn.: Morehouse, 1992); Bernard Botte, *La Tradition apostolique de saint Hippolyte* (Munster: 1963; 4th ed., 1972); Geoffrey J. Cuming, *Hippolytus: A Text for Students* (Bramcote, Notts.: Grove, 1976); and J.M. Hanssens, *La Liturgie d'Hippolyte* I (Rome: 1959, 2nd ed., 1965), II (Rome: 1970). The date, authorship, and provenance of *Apostolic Tradition* is disputed; see Paul F. Bradshaw, *The Search for the Origins of Christian Worship* (New York: Oxford, 1992), pp. 89–92.

11. Some scholars are beginning to question the assumptions that guided the use made of ancient liturgical sources by those involved in the revision of worship materials for churches in the past thirty years. See Bradshaw, *Search for the Origins of Christian Worship*, passim. For a discussion of the effect of modern church bureaucracies on liturgical revision, see Susan J. White, *Christian Worship and Technological Change* (Nashville: Abingdon, 1992), pp. 39-58.

12. Samuel E. West, "Episodes Towards a Recorded History of Associated Parishes for Liturgy and Mission. Episodes IV: Associated Parishes Meets With Dom Gregory Dix, OSB," p. 15.

13. Preface, BCP 1928, p. v.

Chapter One: The Last Cranmerian Liturgy

1. See William Sydnor, *The Story of the Real Prayer Book, 1549–1979* (Wilton, Conn.: Morehouse, revised ed. 1989), pp. 59-61.

2. Alvin W. Skardon, *Church Leader in the Cities: William Augustus Muhlenberg* (Philadelphia: University of Pennsylvania Press, 1971), pp. 194, 199.

3. See Don S. Armentrout and Robert Boak Slocum, *Documents of Witness: A History of the Episcopal Church, 1782-1985* (New York: Church Hymnal Corp., 1994), pp. 208-224; James Thayer Addison, *The Episcopal Church in the United States, 1789-1931* (New York: Charles Scribner's Sons, 1951; reprint ed., Archon Books, 1969), pp. 177-188; Byron D. Stuhlman, *Eucharistic Celebration 1789-1979* (New York: Church Hymnal Corp., 1988), pp. 95-98.

4. Shepherd, *Reform of Liturgical Worship*, p. 19.

5. Stuhlman, *Eucharistic Celebration,* p. 98.

6. See Lesley A. Northup, "The 1892 Book of Common Prayer," *Toronto Studies in Theology 65* (Lewiston/Queenston/Lampeter: Edwin Mellen Press, 1993).

7. Edward Lambe Parsons and Bayard Hale Jones, *The American Prayer Book: Its Origins and Principles* (New York: Charles Scribner's Sons, 1937), p. 57.

8. Massey H. Shepherd, Jr., "The History of the Liturgical Renewal," in *The Liturgical Renewal of the Church*, ed. Massey H.

Shepherd, Jr. (New York: Oxford, 1960), pp. 46–47.

9. On the 1928 Prayer Book see E. Clowes Chorley, *The New American Prayer Book: Its History and Contents* (New York: Macmillan, 1929), pp. 100–133; Parsons and Jones, *The American Prayer Book*, pp. 58–64; Sydnor, *Story of the Real Prayer Book*, pp. 69–83, and p. 120; and Stuhlman, *Eucharistic Celebration*, pp. 105–114.

10. Others were Charles Lewis Slattery, John Wallace Suter, Sr., and Howard B. St. George.

11. *JGC* 1961, pp. 563–564.

12. Ibid., p. 564.

13. DeMille, *Catholic Movement*, pp. 111–112.

14. "Concerning the Service of the Church," BCP 1928, p. vii.

15. Porter, "Toward an Unofficial History of Episcopal Worship," p. 105.

16. Chorley, *New American Prayer Book*, p. 128.

17. Porter, "Toward An Unofficial History of Episcopal Worship," pp. 112, 115.

18. Massey H. Shepherd, Jr., "The Berakah Award: Response," *Worship* 52 (July 1978): 304.

19. See Michael Moriarty, "William Palmer Ladd and the Origins of the Episcopal Liturgical Movement," *Church History* 64 (September 1995): 438–451.

20. William Palmer Ladd, *Prayer Book Interleaves: Some Reflections on How the Book of Common Prayer Might Be Made More Influential In Our English-Speaking World* (New York: Oxford, 1942, 2nd ed., Greenwich, Conn.: Seabury, 1957), pp. 45, 113–114, 157–162, 167.

21. Ibid., pp. iii, 22, 148, 164.

22. A.G. Hebert, *Liturgy and Society: The Function of the Church in the Modern World* (London: Faber and Faber, 1935).

23. Percy Dearmer, *The Parson's Handbook* (London: Grant Richards, 1899; many eds. thereafter by Oxford University Press; 13th ed., 1965, revised and rewritten by Cyril E. Pocknee). See also Nancy Knowles Dearmer, *The Life of Percy Dearmer* (London: Book Club, 1941).

24. Ladd, *Prayer Book Interleaves*, pp. vii–viii.

25. Ibid., p. 167.

26. Ibid., p. 45.

27. Ibid., pp. 113–114.

28. Ibid., pp. 157–162.

29. Ibid., pp. 16, 20–21, 59, 141.

30. Ibid., p. 167.

31. Ibid., p. 23.

32. Ibid., p. 159.

33. Ibid., p. 82.

34. Ibid., p. 4.

35. Ibid., p. 1.

36. Ibid., p. 101.

37. Ibid., p. 2.

38. Ibid., p. 155.

39. Ibid., p. 50.

40. Ibid., pp. 180–184.

41. Ibid., p. 82.

42. Ibid., pp. 55–57.

43. See, for example, ibid., pp. 8, 51, 66, 110, 157, 164.

44. See A.G. Hebert, ed., *The Parish Communion* (London: S.P.C.K., 1937); Donald Gray, *Earth and Altar: The Evolution of the Parish Communion in the Church of England to 1945* (Norwich: Canterbury Press, 1986).

45. Ladd, *Prayer Book Interleaves*, p. 76; see also p. 92.

46. Ibid., p. 80.

47. Ibid., pp. 34, 156.

48. Ibid., p. 156.

49. Urban T. Holmes, "Education for Liturgy: An Unfinished Symphony in Four Movements," in *Worship Points the Way: A Celebration of the Life and Work of Massey Hamilton Shepherd, Jr.*, ed. Malcolm C. Burson (New York: Seabury, 1981), p. 121.

50. Sherman E. Johnson, "Massey Shepherd and the Episcopal Church: A Reminiscence," in *Worship Points the Way: A Celebration of the Life and Work of Massey Hamilton Shepherd, Jr.*, ed. Malcolm C. Burson (New York: Seabury, 1981), pp. 9–10.

51. Massey H. Shepherd, Jr., *The Living Liturgy* (New York: Oxford, 1946), p. 124.

52. Ibid.

53. Massey H. Shepherd, Jr., Letter to the Rt. Rev. Kirkman G. Finlay, Bishop of Upper South Carolina, 26 April 1938, Shepherd Papers, Record Group 237-1-1, The Archives of the Episcopal Church USA, Austin, Texas.

54. Shepherd, *Living Liturgy*, p. 124.

55. Ibid., pp. 124–125.

56. Ibid., p. 125.

57. Theodore Otto Wedel, "The Theology of the Liturgical Renewal," in *The Liturgical Renewal of the Church*, ed. Massey H. Shepherd, Jr. (New York: Oxford, 1960), pp. 3–4.

58. Ibid., pp. 4–5.

59. Gerald Ellard, "Non-Catholic Liturgical Movements," *Thought* XVIII (September 1943): 457–458.

60. Winfred Douglas, *Church Music in History and Practice: Studies in the Praise of God* (New York: Charles Scribner's Sons, 1937; revised ed. by Leonard Ellinwood, New York: Charles Scribner's Sons, 1962); quotations are from the 1937 edition. The lectures that comprise the book originally were delivered in 1935 as the Hale Lectures at Seabury-Western Theological Seminary, Evanston, Ill.

61. Ibid., p. 272.

62. Ibid., pp. 42–43.

63. Shepherd, "History of the Liturgical Renewal," p. 48.

64. Edward Lambe Parsons and Bayard Hale Jones, *The American Prayer Book: Its Origins and Principles* (New York: Charles Scribner's Sons, 1937).

65. *JGC* 1958, p. 491.

66. Parsons and Jones, *American Prayer Book*, p. viii.

67. Ibid., pp. 209–210.

68. Ibid., p. 63.

69. *JGC* 1928, p. 352.

70. *JGC* 1940, pp. 472–473.

71. Ibid., pp. 473–474.

72. *Book of Offices*, eds. of 1940, 1949, 1960; superseded by the *Book of Occasional Services*, eds. of 1979, 1988, 1994.

73. *JGC* 1943, p. 404.

74. Ibid.

75. Ibid., pp. 404, 434.

76. *JGC* 1946, p. 439.

77. Ibid., pp. 439–440.

78. Ibid., p. 440.

79. Since a publisher could not be found willing to take on the series at his own risk, the Church Hymnal Corp. agreed to publish the studies as a service to the church without expectation of profit on the condition that it be guaranteed against loss. The 1949 General Convention appropriated $2,000 for the project. *JGC* 1949, p. 435.

80. *JGC* 1952, p. 375.

81. The titles and dates of the *Prayer Book Studies*, all published by Church Pension Fund, New York, were:

I: Baptism and Confirmation

II: The Liturgical Lectionary (I and II were printed together in one volume published in 1950)

III: The Order for the Ministration to the Sick, 1951

IV: The Eucharistic Liturgy, 1953

V: The Litany, 1953

VI: Morning and Evening Prayer

VII: The Penitential Office (VI and VII were printed together in one volume published in 1953)

VIII: The Ordinal, 1957

IX: The Calendar, 1957

X: The Solemnization of Matrimony

XI: A Thanksgiving for the Birth of a Child (X and XI were printed together in one volume published in 1958)

XII: The Propers for the Minor Holy Days, 1958

XIII: The Order for the Burial of the Dead

XIV: An Office of Institution of Rectors into Parishes (XIII and XIV were printed together in one volume published in 1959)

XV: The Problem and Method of Prayer Book Revision, 1961

XVI: The Calendar and the Collects, Epistles, and Gospels for the Lesser Feasts and Fasts: A Supplementary Revision of Prayer Book Studies IX and XII, 1963

82. For figures, see *JGC*: 1952, pp. 374; 1955, p. 377; 1958, p. 487; 1961, p. 559; 1964, pp. 670–671; 1967, pp. 23.20–23.21.

83. When *PBS IV* was superseded by a further proposed revision in 1966, it had sold 15,771 copies of the study-with-proposed rite, and 26,727 copies of the proposed rite alone.

84. "A Conspectus of Comments on the Rite of Studies IV," no date, Record Group 237-3-14, 15, 16, The Archives of the Episcopal Church, USA, Austin, Texas.

85. *Prayer Book Studies XVII: The Liturgy of the Lord's Supper; a Revision of Prayer Book Studies IV* (New York: Church Pension Fund, 1966), p. iii. For a critique of *PBS IV,* see Stuhlman, *Eucharistic Celebration*, pp. 118–124.

86. Holmes, "Education for Liturgy," p. 122.

87. B.J. Wigan, "The Commissioners' Liturgy," *Episcopal Church-news* CXX, 5 (March 6, 1955), p. 22, quoted in Shepherd, *Reform of Liturgical Worship*, p. 76.

88. Shepherd, "History of the Liturgical Renewal," p. 21.

89. Ibid., p. 22.

90. Among Roman Catholic scholars, for example: Odo Casel, Fernand Cabrol, Henri Leclerq, Louis Duchesne, Pierre Batiffol, Romano Guardini, Joseph Jungmann, Louis Bouyer; among Lutherans: Hans Lietzmann, Peter Brunner, and Luther D. Reed; among Anglicans: Gregory Dix, Percy Dearmer, A. G. Hebert; among Reformed: Oscar Cullman and Jean-Jacques von Allmen.

91. Shepherd, "History of the Liturgical Renewal," p. 27.

92. Gerald Ellard, "The Liturgical Movement in Catholic Circles," *Religion in Life* XVII (Summer 1948): 381.

93. Evelyn Underhill, *Worship* (London: Nisbet & Co., 1936).

94. Ellard, "Non-Catholic Liturgical Movements," pp. 455–456.

95. Evelyn Underhill, *The Mystery of Sacrifice: A Meditation on the Liturgy* (New York: Longmans, 1938).

96. Ellard, "Non-Catholic Liturgical Movements," pp. 456–457.

97. Marx, *Virgil Michel*, p. 381.

98. Shepherd, *Living Liturgy*, p. 125.

99. Ladd, *Prayer Book Interleaves*, pp. 117–122.

100. Ibid., p. 114.

101. Ibid., p. 117.

102. For an overview of the liturgical movement among Protestants in the United States and Europe from after World War I to the eve of Vatican II, see Arthur Carl Piepkorn, "The Protestant Worship Revival and the Lutheran Liturgical Movement," in *The Liturgical Renewal of the Church*, ed. Massey H. Shepherd, Jr. (New York: Oxford, 1960).

103. Ladd, *Prayer Book Interleaves*, pp. 64, 155, 157.

104. Shepherd, "History of the Liturgical Renewal," p. 22.

105. Ibid., pp. 22–23.

106. Ibid., p. 23.

107. See Peter J. Jagger's two books, *Bishop Henry de Candole: His Life and Times, 1895–1971* (Leighton Buzzard, Beds.: Faith, 1975); and *A History of the Parish and People Movement* (Leighton Buzzard, Beds.: Faith, 1978).

108. Jagger, *History of the Parish and People Movement*, pp. 52, 57, 85, 90–91, 108, 131.

109. Ibid., pp. 16, 49–50.

Chapter Two: Associated Parishes' Divine Discontent

1. Henry H. Breul, "AP At Notre Dame: The Recovery of Despair," *Open* (Summer 1984): 9.

2. Patterson was born Feb. 29, 1908, in Goldfield, Nev., the son of Oliver Macrae Patterson and Mary Martin. After attending the University of Illinois at Chicago and MIT, Patterson prepared for the priesthood at Seabury-Western Theological Seminary, Evanston, Ill., and was ordained deacon in April 1934 and priest in November of that year. In 1936 Patterson married Elizabeth Andrews; they had four children. He received a D.D. from Seabury-Western in 1951 and an S.T.D. from Hobart College, Geneva, N.Y., in 1961.

Patterson began his priestly ministry as priest-in-charge of St. Ansgarius Church, Chicago, 1933–1937. He was rector of St. Mary's Church, Mitchell, S.D., 1937–1941, and rector of Grace Church, Madison, Wisc., 1941–1949. From 1949 to 1962 he was rector and headmaster at Kent School, Kent, Conn. In 1962 he became the founder, rector, and headmaster of St. Stephen's School, Rome, Italy, and served there until 1970. Patterson retired in 1970, but continued to live in Rome; from 1971 to 1979 he was an associate priest at St. Paul's Church in Rome. He then moved to San Francisco and served as an associate priest at St. James's Church from 1982 until his death in 1988.

3. West, "Episodes III: A Friend's Profile of John O. Patterson," p. 10.

4. Ibid.

5. West, "Episodes II: Associates [*sic*] Parishes—The Dream and Hope: A Personal Recall," p. 5.

6. Ibid., p. 6.

7. Ibid.

8. Ibid.

9. Sam West, "Massey Shepherd: A Personal Memoir," *Open* (Summer 1990):11.

10. Besides Shepherd, Keene, and West, the letter went to Thaddeus Clapp, Worcester, Mass.; Robert Reister, Appleton, Wisc.; William Spicer, Syracuse, N.Y.; and Theodore Wedel, Washington, D.C.

11. John Patterson, "The Founding Letter: 1946," in West, "Episodes Towards a Recorded History of Associated Parishes," p. 5.

12. Ibid., pp. 5–6.

13. Associated Parishes, "Notes on Material Presented by the Reverend John O. Patterson at the Conference of the Associated Parishes, College of Preachers, Washington, D.C.," Minutes of the Initial Conference, November 4–8, 1946, Record Group 272-1, The Archives of the Episcopal Church USA, Austin, Texas.

14. In addition to Patterson, Shepherd, Keene, and West, the original members of A.P. were: Thaddeus Clapp, Worcester, Mass.;

William F. Donnelly, Madison, Wisc.; James Joseph, Pittsburgh, Pa.; Warren McKenna, Boston, Mass.; Noble Powell, Baltimore, Md.; Robert Reister, Appleton, Wisc.; William Spicer, Syracuse, N.Y.; and Stephen Walke, Lookout Mountain, Tenn.

15. Massey H. Shepherd, Jr., "A Response to Henry Breul," *Open* (July 1983): 2.

16. West, "Massey Shepherd: A Personal Memoir," p. 10.

17. John O. Patterson, "Forty Years On," *Open* (May 1986): 2–3.

18. Ibid.

19. Ibid., p. 2.

20. Ibid.

21. Associated Parishes, "The Accepted Corporate Program," Minutes of the Initial Conference, November 4–8, 1946, Record Group 272-1, The Archives of the Episcopal Church USA, Austin, Texas. The program was revised several times and served as a guideline for A.P.'s work in parishes until the mid-1960s, when it fell into abeyance as the beginning of trial use of new liturgies bypassed the situation it was speaking to.

22. "Notes on Material Presented by ... John O. Patterson," Minutes of the Initial Conference.

23. Ibid.

24. Ibid.

25. Patterson, "Forty Years On," p. 2.

26. Ibid.

27. Holmes, "Education for Liturgy," p. 123, who was a friend of A.P., said A.P.'s early members were "prayer book fundamentalists" who "believed that if we followed the rubrics strictly and used the whole book we would discover an enlivened worship which would enable us to be what the theology of the liturgical movement believed the church to be."

28. Patterson, "Forty Years On," p. 2.

29. West, "Episodes I: Origins," pp. 2–3.

30. "Accepted Corporate Program," 1946.

31. Holmes said that A.P. "was in the beginning a secret organization. If they were going to educate the church, it was to be in a

clandestine fashion. ... Associated Parishes was not only a secret organization, it was an unofficial body." (Holmes, "Education for Liturgy," p. 123.) "Clandestine" is not the word for a group that meets under the eye of official Episcopalianism at the College of Preachers, enlists a bishop as one of its founding members, publicly demonstrates its ideas in parishes across the nation, and begins issuing pamphlets within four years of its founding.

32. Minutes of the Business Meeting, May 8, 1947.

33. Minutes of the November 3–7, 1947, Meeting.

34. Minutes of the Executive Session of the Council, April 8, 1970.

35. "Accepted Corporate Program (Draft and Revision #3)," Minutes of the November 3–7, 1947, Meeting.

36. Ibid.

37. "Accepted Corporate Program," *Rearvue* Vol. I, No. 2, no date.

38. West, "Episodes IV: Associated Parishes Meets with Dom Gregory Dix, OSB," p. 15.

39. Ibid. Unfortunately, the rest of the substance of that encounter between one of Anglicanism's most prominent liturgical scholars and some representatives of the liturgical movement in the Episcopal Church is lost. West's unpublished reminiscences are the only record. It was West whom A.P. commissioned to contact Dix at Seabury-Western Theological Seminary in Evanston, Ill., where Dix was lecturing at the time.

40. West, "Episodes IV: Associated Parishes Meets with Dom Gregory Dix, OSB," p. 16.

41. West, "Episodes V: A.P. Meets With Father Hebert," p. 23.

42. A.G. Hebert, *The Bible From Within* (New York: Oxford, 1950), pp. 1, 3.

43. West, "Episodes V: A.P. Meets With Father Hebert," p. 21.

44. *Revue* (June 1952). No copies of any of the mimeographed courses developed and used by A.P. over the years exists in the A.P. archives or in the Archives of the Episcopal Church, USA, in Austin, Texas. But a 1957 A.P. financial report gives the titles of five

of these courses: "The Creed, the Lord's Prayer, and the Ten Commandments;" "The Prayer Book;" "The New Testament;" "The Old Testament;" and "Personal Christian Living." ("The Development of the Associated Parishes and Its Present Financial Status," May 1, 1957.)

45. Minutes of the November 1954, Meeting.

46. "Report to the Associated Parishes from J.H. Keene, Christian Education Committee, November 1956," Minutes of the November 5–8, 1956, Meeting.

47. Minutes of the April 25–28, 1966, Meeting.

Chapter Three: The Shape of Things to Come

1. Associated Parishes, *The Parish Eucharist* (Madison, Wisc.: Associated Parishes, 1955), inside back cover. The statement explaining what the liturgical revival and what A.P. were began to appear in 1953 in A.P.'s brochures and journal.

2. Massey H. Shepherd, Jr., *The Liturgical Movement and the Prayer Book; The Twenty-Ninth Annual Hale Memorial Sermon* (Evanston, Ill.: Seabury-Western Theological Seminary, 1946), pp. 21-29.

3. Ibid., pp. 20-21.

4. Ibid., p. 21.

5. Ibid.

6. Paul Z. Hoornstra to the author, 23 October 1992.

7. Minutes of the May 1948 Meeting.

8. "Minutes and Motions—Meeting, May 1949" (newsletter).

9. Minutes of the May 24, 1950, Business Meeting.

10. Francis F. Bowman, Jr., to Members of A.P., 1 November 1952.

11. Minutes of the November 1953 Meeting.

12. Minutes of the November 5–8, 1956, Meeting.

13. "Some Facts About the Associated Parishes, Incorporated, A Small Fellowship of the Episcopal Church in Need of $75,000," p. 2.

14. Ibid., p. 1.

15. Ibid., p. 8.

16. Massey H. Shepherd, Jr., "What Is the Associated Parishes?" *Sharers* V (Fall 1959): 1–5.

17. Frederick W. Putnam, "From the Editor," *Sharers* VII (Late Trinity, 1961): 13–14.

18. They were: *The Parish Eucharist*, 1950; *Christian Initiation, Part I: Holy Baptism*, 1953; *Christian Initiation, Part II: Confirmation*, 1954; *"In Newness of Life:"* A Guide for Self-Examination, 1954; *Christian Burial*, 1955; *The Christian Meaning of Work*, 1959; *Holy Matrimony and the Christian Family*, 1960; *The Daily Offices*, 1963.

Each was 8½ by 11 inches, typically 14 to 24 pages, and sold for 35 cents apiece from 1950 to 1955, when the price went up to 50 cents. Holmes, "Education for Liturgy," p. 126 says these pamphlets "made money for the AP." They didn't make much, though. A 1957 financial report shows A.P. made about $2,925 on its brochures from 1951 to 1957. In 1961, treasurer Frank Bowman reported that sale of brochures, royalties from books, and donations combined brought in only about $2,000 a year. ["The Development of the Associated Parishes and Its Present Financial Status," May 1, 1957; "Treasurer's Report," Minutes of the November 1961 Meeting.]

19. "Parishes Using Associated Parishes Material as of November 1960."

20. Francis Bowman to the Members of A.P., no date [but 1961].

21. Book Review, *TLC* 121 (Oct. 8, 1950): 19.

22. By 1953 the original 1950 edition of 10,000 copies of *The Parish Eucharist* had sold out and a slightly revised edition of 3,000 was printed. By 1955, the brochure had sold 17,300 copies. [Minutes of the Spring 1953 Meeting; Minutes of the November 1955, Meeting.]

23. *Parish Eucharist*, p. 20.

24. Ibid., pp. 4, 14, 15.

25. Ibid., p. 14.

26. Ibid., pp. 10–11.

27. Massey H. Shepherd, Jr., *The Oxford American Prayer Book Commentary* (New York: Oxford, 1950), p. 81–82.

28. *Parish Eucharist*, p. 18.

29. *Holy Baptism*, pp. 2–3, 16; *Confirmation*, pp. 2, 9, 13.

30. *Holy Baptism*, pp. 1, 4, 8, 11.

31. A.P. members needed to keep in touch with one another between meetings, not just to share news but for mutual encouragement and support. The earliest evidence of an A.P. newsletter is a mimeographed sheet called *Action* dated Epiphany 1949. If this news sheet had any predecessors, or if more than one issue of it was ever published, no copies survive in A.P.'s archives.

In May 1949 secretary Samuel West sent out a single newsletter reporting on a recent meeting, "Minutes and Motions—Meeting, May 1949." A copy or two of another mimeographed newsletter called *Rearvue* exists in A.P.'s files, apparently from 1950 or 1951. By Dec. 1, 1952, these initial gropings had coalesced into the first issue of *Sharers in A.P.*, a monthly legal-sized mimeographed sheet.

32. Subscriptions were $1.00 a year. By 1962 when A.P. closed the magazine, it was costing $1,200 a year in subsidy, which was prohibitive for A.P.'s hand-to-mouth finances. Minutes of the November 6–10, 1961, Meeting; Frederick W. Putnam, "The End of *Sharers*," *Sharers* VIII (December 1962): 18.

33. Howard Kunkle, "Segregation and the Eucharist," *Sharers* I (May 1955); John O. Patterson, "What Can the Parish Do? At Work—at Worship—in the World," *Sharers* II (Spring 1957); Carl R. Sayers, "Holy Society: Some Reflections on the Theology of F.D. Maurice in Relation to the Prayer for the Whole State of Christ's Church," *Sharers* VI (Trinity 1960): 9–17; Jules L. Moreau, "The Church and Society: An Ascension Day Address," *Sharers* VII (Easter 1961); Carl R. Sayers, "Catholic Eucharist and Mission for the Congregation," *Sharers* VII (Easter 1961); Hugh White, "The Detroit Industrial Mission," *Sharers* VII (Advent 1961): 1–10; C. Kilmer Myers, "Thinking About the Urban Church," *Sharers* VII (Advent 1961): 11–17.

34. Henry H. Breul, "The Building of a New Church," *Sharers* VIII (Lent 1962): 13.

35. Alfred R. Shands, "A Report on the Continental Liturgical Movement," *Sharers* III (Fall 1957); H. Boone Porter, "A Sunday in

South India," *Sharers* VI (Trinity 1960): 1–5.

36. J.H. Cranswick and R.O. Herde, "The Need to Develop the Liturgical Movement in Australia," *Sharers* V (Spring 1959); R.B. MacDonald "Rhodes '61," *Sharers* VII (Christmas 1961): 1–3; Archie C. Stapleton, "The Spirit Moves in Manila," *Sharers* VIII (Trinity 1962): 20–22; Frederick W. Putnam, "Liturgy Around the World," *Sharers* VII (Late Trinity 1961): 3–10.

37. Massey H. Shepherd, Jr., "Rubrical Observances," *Sharers* (no date, c. late 1950s); William Spicer, "The Order for Daily Morning and Evening Prayer," *Sharers* (no date, c. late 1950s); Howard R. Kunkle, "Observing Pentecost in a Parish Church," *Sharers* VII (Late Trinity 1961): 1–3; John Robert Bill, "The Processional at Rogationtide," *Sharers* VIII (Lent 1962): 1–4; Paul Z. Hoornstra "The Mechanics of the Offertory Procession," *Sharers* VIII (December 1962): 1–8.

38. William H. Nes, "Let Us Think Further About the Laity," *Sharers* V (Summer 1959): 1–2; H. Boone Porter, "The Liturgical Movement and the Sacred Ministry," *Sharers* IV (Spring 1958); Carl R. Sayers, "Lay Apostolate," *Sharers* VI (Advent 1960); Frank S. Cellier, "The Liturgical Movement and the Laity," *Sharers* V (Spring 1959); H. Boone Porter, "Oil in Church," *Sharers* V (Summer 1959): 5–9; Howard R. Kunkle, "I Prefer To Go To the Early Service," *Sharers* (Easter 1961); Robert A. Reister, "The Parish Eucharist in an Expanding Parish," *Sharers* IV (Winter 1958); William H. Boar, "College Work and the Liturgical–Theological Revival," *Sharers* IV (Winter 1958); William H. Nes, "Towards a Theology of Sickness, Health and Healing," *Sharers* V (Fall 1959): 8–10; Robert F. Cavitt, "I Treat, But God Heals," *Sharers* VII (Late Trinity 1961): 10–13; Edward A. Heffner and Christine E. Heffner, "Sacramental Restoration," *Sharers* VIII (Trinity 1962): 1–13.

39. Massey H. Shepherd, John H. Keene, John O. Patterson, and John R. Bill, eds., with the assistance of other members of the Associated Parishes, Inc., *Before the Holy Table: A Guide to the Celebration of the Holy Eucharist, Facing the People, According to the Book of Common Prayer* (Greenwich, Conn.: Seabury, 1956).

40. Minutes of the April 26–29, 1955, Meeting.

41. Massey H. Shepherd, Jr., ed., For the Associated Parishes, Incorporated, *Holy Week Offices* (Greenwich, Conn.: Seabury, 1958), p. iii.

42. Ibid.

43. Ibid., pp. vii–viii.

44. Minutes of the November 2–5, 1954, Meeting.

45. Leonard, "The Liturgical Movement in the United States," pp. 302–303.

46. Ladd, *Prayer Book Interleaves*, pp. 117–122.

47. David L. Taylor, "The Order of St. Luke and *The Versicle*, A Resume: 1946–1961," *Doxology* 3 (1986): 48–56.

48. The papers of the 1958 conference were published as Massey H. Shepherd, Jr., ed., *The Liturgical Renewal of the Church* (New York: Oxford, 1960). The addresses from the 1959 conference were published as Massey H. Shepherd, Jr., ed., *The Eucharist and Liturgical Renewal* (New York: Oxford, 1960). The 1962 conference's papers were published as Frank S. Cellier, ed., *Liturgy Is Mission* (New York: Seabury, 1964).

49. "Registrations for the Liturgical Conference at Grace Church, Madison, Wisconsin, May 19–21, 1958."

50. Odo Casel, *The Mystery of Christian Worship and Other Writings* (Westminster, Md.: Newman, 1962).

51. Shepherd, "Foreword," *Liturgical Renewal of the Church*, pp. viii–ix.

52. The conference cost A.P. $7,800, but there is no indication whether it made any profit.

53. A.P. realized a modest financial gain from the Wichita conference. The conference cost slightly more than $10,500 to mount. Of the almost $3,000 surplus, A.P. received half. ("The Wichita Liturgical Conference, Final Balance Sheet, Dec. 7, 1962.")

54. Cellier, "Introduction," *Liturgy Is Mission*, pp. 30–31.

55. Frederick W. Putnam to James Joseph, 11 December 1962.

56. Arthur E. Walmsley to James Joseph, 22 May 1961.

57. "Principles Concerning the Christian Use of Property Adopt-

ed at the Associated Parishes Meeting, June 18–22, 1951," Minutes of the June 18–22, 1951, Meeting.

58. Ibid.

59. Ibid.

60. *Christian Meaning of Work*, pp. 3, 12.

61. Ibid., pp. 10, 12.

62. "Accepted Corporate Program," 1962.

63. Ibid.

64. Martin Luther King, Jr., "Who Is Their God?" *The Nation* (13 October 1962): 210, quoted in James H. Cone, *Martin & Malcolm & America: A Dream or a Nightmare* (Maryknoll, N.Y.: Orbis, 1991), p. 138.

65. "Letter to Dr. King," reprinted in *New Leader* XLVI (24 June 1963): 5, quoted in Cone, p. 138.

66. See "Integration Crisis at Sewanee, 1952," pp. 493–497; "Racial Cooperation, 1955," pp. 500–501; "American Martyr: The Jon Daniels Story, 1965," pp. 505–508; "John Hines, Sermon, 1967," pp. 508–510; "Jenny Moore, The People on Second Street, 1968," pp. 511–513; "Journey Toward Justice, 1979," pp. 518–520; "Nathan Wright, Jr., Self-Development and Self-Respect," pp. 525–529, in Armentrout and Slocum, *Documents of Witness*.

67. Robert W. Prichard, *A History of the Episcopal Church* (Harrisburg, Pa.: Morehouse, 1991), pp. 215, 243, 261, 263; David L. Holmes, *A Brief History of the Episcopal Church* (Valley Forge, Pa.: Trinity, 1993), p. 164.

68. Minutes of the November 1962 Meeting.

69. Samuel E. West to James Joseph, 13 December 1962.

70. Minutes of the November 1962 Meeting.

71. Ibid.

72. Samuel E. West to James Joseph, 13 December 1962.

73. Trevor Huddleston, "Africa and You," *Sharers* VII (Christmas 1961): 12–13; emphasis in original.

74. Ibid., p. 15; emphasis in original.

75. The Church of South India, *The Book of Common Worship As Authorized by the Synod 1962* (London: Oxford, 1963).

76. T.S. Garrett, *Worship in the Church of South India*, Ecumenical Studies in Worship, no. 2 (Richmond: John Knox, 1958), p. 6.

77. See Dorothy L. Braun, "A Historical Study of the Origin and Development of the Seabury Series of the Protestant Episcopal Church," (Ph.D. dissertation, New York University, 1960).

78. Minutes of the November 5–8, 1956, Meeting, pp. 3–4.

79. Ibid., pp. 4, 6.

80. G. Cope, J.G. Davies, and D.A. Tytler, *An Experimental Liturgy*, Ecumenical Studies in Worship, no. 3 (Richmond: John Knox, 1958); John A.T. Robinson, *Liturgy Coming To Life* (London: A.R. Mowbray, 1960; 2nd ed. 1963).

81. *The Eucharistic Liturgy of Taizé*, with an introductory essay by Max Thurian (London: Faith, 1962).

82. *Prayer Book Studies XVII: The Liturgy of the Lord's Supper*, pp. 14–16.

83. J.P. Donovan, "Were Our Own Liturgists Afoul?" *Homiletic and Pastoral Review* XXXIX (1949): 750–751.

84. Gerald Ellard, *The Dialog Mass: A Book for Priests and Teachers of Religion* (New York: Longmans, Green and Co., 1942).

85. Susan J. White, *Art, Architecture, and Liturgical Reform: The Liturgical Arts Society (1928–1972)* (New York: Pueblo, 1990); Lawrence Madden, "The Liturgical Conference of the United States of America: Its Origin and Development, 1940–1968" (Ph.D. dissertation, Trier, 1969); Joel P. Garner, "The Vision of a Liturgical Reformer: Hans Ansgar Reinhold, American Catholic Educator" (Ph.D. dissertation, Columbia University, 1972), pp. 206–227.

86. Gerald Ellard, *The Mass of the Future* and *The Mass in Transition* (both Milwaukee: Bruce).

87. Gregory Dix, *The Shape of the Liturgy* (London: Dacre, 1945; new edition with additional notes by Paul V. Marhsall, New York: Seabury, 1982). See also Kenneth W. Stevenson, *Gregory Dix—Twenty-Five Years On*, Grove Liturgical Study No. 10 (Bramcote, Notts.: Grove, 1977).

88. See Stuhlman, *Eucharistic Celebration*, pp. 126–127.

89. Robert J. Kennedy, *Michael Mathis: American Liturgical Pioneer*,

American Essays in Liturgy 5 (Washington, D.C.: Pastoral Press, 1987), pp. 11–18.

90. Josef A. Jungmann, *The Mass of the Roman Rite: Its Origins and Development (Missarum Sollemnia)*, 2 vols. (New York: Benziger, 1951).

91. Ladd, *Prayer Book Interleaves*, p. 133.

92. Holmes, "Education for Liturgy," p. 127.

93. Ibid., p. 128.

94. See Ralph N. McMichael, Jr., ed., *Creation and Liturgy: Studies in Honor of H. Boone Porter* (Washington, D.C.: Pastoral Press, 1993).

95. *The Lambeth Conference 1958: The Encyclical Letter from the Bishops together with the Resolutions and Reports* (Greenwich, Conn.: S.P.C.K. and Seabury, 1958), pp. 2.78–2.79.

96. The Bohlen Lectures, delivered in the Church of the Holy Trinity, Philadelphia, April 26–28, 1959; published as *The Reform of Liturgical Worship, Perspectives and Prospects* (New York: Oxford, 1961).

97. Ibid., p. viii.

98. Shepherd, *The Liturgical Movement and the Prayer Book*, p. 14.

99. Shepherd, *Reform of Liturgical Worship*, pp. 69–70.

100. Ibid.

101. Ibid., pp. 73–74.

102. Ibid., pp. 76–77.

103. *The Lambeth Conference 1958*, p. 1.48.

104. *PBS XVII*, p. 16.

105. Ibid., pp. 58–59.

Chapter Four: The Turning Point

1. *JGC* 1955, pp. 377–379.

2. Holmes, "Education for Liturgy," p. 125.

3. *PBS XV: The Problem and Method of Prayer Book Revision*, p. 14.

4. Ibid., p. 18.

5. "A Form of Memorial to the General Convention."

6. James Joseph to Massey Shepherd, 2 March 1961.

7. Holmes, "Education for Liturgy," p. 125.

8. Ibid., pp. 125–126.

9. Shepherd, "What Is the Associated Parishes," p. 4.

10. Minutes of the November 16–20, 1959, Meeting.

11. Paul Z. Hoornstra to the author, 23 October 1992.

12. H. Boone Porter to James Joseph, 27 June 1962.

13. Telephone interview with Henry H. Breul, 26 August 1992. Holmes's information about A.P. on pp. 129–130 of "Education for Liturgy" mistakes dates, places of meetings, conflates at least three separate events in A.P.'s history, and misgauges A.P.'s relation to the instigation of official Prayer Book revision.

14. Samuel E. West to the author, 29 October 1992; emphasis in the original.

15. Paul Z. Hoornstra to the author, 23 October 1992.

16. Bonnell Spencer, O.H.C., to the author, 5 September 1992.

17. Ibid.

18. Frederick W. Putnam, "Epistle General to the Associated Parishes from the President," 25 March 1963.

19. Frederick W. Putnam, "News Letter to People Interested in Liturgical Renewal," June 1963, p. 2.

20. Ibid.

21. Ibid., p. 1.

22. Paul Z. Hoornstra to the author, 23 October 1992.

23. *A Parish Program for Liturgy and Mission* (Madison, Wisc.: Associated Parishes, 1964).

24. Putnam, "News Letter to People Interested in Liturgical Renewal," pp. 1–2.

25. Paul Z. Hoornstra to the author, 23 October 1992. The minutes for the Spring 1969 Council meeting show that when A.P.'s constitution was revised that year the words "for Liturgy and Mission" were added to the name. But that does not indicate the name was changed in that year; it may have occurred earlier, with the constitution only then catching up with the change. (Minutes of the April 14–17, 1969, Meeting.)

26. *JGC* 1964, p. 349.

27. Ibid.

28. The role of the SLC; use of liturgical consultants; designation of a coordinator for Prayer Book revision; financing; trial use; and target dates. (*JGC* 1967, Appendix 23.5–23.7.

29. A list of all the consultants' names for the 1970–1973 triennium is on pp. 518–521, *JGC* 1970. The names of more than 300 consultants for the 1974–1976 triennium are listed on pp. AA-295–AA-299, *JGC* 1976.

A list of the drafting committees and their membership appears on pp. 517–518, *JGC* 1970. By 1976 the number of drafting committees had grown to 27; they and their membership are listed on pp. AA-288–AA-291, *JGC* 1976.

30. *JGC* 1970, pp. 491–492.

31. *JGC* 1969, pp. 325–326.

32. *Associated Parishes Newsletter* (July 1967): 2.

33. Ibid. Emphasis in the original.

34. Ibid., p. 3.

35. *JGC* 1967, Appendix 23.4.

36. Ibid.

37. Ibid., Appendix 23.5.

38. The vote in the House of Deputies was a landslide. The tallies, by orders and dioceses, were: Clerical—Ayes 84½, Noes 0, Divided 1. Lay—Ayes 83¾, Noes ¼, Divided 1. (*JGC* 1967, pp. 458–460.)

39. Ibid., Appendix 23.10.

40. There had been an unsuccessful skirmish in the House of Deputies to have the Penitential Order printed in the body of the new rite. The penitential order was referred to by rubric in *The Liturgy of the Lord's Supper,* immediately after the creed, but one had to flip to the back of the book to find it. The penitential order also could be said before the liturgy, or after the Summary of the Law. Its use was mandatory on five days a year (First Sunday in Advent, Ash Wednesday, First Sunday in Lent, Passion Sunday, First Sunday after Trinity), and optional at other times.

Proponents of printing the penitential order within the text of the service said they were not against trial use, but that it was "simply a matter of fair play" to print the order in place "for the convenience of those who want to use it." If they thought that the new rite slighted recognition of human sinfulness, they chose not to launch that doctrinal debate at this point, when the issue before General Convention simply was trial use. (*JGC* 1967, pp. 459–460.)

The SLC's position was that there was "sufficient weight of opinion" among SLC members to warrant testing whether penitential material in the eucharist ought not to be optional except on a very few specific occasions. Printing the penitential order at the end of the rite, and allowing its insertion at several points in the service, "is the only practical way to leave the Church free, through actual experimentation, to determine how frequently the material should be used, and which of the several positions is the best." (*JGC* 1967, Appendix 23.11.)

41. *PBS XVII*, p. iii.

42. *JGC* 1967, Appendix 23.10.

43. *PBS XVII*, p. iii.

44. Ibid., p. 13.

45. Chilton Powell to Massey H. Shepherd, Jr., 24 September 1965, Record Group 237-1-9, The Archives of the Episcopal Church USA, Austin, Texas.

46. *PBS XVII*, p. 17.

47. Ibid., p. 54.

48. *PBS XVII*, pp. 46–48.

49. Ibid., p. 40. This was not the first Anglican rite to use a litany structure for this prayer, the SLC noted. That distinction belongs to the Ceylon Liturgy of 1933. (Ibid., p. 39.)

50. Alfred R. Shands, III, "What Sunday Morning Is Coming To," *The Episcopalian* 133 (November 1968):8.

51. *PBS XVII*, p. 22.

52. Ibid., p. 2.

53. Ibid., p. 57.

54. Ibid., p. 22.

55. Edward T. Martin, St. Petersburg, Fla., "COCU Service," *TLC* 160 (April 12, 1970): 5.

56. Robert J. McCloskey, Jr., Rector of St. James' Church, West

Somerville, Mass., "Massachusetts Installation," *TLC* 160 (June 14, 1970): 6.

57. *Prayer Book Studies 21: The Holy Eucharist; the Liturgy for the Proclamation of the Word of God and Celebration of the Holy Communion* (New York: Church Hymnal Corp., 1970), p. 2.

58. Ibid.

59. Minutes of the November 11–14, 1968, Meeting.

60. Transcript of the August 27, 1969, Membership Meeting.

61. Roderic D. Wiltse, Rector of Holy Trinity Parish, Wyoming, Mich., "Trial Liturgy," *TLC* 157 (August 18, 1968): 4. Wiltse said he was told of this incident occurring in another parish.

62. Alan A. Snow, Beverly Hills, Cal., "'Newspaper-Language' Liturgy," *TLC* 157 (July 28, 1969): 2.

63. Herbert J. Mainwaring, Natick, Mass., "Praise of BCP," *TLC* 160 (January 18, 1970): 8–9.

64. C.O. Jensen, Hartland, Wisc., "Worship Forum," *The Episcopalian* 133 (May 1968): 4.

65. Paulea Patterson, Houston, Tex., "Trial Liturgy," *TLC* 157 (August 18, 1968): 4.

66. The Rev. George A.J. Porthan, Calumet, Mich., "Worship Forum," *The Episcopalian* 133 (October 1968): 6.

67. Jean Helen Selch, St. Martin's Parish, Providence, R.I., "Trial Liturgy, *Si*," *TLC* 157 (September 15, 1968): 4.

68. Heather Huyck, San Jose, Costa Rica, "Worship Forum," *The Episcopalian* 133 (September 1968): 43.

69. W. Francis B. Maguire, Bonita, Cal., "Worship Forum," *The Episcopalian* 133 (May 1968): 4.

70. John H. Young, Ft. Wayne, Ind., "Updating the Creed," *TLC* 157 (July 21, 1968): 5.

71. John H. Young, Fort Wayne, Ind., "Worship Forum," *The Episcopalian* 133 (September 1968): 42.

72. John H. Young, Fort Wayne, Ind., "Worship Forum," *Episcopalian* 133 (September 1968): 42.

73. Wilma L. Tague, Kenosha, Wisc., "Trial Liturgy," *TLC* 157 (November 17, 1968): 4.

74. W. Francis B. Maguire, Bonita, Cal., "Worship Forum," *The Episcopalian* 133 (May 1968): 4.

75. Mrs. Copeland Kell, Beaufort, N.C., "Worship Forum," *The Episcopalian* 133 (October 1968): 61.

76. Mrs. Charles C. Rettew, Charles Summit, Pa., *The Episcopalian* 133 (April 1968): 4.

77. Eldon W. Borell, Martin's Ferry, Ohio, *The Episcopalian* 133 (June 1968): 4.

78. Paula Chandler, Philadelphia, Pa., *The Episcopalian* 133 (May 1968): 5.

79. Ruth H. McLarnan, Chicago, "Repeal of BCP," *TLC* 157 (August 25, 1968): 12.

80. Edward S. Gray, Rector of St. Mark's Church, Denver, Col., "Whither PECUSA," *TLC* 164 (June 18, 1972): 3.

81. West, "Episodes VII: A.P. in a Diocese," p. 36.

82. Georgianna F. King, Kansas City, Mo., "Worship Forum," *The Episcopalian* 133 (October 1968): 61.

83. G.W. Martin, Iowa City, Ia., "Trial Liturgy," *TLC* 157 (November 17, 1968): 4.

84. Florence Marquardt, Whitefish Bay, Wisc., "Prayer Book and Change," *TLC* 161 (September 20, 1970): 3.

85. Mary Jane Coffey, Dedham, Mass., "Preoccupation with Liturgy," *The Churchman* CLXXXIII (April 1969): 2.

86. John Clark, Poughkeepsie, N.Y., "B.C.P., R.I.P.," *TLC* 157 (July 7, 1968): 5.

87. Darwin Kirby, Rector of St. George's Church, Schenectady, N.Y., "For Liturgical Variety," *TLC* 157 (September 29, 1968): 3.

88. Ronald B. Nicholson, Rector of Karkloof, Natal, South Africa, "Experimental Services," *TLC* 160 (June 14, 1970): 5.

89. *JGC* 1970, p. 509. Final sales figures in 1976 were slightly higher: 54,170 copies of *PBS XVII*, 716,441 copies of the pew edition, and 5,523 copies of the altar edition. (*JGC* 1976, p. AA-283.)

90. Minutes of the November 7–11, 1966, Meeting.

91. Associated Parishes, *The Liturgy of the Lord's Supper; Leader's*

Guide and Workbook For a Five-Session Study Course in Conjunction With Prayer Book Studies No. XVII (Madison, Wisc.: Associated Parishes, 1967). The study guide conformed in style to A.P.'s brochure series. It was 8½ x 11 inches, 52 pages, and sold for $1.00. Its dark green cover complemented the cover of *PBS XVII*.

A.P. published a second edition in 1971 which took into account the new eucharistic rites which had been proposed by then: David Babin, for the Associated Parishes, *Making Use of Trial Use; A Leader's Guide for a Five-Session Study Course of the Holy Eucharist* (No place of publication, Associated Parishes, 1971).

92. *The Liturgy of the Lord's Supper; Leader's Guide and Workbook,* p. 43.

93. Chilton Powell to All Bishops, 6 February 1968, Records of the Standing Liturgical Commission in the personal possession of the Rev. Dr. James F. White, South Bend, Indiana.

94. Minutes of the November 11–14, 1968, Meeting.

95. Shepherd, "A Response to Henry Breul," p. 2.

96. Transcript of the August 27, 1969, Membership Meeting.

97. Minutes of the April 24–26, 1968, Meeting. No copies of *Music for The Liturgy of the Lord's Supper,* written by A.P. Council member Richard Forrest Woods, survive in A.P.'s archives, but the $1.00 brochure was announced in an untitled, undated news release in the archives.

98. *The Parish Eucharist* (Madison, Wisc.: Associated Parishes, no date). The decision not to rewrite the brochure now but to simply insert new material in order to get the booklet into circulation quickly was made at A.P.'s November 11–14, 1968, meeting.

99. Ibid., p. 26.

100. Minutes of the November 6–10, 1967, Meeting.

101. Transcript of the August 27, 1969, Membership Meeting.

102. Minutes of the April 25–28, 1966, Meeting.

103. Minutes of the April 24–26, 1968, Meeting.

104. Ibid.

105. Charles's appointment was the subject of an A.P. news release (no headline or date) and an article, "Meet the Executive

Secretary," in the *Associated Parishes Newsletter* (no volume no. or date): 1.

106. Minutes of the April 24–26, 1968, Meeting.

107. Minutes of the April 6–9, 1970, Meeting.

108. Associated Parishes, Untitled, undated news release.

109. Minutes of the November 11–14, 1968, Meeting.

110. Associated Parishes, Untitled news release, 10 March 1969.

111. "A.P. Launches New Program for Renewal," *Associated Parishes Newsletter* (no date): 1.

112. Associated Parishes, Untitled, undated news release. The consultants were: the Rev. Norman Mealy, Church Divinity School of the Pacific, Berkeley, Cal.; the Rev. William Petersen, University of California, Berkeley; Mr. Jack C. Miller, Claremont College; Miss Janet deCoux, Gibsonia, Pa.; Mr. Ronald Haines, Glastonbury, Conn.; the Rev. Peter Norman, Rochester, N.Y.; Mr. Arthur C. Greene, University of Virginia, Charlottesville, Va.; the Rev. Eugenio Ayala, St. Andrew's Church, Mayaguez, Puerto Rico; the Rev. Edwin Hoover, Memphis State University, Memphis, Tenn.; the Rev. Barry Evans, Church of St. Stephen and the Incarnation, Washington, D.C.; the Rev. William Crews, University of New Mexico, Albuquerque, N.M.; and the Rev. Frederick Phinney, Church of the Holy Spirit, Lake Forest, Ill. Unfortunately, there is no record of the consultants' activities.

113. Otis Charles to Chester Byrns, 20 November 1970.

114. Transcript of the August 27, 1969, Membership Meeting.

115. Transcript of the April 14–17, 1969, Meeting.

116. Ibid.

117. Minutes of the Meeting of the Executive Committee, July 6–8, 1971. The name of the other council member opposed is not recorded.

118. Ibid.

119. Minutes of the Meeting of the Executive Committee, September 18, 1971.

120. Minutes of the April 9–10, 1972, Meeting.

121. Minutes of the November 11–14, 1968; April 14–17, 1969;

August 27, 1969; and December 7, 1972, Council Meetings.

122. *JGC* 1976, pp. AA-287–AA-288.

123. Ibid., p. AA-288.

124. *JGC* 1970, pp. 517–518.

125. *JGC* 1976, pp. AA-288–AA-291.

126. West, "Massey Shepherd: A Personal Memoir," p. 11.

127. *A.P. Newsletter,* 7 October 1965.

128. Thomas J. Talley, "The Year of Grace," in *The Identity of Anglican Worship*, ed. Kenneth Stevenson and Bryan Spinks (Harrisburg, Pa.: Morehouse, 1991), p. 30.

129. *An Order of Worship for the Proclamation of the Word of God and the Celebration of the Lord's Supper with Commentary* (Cincinnati: Forward Movement, 1968).

130. "Letter from the President," *Sharers in A.P.* 1 (Dec. 1, 1952): no page number.

131. Minutes of the November 7–11, 1966, Meeting.

132. Minutes of the November 6–10, 1967, Meeting.

133. Minutes of the November 11–14, 1968, Meeting.

134. Minutes of the Executive Session of the Council, April 9, 1972.

135. West, "Massey Shepherd: A Personal Memoir," p. 11.

136. Frederick W. Putnam, *Manual For Regional Liturgical Conferences Sponsored By The Associated Parishes, Inc.,* p. 2.

137. Transcript of the April 14–17, 1969, Meeting.

138. Transcript of the November 11–14, 1968, Meeting.

139. James F. White, communication with author, 4 March 1996.

140. *Open* 1 (1971): 1.

141. *Open* 5 (1969).

142. Robert McClernon, "House Church," broadsheet published by A.P.

143. Transcript of the November 11–14, 1968, Meeting.

144. "Formal presentation of Mr. Jim Colliani [*sic*] at A.P. Council meeting, St. Louis, April 15, 1969;" Minutes of the April 14–17, 1969, Meeting.

145. Transcript of the April 14–17, 1969, Meeting.

146. Minutes of the August 25–28, 1969, Meeting.

147. Minutes of the May 23–26, 1983, Meeting.

148. Minutes of the Meetings of November 7–11, 1966; April 24–26, 1968; May 26–30, 1975; May 26–30, 1976.

149. David L. Holmes, *Brief History of the Episcopal Church*, p. 172.

150. In addition to the *Journal* of this convention, see *The Episcopalian* 134 (October 1969): Special Convention Issue.

151. *JGC* 1969, p. 326, 329; see also *JGC* 1970, pp. 512–517.

152. Transcript of the April 14–17, 1969, Meeting.

153. See Prichard, *History of the Episcopal Church*, pp. 261–263; David Holmes, *A Brief History of the Episcopal Church,* pp. 164–167; 174–175; "John Hines, Sermon, 1967," in Armentrout and Slocum, *Documents of Witness*, pp. 508–510.

154. *National Catholic Reporter*, 10 September 1969, p. 1.

155. Minutes of the August 25–28, 1969, Meeting.

156. Henry Breul, "A Report from Henry Breul on A.P. at Milwaukee and GCII or Associated Parishes Rides Again," *Open* 4 (1969); no page number.

157. Prichard, *History of the Episcopal Church*, p. 262.

158. Breul, "A Report from Henry Breul," no page number.

159. Ibid.

160. Ibid.

161. For example, on Sunday night the Rev. Fred Williams, Chairman of the Black Clergy and Laity, celebrated a eucharist following their "dramatic demonstration before the Convention." Monday night, Dick York led a eucharist using one of the rites of the Free Church of Berkeley that included a discussion by the young people present as the service of the word. Wednesday night's liturgy led by the chaplain and students from Ann Arbor, Michigan, was based on the theme of the circus and used a multi-media approach. (Breul, "A Report From Henry Breul," no page number.)

162. Breul, "A Report From Henry Breul," no page number.

163. "The most heroic moment came when we ... rented a flat-bed truck from Hertz to transport it," Henry Breul reported. "Those who saw Bill Wendt climb into the cab of the Behemoth witnessed

a moment of true heroism for the cause of liturgical renewal." (Breul, "A Report from Henry Breul," no page number.)

164. Jeffrey Cave, "God Box With A Difference," *Open* 4 (1969): no page number.

165. Ibid.

166. Breul, "A Report from Henry Breul," no page number.

167. Ibid. Another A.P. report noted "bishops balancing soap bubbles on their noses." Perhaps it was only hyperbole. (Jan Chishom, Untitled article, *Open* 5 (1969): 4.)

168. Transcript of the A.P. Membership Meeting, August 27, 1969.

169. Membership recruitment flyer, no date but c. 1970.

170. Chishom, Untitled article, *Open* 5 (1969): 4.

171. Marty Smith, "Focus #4," *Open* 4 & 5 (1970): 8; emphasis in the original.

172. Untitled press release, 25 November 1969; Smith, "Focus #4," *Open* 4 & 5 (1970): 8.

173. Minutes of the April 6–9, 1970, Meeting; Transcript of the April 14–17, 1969, Meeting.

174. Transcript of the November 11–14, 1968, Meeting.

175. Ibid.

176. Name Withheld, "Ah, Relevance," *TLC* 158 (May 18, 1969): 4.

177. Larry Rouillard, *A.P. Newsletter* (Lent 1966): 6. The newsletter did not mention the text used, but since *The Liturgy of the Lord's Supper* was not published until 1966 and not authorized for trial use until 1967, A.P.'s 1965 liturgical celebration presumably used the 1928 rite, rearranged and adapted.

178. Larry Rouillard, "The Living Room Concelebration," *A.P. Newsletter* (Whitsuntide 1966): 8–9.

179. Larry Rouillard, "Comments on Worship at Chicago," *A.P. Newsletter* (July 1967): 4.

180. Ibid.

181. Ibid., p. 5.

182. Minutes of the April 24–26, 1968, Meeting.

183. Minutes of the November 11–14, 1968, Meeting.

184. Minutes of the April 14–17, 1969, Meeting.

185. Minutes of the April 6–9, 1970, Meeting.

186. *PBS 21*, pp. 1, 3. That decision was made as early as October 1968 at the second session of the Drafting Committee on the Eucharist. (Drafting Committee on the Eucharist, *Report DC-V/2*, "Report of the Chairman," 15 October 1968, p. 2.)

187. Minutes of the November 11–14, 1968, Meeting.

188. *PBS 21*, pp. 8–9.

189. Drafting Committee on the Psalter, Report by Chairman, 27 December 1968, DC-XI/2.

190. Hancock, who was dean of St. Mark's Cathedral, Minneapolis, Minn., died March 24, 1970. His obituary notice in the SLC's report to the 1970 General Convention noted Hancock's love for the language of the Prayer Book and his "keen sense of its poetry." (*JGC* 1970, p. 491.)

191. Shepherd, "A Response to Henry Breul," p. 2.

192. *PBS 21*, pp. 29–30.

193. Minutes of the November 11–14, 1968, Meeting, and Transcript of the April 14–17, 1969, Meeting.

194. Edith M. Docker, Fresno, Cal., "'Thou' or 'You'?" *TLC* 163 (September 12, 1971): 6.

195. Wesley Mansfield, Organist at Christ Church, Chattanooga, Tenn., "'Thou,' etc.," *TLC* 166 (April 29, 1973): 4.

196. William D. Loring, Rector of St. John's Church, Sandy Hook, Conn., "'Thou,' etc.," *TLC* 166 (April 29, 1973): 3.

197. R. Scoon, Fuller Theological Seminary, "The Thirty-nine Articles," *TLC* 164 (January 30, 1972): 5.

198. Lynn Chester Edwards, Rector of Church of the Good Shepherd, Pittsburgh, Pa., "Liturgical Coercion?" *TLC* 164 (February 27, 1972): 4.

199. Edgar M. Tainton, Jr., Vicar of St. Thomas' Church, Eugene, Ore., "Too Late to Ask," *TLC* 163 (August 29, 1971): 9.

200. Alston Watkins, Wilmington, N.C., "Prayer Book Revision," *TLC* 166 (January 21, 1973): 4.

201. Harry W. Shipps, Rector of St. Alban's Church, Augusta, Ga., "Trial Use," *TLC* 165 (July 2, 1972): 4.

202. Holmes, "Education for Liturgy," p. 131.

203. Ibid., p. 134.

204. Shepherd, "A Response to Henry Breul," p. 2.

205. Harold L. Weatherby, Nashville, Tenn., "SPBCP," *TLC* 163 (September 19, 1971): 5.

206. George Stamm, Vicar of the Lake Missions, Clear Lake, Wisc., "Why Be an Episcopalian?" *TLC* 166 (May 6, 1973): 4.

207. Harold T. Lewis, St. John's College, Cambridge, England, "The Fraction," *TLC* (February 4, 1973): 3–4.

208. The Academic Council of the School of Theology, "SPBCP," *TLC* 163 (November 21, 1971): 6.

209. Grace V. Dillingham, Brooklyn, N.Y., "Prayer Book Revision," *TLC* 166 (April 15, 1973): 3.

210. Richard R. Worden, Black River, N.Y., "The Prayer Book," *TLC* 165 (July 30, 1972): 5.

Chapter Five: The Creation of the 1979 Prayer Book

1. Transcript of the November 11–14, 1969, Meeting.

2. Smith, "Focus #4," *Open* 4 & 5 (1970): 8.

3. *Open*, 4 & 5 (1970): 9.

4. Published in New York by Church Hymnal Corp., they were:

Prayer Book Studies 18: On Baptism and Confirmation; Holy Baptism with the Laying-On-of-Hands.

Prayer Book Studies 19: The Church Year; the Calendar and the Proper of the Sundays and Other Holy Days Throughout the Church Year.

Prayer Book Studies 20: The Ordination of Bishops, Priests, and Deacons.

Prayer Book Studies 21: The Holy Eucharist: the Liturgy for the Proclamation of the Word of God and Celebration of the Holy Communion.

Prayer Book Studies 22: The Daily Office: Morning and Evening Prayer, Services for Noonday and Close of Day, Daily Devotions.

Prayer Book Studies 23: The Psalter, Part I: A Selection of the Most

Frequently Appointed Psalms.

Prayer Book Studies 24: Pastoral Offices: Marriage, Thanksgiving for a Child, Commitment to Service, Ministry to the Sick, Reconciliation, Anointing of the Sick, Private Communions, Prayers for the Dying, Burial of the Dead.

The 1970 convention also took the unusual step of authorizing for trial use a Prayer Book Study not yet published—number 25, *Prayers, Thanksgivings, and Litanies*—on the ground that the study was not an alternative for any existing service, office, or rite currently in the Prayer Book. [*"Prayer Book Studies 'In,'" Open* 4 & 5 (1970): 5.]

5. *Services for Trial Use; Authorized Alternatives to Prayer Book Services* (New York: Church Hymnal Corp., 1971).

6. Holmes, "Education for Liturgy," p. 133.

7. Shepherd, "A Response to Henry Breul," p. 2.

8. The Rev. Edmund W. Olifiers, Jr., Lindenhurst, N.Y., "Trial Use," *TLC* 165 (July 16, 1972): 3.

9. Frederick Cooper, Wynnewood, Pa., "Greenbookery," *TLC* 166 (June 10, 1973): 7.

10. The Rev. Kenneth E. Trueman, Rector of Trinity Church, Wauwatosa, Wis., "Preparation for Trial Use," *TLC* 165 (June 11, 1972): 3.

11. Frances Beardmore, Manhatten, Kan., "The Green Book," *TLC* 166 (April 29, 1973): 4.

12. The Rev. Harris C. Mooney, Rector of All Saints Church, Indianapolis, Ind., "TLC, June 11," *TLC* 165 (August 6, 1972): 3.

13. The Rev. William L. Hicks, Rector of the Church of the Resurrection, Greenwood, S.C., "Trial Use," *TLC* 165 (July 16, 1972): 3; The Rev. V.L. Livingston, Rector of St. David's Church, Portland, Ore., ibid.

14. The Rev. Donald K. White, Rector of Christ Church, Castle Rock, Colo., "The Second Service," *TLC* 164 (June 11, 1972): 6.

15. The Rev. William B. Olnhausen, Vicar of St. Boniface Church, Mequon, Wis., "Trial Usage," *TLC* 165 (May 28, 1972): 4.

16. Minutes of the Executive Council Meeting, November 8, 1973.

17. Minutes of the Executive Committee Meeting, June 26–27, 1973.

18. All published by Church Hymnal Corp., New York, 1973, they were:

Prayer Book Studies 26: Holy Baptism, together with A Form for Confirmation or the Laying-On of Hands by the Bishop with the Affirmation of Baptismal Vows.

Holy Baptism, together with A Form for the Affirmation of Baptismal Vows with the Laying-On of Hands by the Bishop, also called Confirmation; Supplement to Prayer Book Studies 26.

Prayer Book Studies 27: The Daily Office Revised.

Prayer Book Studies 28: Dedication and Consecration of a Church; Celebration of a New Ministry.

19. *JGC* 1973, p. 616.

20. *Authorized Services, 1973*, Pew Edition (New York: Church Hymnal Corp., 1973) and *Authorized Services, 1973*, Expanded Edition (New York: Church Hymnal Corp, 1973).

21. Minutes of the Meetings of May 26–30, 1975, and May 26–30, 1976.

22. West, "Episodes VIII: A.P. & A Key Prayer Book Revision Committee," pp. 43–44.

23. *Prayer Book Studies 29: Introducing the Proposed Book*, p. 9.

24. Bradshaw, *Search for the Origins of Christian Worship*, p. 161.

25. Westminster: Dacre Press.

26. Ruth A. Meyers, "The Renewal of Christian Initiation in the Episcopal Church 1928–1979," (Ph.D. dissertation, University of Notre Dame, 1992), p. 138.

27. Geoffrey W.H. Lampe, *The Seal of the Spirit: A Study in the Doctrine of Baptism and Confirmation in the New Testament and the Fathers* (London: Longmans, Green, and Co., 1951; 2nd ed., London: S.P.C.K., 1967).

28. Meyers, "Renewal of Christian Initiation," pp. 167–169.

29. Louis Weil, *Christian Initiation: A Theological and Pastoral Commentary on the Proposed Rites* (Alexandria, Va.: Associated Parishes, n.d.), p. 3.

30. The English BCP 1662 added an explicit public affirmation of faith to confirmation.

31. Extra-rubrical use of chrismation was widespread before adoption of the 1979 Prayer Book. With the BCP 1928, clergy often anointed with chrism at baptism and bishops sometimes anointed with chrism at confirmation. The BCP 1979 suggests use of chrism at baptism but not at confirmation.

32. Meyers, "Renewal of Christian Initiation," pp. 192–193.

33. Massey H. Shepherd, Jr., *Liturgy and Education* (New York: Seabury, 1965), pp. 106–107.

34. "Statement Issued by the Council of Associated Parishes on the Admission of Children to Communion," November 15, 1968.

35. "Episcopal History Made," *Boston Globe*, 4 October 1969, pp. 1, 16; Associated Parishes, untitled, undated news release.

36. Leonel L. Mitchell, *Baptismal Anointing* (London: S.P.C.K., 1966).

37. See Meyers, "Renewal of Christian Initiation," pp. 181–186; quote is on p. 185.

38. Transcript of the April 14–17, 1969, Meeting.

39. See Meyers, "Renewal of Christian Initiation," pp. 200–232.

40. Transcript of the April 14–17, 1969, Meeting.

41. Meyers, "Renewal of Christian Initiation," pp. 203–204, 207.

42. Holmes, "Education for Liturgy," p. 133.

43. *PBS 24*, p. 10.

44. *JGC* 1973, pp. 1072–1073.

45. *PBS 26: Holy Baptism*, pp. 2–5.

46. New York: Church Hymnal Corp., 1973.

47. New York: Church Hymnal Corp., 1973.

48. New York: Church Hymnal Corp., 1975.

49. *JGC* 1976, p. B-112.

50. *Proposed BCP 1976*, p. 412; BCP 1979, p. 412.

51. *Proposed BCP 1976*, p. 412; BCP 1979, p. 412.

52. BCP 1979, p. 298.

53. BCP 1979, pp. 307–308.

54. Ibid., pp. 416, 418.

55. Weil, "Christian Initiation: A Theological and Pastoral Commentary on the Proposed Rites," *Nashotah Review* 14 (1975): 206.

56. Frederick J. Warnecke, "Let's Change Confirmation," *The Episcopalian* 134 (March 1969): 21–23.

57. See *The Episcopalian* 134 (May 1969): 45–46; (June 1969): 6,8; (July 1969): 6,35.

58. Wm. Thomas Martin, Newton Centre, Mass., "Confirmation Forum," *The Episcopalian* 134 (June 1969): 6,8.

59. Mrs. Nadine Ermolaeff, Pittsfield, Mass., "Confirmation Forum," *The Episcopalian* 134 (May 1969): 45.

60. Henry H. Breul,"Initiation Rite," *TLC* 161 (Sept. 6, 1970): 5.

61. "Editorials: A Plea to Convention," *TLC* 161 (Sept. 6, 1970): 11.

62. Robert L. Ladehoff, Rector of St. Christopher's Church, Charlotte, N.C., *"PBS 18,"* *TLC* 161 (Oct. 25, 1970): 7.

63. Henry I. Louttit, Jr., Rector of Christ Church, Valdosta, Ga., *"PBS 18,"* *TLC* 161 (Oct. 25, 1970): 7.

64. "Editorials: Holy Baptism Bowdlerized," *TLC* 163 (Sept. 12, 1971): 17.

65. Lee A. Belford, Chairman of the Department of Religious Education, New York University, New York City, "Holy Baptism Bowdlerized," *TLC* 163 (Oct. 24, 1971): 5.

66. Oliver N. Quigley, Los Angeles, "Holy Baptism Bowdlerized," *TLC* 163 (Oct. 24, 1971): 6.

67. *Ministry I: Holy Baptism* (Alexandria, Va.: Associated Parishes, 1978), pp. 1, 10.

68. *Celebration: Community and Communion; A Program of Continuing Education for Those Baptized & Admitted to Communion at an Early Age* (No place of publication given: Associated Parishes, 1971). The course was prepared by the Diocese of Central New York and published and distributed by A.P.

69. Minutes of the November 6–10, 1967, and April 24–26, 1968, Meetings, and Transcript of the November 11–14, 1968, Meeting.

70. Transcript of the November 11–14, 1968, Meeting.

71. Transcript of the November 11–14, 1968, Meeting.

72. Minutes of the April 14–17, 1969, Meeting.

73. Transcript of the April 14–17, 1969, Meeting.

74. Transcript of the August 27, 1969, Membership Meeting.

75. Minutes of the April 6–9, 1970, Meeting.

76. Minutes of the November 18–19, 1970, Meeting.

77. "Initial Report of the Drafting Committee on the Catechism, Offices of Instruction, and the 39 Articles," 14 August 1968.

78. Transcript of the April 14–17, 1969, Meeting; "Request to Associated Parishes," Drafting Committee on Catechism and Offices of Instruction, DC-VII/3, 29 May 1969; Transcript of the Membership Meeting, August 27, 1969.

79. Charles M. Guilbert to William Gray, 3 January 1972.

80. William Gray to George H. Woodward, 18 January 1973.

81. Robert R. Parks to William Gray, 6 April 1973.

82. "Ad Hoc Committee Report About Consultant in Liturgical Education Approved and Adopted by Associated Parishes Council on May 14, 1973."

83. Minutes of the May 3–7, 1974, Meeting.

84. Minutes of the May 26–30, 1975, Meeting.

85. Minutes of the Executive Committee Meeting, September 25, 1974.

86. Minutes of the May 26–30, 1975, Meeting.

87. Michael Merriman, Consultant's Report, May 1976.

88. Minutes of the Executive Committee Meeting, November 8, 1973.

89. Minutes of the Executive Session, May 3–7, 1974.

90. Minutes of the May 26–30, 1975, Meeting.

91. West. "Episodes (cont): Conflict Resolution before Minneapolis Gen'l Convention," no page no.

92. Minutes of the May 26–30, 1976, Meeting.

93. Ibid.; West, "Episodes (cont): Conflict Resolution before Minneapolis Gen'l Convention," no page no.

94. Minutes of the November 6–10, 1967, Meeting.

95. Minutes of the Executive Session of the Council, April 22, 1971.

96. West, "Episodes VI: Guests, Several Times, Orleton Farms, Ohio," p. 32.

97. West, "Episodes VII: A.P. in a Diocese; The Baptismal Ministry: Liturgical Leadership, by Clergy AND Laity?" p. 33.

98. Holmes, "Education for Liturgy," p. 132.

99. Minutes of the April 6–9, 1970, Meeting.

100. Minutes of the November 18–19, 1970, Meeting; "A.P. Council & Lit Chairmen Meet," *Open* 4 & 5 (1970): 7,9.

101. Minutes of the Executive Committee Meeting, September 30, 1973.

102. Minutes of the Executive Committee Meeting, November 8, 1973.

103. Minutes of the November 8, 1973, Meeting; "A Report to the Membership of Associated Parishes," undated.

104. Minutes of the May 26–30, 1975, Meeting.

105. Minutes of the May 14–18, 1979, Meeting.

106. *JGC* 1979, pp. C-8–C-10.

107. Sydnor, *Story of the Real Prayer Book*, p. 105.

108. West, "Episodes (cont): Conflict Resolution Before Minneapolis Gen'l Convention," no page no.

109. Ibid.

110. Minutes of the May 26–30, 1976, Meeting.

111. Minutes of the April 3–7, 1967, and November 6–10, 1967, Meetings; Minutes of the April 14–17, 1969, Meeting.

112. *The Holy Eucharist, Rite Two: A Commentary* (Alexandria, Va.: Associated Parishes, 1976), p. 1.

113. Minutes of the May 26–30, 1976, Meeting.

114. *Holy Eucharist, Rite Two*, p. 3.

115. Parish Eucharist, p. 2.

116. Ibid., p. 1.

117. Ibid., p. 14.

118. Ibid., p. 10.

119. Ibid., pp. 10–11.

120. *Ministry I: Holy Baptism*, p. 1; and *Ministry II: Laity, Bishops, Priests, and Deacons* (Alexandria,Va.: Associated Parishes, 1978), p. 1.

121. *Ministry I: Holy Baptism*, pp. 1, 9.

122. Ibid., p. 1.

123. Ibid., pp. 8,9.

124. *Ministry II: Laity, Bishops, Priests, and Deacons*, p. 1.

125. Ibid., p. 2; emphasis in the original.

126. Ibid., p. 6.

127. Ibid.

128. "The Wewoka Statement," Wewoka, Oklahoma, April 1977; *Ministry II*, p. 7.

129. "The Waverly Statement," Waverly, Georgia, May 1981.

130. "The Toronto Statement," Toronto, May 1992.

131. Louis Weil, *Christian Initiation*, pp. 4, 14, 15.

132. "Resolution 1982," Mississauga, Ontario, April 1982. A.P.'s appeal was addressed to both the Episcopal Church and the Anglican Church of Canada.

133. Minutes of the May 20–23, 1985, Meeting.

134. *Holy Baptism: A Liturgical and Pastoral Commentary* (Alexandria, Va.: Associated Parishes, 1987), p. 14.

135. Minutes of the May 20–23, 1985, Meeting; Minutes of the May 13–17, 1987, Meeting.

136. *The Catechumenate: Formation for Church Membership* (Alexandria, Va.: Associated Parishes, 1991).

137. *Holy Orders: The Ordination of Bishops, Priests, and Deacons* (Alexandria, Va.: Associated Parishes, 1991), pp. 15, 4.

138. Ibid., pp. 3–5.

139. Ibid., p. 15.

140. Ibid., p. 4.

141. *Great Vigil of Easter*, pp. 2–4; *Holy Baptism*, p. 5.

142. *Burial of the Dead*, pp. 1, 5, and passim.

143. *Parish Worship Committee*, p. 18.

144. *Commentary on Prayer Book Studies 30, Containing Supplemental Liturgical Texts* (New York: Church Hymnal Corp., 1989).

145. Henry Breul, "A Commentary: Benign Anarchy," *Open*

(September 1989): 8.

146. Henry I. Louttit, Jr., "Tolerance and Truth," *Open* 37 (Summer 1991): 14.

147. Joe Morris Doss, "Inclusive Language and General Convention," *Open* 37 (Fall 1991): 5. See also a response to Doss by Gregory M. Howe, "Inclusive Language: A Response," *Open* 38 (Spring 1992): 13.

148. John E. Hines, "A Birthday Greeting From the 'PB,'" *Open* (no number or date, but 1971).

149. Charles Mortimor [*sic*] Guilbert, "From the Prayer Book's Official 'Watchdog,'" *Open* (no number or date, but 1971).

150. John O. Patterson, "Forty Years On," p. 3.

151. Massey H. Shepherd, Jr., "And From An Old & Dear Friend," *Open* (no number or date, but 1971).

Chapter Six: A Prayer for a Post-Christendom Church

1. Ladd, *Prayer Book Interleaves*, pp. 2, 101.

2. Porter, "Toward An Unofficial History of Episcopal Worship," p. 110.

3. Shepherd, "History of the Liturgical Renewal," pp. 21–22, 27.

4. I am indebted to Peter E. Fink, S.J., for the models of God in the following paragraphs.

5. Massey H. Shepherd, Jr., "The Dimension of Liturgical Change," *Anglican Theological Review* 51 (October 1969): 251–252.

6. Holmes, "Education for Liturgy," p. 131.

7. Ibid.

8. BCP 1979, p. 291.

Bibliography

Associated Parishes Publications
(In chronological order)

Brochures:

The Parish Eucharist. Madison, Wisc.: Associated Parishes, 1950.

Christian Initiation, Part I: Holy Baptism. Madison, Wisc.: Associated Parishes, 1953.

Christian Initiation, Part II: Confirmation. Madison, Wisc.: Associated Parishes, 1954.

"In Newness of Life:" A Guide for Self-Examination. Madison, Wisc.: Associated Parishes, 1954.

Christian Burial. Madison, Wisc.: Associated Parishes, 1955.

The Christian Meaning of Work. Madison, Wisc.: Associated Parishes, 1959.

Holy Matrimony and the Christian Family. Madison, Wisc.: Associated Parishes, 1960.

The Daily Offices. Madison, Wisc.: Associated Parishes, 1963.

The Parish Eucharist. Madison, Wisc.: Associated Parishes, revised ed., c. 1966.

The Holy Eucharist, Rite Two: A Commentary. Alexandria, Va.: Associated Parishes, 1976.

Parish Eucharist. Alexandria, Va.: Associated Parishes, 1977.

The Great Vigil of Easter: A Commentary. Alexandria. Va.: Associated Parishes, 1977.

Ministry I: Holy Baptism. Alexandria, Va.: Associated Parishes, 1978.

Ministry II: Laity, Bishops, Priests, and Deacons. Alexandria, Va.: Associated Parishes, 1978.

Celebrating Redemption: The Liturgies of Lent, Holy Week, and the Great Fifty Days. Alexandria, Va.: Associated Parishes, 1980.

The Burial of the Dead: A Commentary. Alexandria, Va.: Associated Parishes, 1980.

The Daily Office: A Guide for Individual and Group Recitation. Alexandria, Va.: Associated Parishes, 1981.

Holy Baptism: A Liturgical and Pastoral Commentary. Alexandria, Va.: Associated Parishes, 1987.

The Celebration and Blessing of a Marriage: A Liturgical and Pastoral Commentary. Alexandria, Va.: Associated Parishes, 1987.

The Parish Worship Committee. Alexandria, Va.: Associated Parishes, 1988.

Holy Orders: The Ordination of Bishops, Priests, and Deacons. Alexandria, Va.: Associated Parishes, 1991.

The Catechumenate: Formation for Church Membership. Alexandria, Va.: Associated Parishes, 1991.

Books:

Shepherd, Massey Hamilton, Jr., ed. *The Liturgical Renewal of the Church; Addresses of the Liturgical Conference Held in Grace Church, Madison, May 19–21, 1958.* New York: Oxford University Press, 1960.

———, ed. *The Eucharist & Liturgical Renewal; Addresses of the Liturgical Conference Held in St. Paul's Church, San Antonio, November 16–18, 1959.* New York: Oxford University Press, 1960.

Cellier, Frank Stephen, ed. *Liturgy Is Mission.* New York: Seabury, 1964.

Other Publications:

Shepherd, Massey H., Jr.; Keene, John H.; Patterson, John O.; Bill, John R., eds. *Before the Holy Table: A Guide to the Celebration of the Holy Eucharist, Facing the People, According to the Book of Common Prayer.* Greenwich, Conn.: Seabury, 1956.

Shepherd, Massey H., Jr. *Fasting Among Churchmen*. Madison, Wisc.: Associated Parishes, 1958.

This Our Bounden Duty and Service. Madison, Wisc.: Associated Parishes, no date.

A Parish Program for Liturgy and Mission. Madison, Wisc.: Associated Parishes, 1964.

Calvin, Susan. *"Orleton" Mass*. [Music for the Holy Communion, dedicated to Associated Parishes.] Madison, Wisc.: Associated Parishes, 1966.

The Liturgy: A Celebration of Worldly Men. No place of publication: Associated Parishes, 1968.

"House Church." Alexandria, Va.: Associated Parishes, no date but c. 1969.

The Liturgy of the Lord's Supper; Leader's Guide and Workbook For a Five-Session Study Course in Conjunction With Prayer Book Studies No. XVII. Madison, Wisc.: Associated Parishes, 1967. Revised ed., David Babin for the Associated Parishes. *Making Use of Trial Use; A Leader's Guide for a Five-Session Study Course of the Holy Eucharist*. No place of publication: Associated Parishes, 1971.

Woods, Richard Forrest. *Music for The Liturgy of the Lord's Supper*. Associated Parishes, 197–?

Celebration: Community and Communion; A Program of Continuing Education for Those Baptized & Admitted to Communion at an Early Age. New York: Associated Parishes, 1971.

A Deacon is a . . . What? Washington, D.C.: Associated Parishes, no date, but c. 1976.

Weil, Louis. *Christian Initiation: A Theological and Pastoral Commentary on the Proposed Rites*. Alexandria, Va.: Associated Parishes, no date.

Liturgical Texts:

Shepherd, Massey H., Jr., ed. *Holy Week Offices*. Greenwich, Conn.: Seabury, 1958.

Create and Celebrate. No place or date of publication.

Periodicals:

Sharers. Madison, Wisc., c. 1954–1962.

Open. New York, Alexandria, Va., and South Bend, Ind., 1968–1996.

Unpublished Archival Material

Associated Parishes. Minutes of Meetings, Correspondence, and Other Materials, 1946–1991. Archives of the Associated Parishes, Alexandria, Virginia.

Associated Parishes. Minutes of Meetings and Publications, 1946–1970. Record Group 272. Archives of the Episcopal Church USA, Austin, Texas.

Malania, Leo. Drafting Committee Reports and Correspondence, 1968–1970. Records in the personal possession of James F. White, South Bend, Indiana.

Shepherd, Massey Hamilton, Jr. General Correspondence, Associated Parishes Materials, and Other Materials, 1936–1985. Record Group 237. Archives of the Episcopal Church USA, Austin, Texas.

Liturgical Texts

Authorized Services 1973. New York: Church Hymnal Corp., 1973. Expanded ed., 1973.

The Book of Common Prayer and Administration of the Sacraments and Other Rites and Ceremonies of the Church According to the Use of the Protestant Episcopal Church in the United States of America Together with The Psalter or Psalms of David. (1928). New York: Church Pension Fund, 1968.

The Book of Common Prayer and Administration of the Sacraments and Other Rites and Ceremonies of the Church Together with The Psalter or Psalms of David According to the use of The Episcopal Church. (1979). New York: Church Hymnal Corp., 1979.

Book of Offices: Services for Certain Occasions not provided for in the Book of Common Prayer; Compiled by the Liturgical Commission and commended for use by General Convention. New York: Church Pension Fund, 1940. 2nd ed., 1949. 3rd ed., 1960.

The Book of Occasional Services. New York: Church Hymnal Corp., 1979. 2nd ed., 1988. 3rd ed., 1994.

The Draft Proposed Book of Common Prayer and Administration of the Sacraments and Other Rites and Ceremonies of the Church According to the use of the Protestant Episcopal Church in the United States of America otherwise known as The Episcopal Church Together with The Psalter or Psalms of David. New York: Church Hymnal Corp., 1976.

The Hymnal of the Protestant Episcopal Church in the United States of America 1940. New York: Church Pension Fund, 1940, 1943.

Prayer Book Studies I: Baptism and Confirmation. New York: Church Pension Fund, 1950.

Prayer Book Studies II: The Liturgical Lectionary. New York: Church Pension Fund, 1950.

Prayer Book Studies III: The Order for the Ministration to the Sick. New York: Church Pension Fund, 1951.

Prayer Book Studies IV: The Eucharistic Liturgy. New York: Church Pension Fund, 1953.

Prayer Book Studies V: The Litany. New York: Church Pension Fund, 1953.

Prayer Book Studies VI: Morning and Evening Prayer. New York: Church Pension Fund, 1953.

Prayer Book Studies VII: The Penitential Office. New York: Church Pension Fund, 1953.

Prayer Book Studies VIII: The Ordinal. New York: Church Pension Fund, 1957.

Prayer Book Studies IX: The Calendar. New York: Church Pension Fund, 1957.

Prayer Book Studies X: The Solemnization of Matrimony. New York: Church Pension Fund, 1958.

Prayer Book Studies XI: A Thanksgiving for the Birth of a Child. New York: Church Pension Fund, 1958.

Prayer Book Studies XII: The Propers for the Minor Holy Days. New York: Church Pension Fund, 1958.

Prayer Book Studies XIII: The Order for the Burial of the Dead. New York: Church Pension Fund, 1959.

Prayer Book Studies XIV: An Office of Institution of Rectors into Parishes. New York: Church Pension Fund, 1959.

Prayer Book Studies XV: The Problem and Method of Prayer Book Revision. New York: Church Pension Fund, 1961.

Prayer Book Studies XVI: The Calendar and the Collects, Epistles, and Gospels for the Lesser Feasts and Fasts: A Supplementary Revision of Prayer Book Studies IX and XII. New York: Church Pension Fund, 1963.

Prayer Book Studies XVII: The Liturgy of the Lord's Supper; A Revision of Prayer Book Studies IV. New York: Church Pension Fund, 1966.

Prayer Book Studies 18: On Baptism and Confirmation; Holy Baptism with the Laying-On-of-Hands. New York: Church Pension Fund, 1970.

Prayer Book Studies 19: The Church Year; The Calendar and the Proper of the Sundays and Other Holy Days throughout the Church Year. New York: Church Hymnal Corp., 1970.

Prayer Book Studies 20: The Ordination of Bishops, Priests, and Deacons. New York: Church Hymnal Corp., 1970.

Prayer Book Studies 21: The Holy Eucharist; the Liturgy for the Proclamation of the Word of God and Celebration of the Holy Communion. New York: Church Hymnal Corp., 1970.

Prayer Book Studies 22: The Daily Office; Morning and Evening Prayer, Services for Noonday and Close of Day, Daily Devotions. New York: Church Hymnal Corp., 1970.

Prayer Book Studies 23: The Psalter, Part I. New York: Church Hymnal Corp., 1970.

Prayer Book Studies 24: Pastoral Offices; Marriage, Thanksgiving for a Child, Commitment to Service, Ministry to the Sick, Reconciliation, Anointing of the Sick, Private Communions, Prayers for the Dying, Burial of the Dead. New York: Church Hymnal Corp., 1970.

Prayer Book Studies 25: Prayers, Thanksgivings, and Litanies. New York: Church Hymnal Corp., 1973.

Prayer Book Studies 26: Holy Baptism together with A Form for Confirmation or the Laying-On of Hands by the Bishop with the Affirmation of Baptismal Vows. New York: Church Hymnal Corp., 1973.

Supplement to Prayer Book Studies 26: A Form for the Affirmation of Baptismal Vows with the Laying-On of Hands by the Bishop also called Confirmation. Prepared for The Standing Liturgical Commission by Daniel B. Stevick. New York: Church Hymnal Corp., 1973.

Prayer Book Studies 27: The Daily Office Revised. New York: Church Hymnal Corp., 1973.

Prayer Book Studies 28: Dedication and Consecration of a Church, Celebration of a New Ministry. New York: Church Hymnal Corp., 1973.

Prayer Book Studies 29, Revised: Introducing the Proposed Book; A Study of the Significance of the Proposed Book of Common Prayer for the Doctrine, Discipline, and Worship of the Episcopal Church. By Charles P. Price for the Standing Liturgical Commission. New York: Church Hymnal Corp., 1976.

Commentary on Prayer Book Studies 30, containing Supplemental Liturgical Texts. New York: Church Hymnal Corp., 1989.

Proposed The Book of Common Prayer and Administration of the Sacraments and Other Rites and Ceremonies of the Church Together with The Psalter or Psalms of David According to the use of The Episcopal Church. New York: Church Hymnal Corp. and Seabury, 1976.

Services for Trial Use: Authorized Alternatives to Prayer Book Services. New York: Church Hymnal Corp., 1971.

Official Reports and Publications

Constitution & Canons for the Government of the Protestant Episcopal Church in the United States of America Otherwise Known as The Episcopal Church Adopted in General Conventions 1789–1991 together with the Rules of Order Revised by the Convention 1991.

Journal of the General Convention of the Protestant Episcopal Church in the United States of America. 1940–1991.

Books and Monographs

Addison, James Thayer. *The Episcopal Church in the United States, 1789–1931.* No place of publication: Archon Books, 1969; reprint of 1951 ed.

An Order of Worship for the Proclamation of the Word of God and the Celebration of the Lord's Supper with Commentary. Cincinnati: Forward Movement, 1968.

Armentrout, Don S., and Slocum, Robert Boak. *Documents of Witness: A History of the Episcopal Church, 1782–1985.* New York: Church Hymnal, 1994.

Bradshaw, Paul F. *The Search for the Origins of Christian Worship: Sources and Methods for the Study of Early Liturgy.* New York: Oxford, 1992.

Burson, Malcolm C., ed. *Worship Points the Way: A Celebration of the Life and Work of Massey Hamilton Shepherd, Jr.* New York: Seabury, 1981.

Casel, Odo. *The Mystery of Christian Worship and Other Writings.* Westminster, Md.: Newman, 1962.

Chorley, E. Clowes. *The New American Prayer Book: Its History and Contents.* New York: Macmillan, 1929.

Cone, James H. *Martin & Malcolm & America: A Dream or a Nightmare.* Maryknoll, N.Y.: Orbis, 1991.

Cope, G., Davies, J.G., and Tytler, D.A. *An Experimental Liturgy*. Ecumenical Studies in Worship, No. 3. Richmond, Va.: John Knox, 1958.

Davies, Horton. *Worship and Theology in England*. Vol. IV: *From Newman to Martineau, 1850–1900*. Princeton University Press, 1962.

Dearmer, Percy. *The Parson's Handbook*. London: Grant Richards, 1899; many eds. thereafter published by Oxford University Press; 13th edition revised, rewritten, and abbreviated by Cyril E. Pocknee, 1965.

DeMille, George E. *The Catholic Movement in the American Episcopal Church*. Philadelphia: Church Historical Society, 1941.

Dix, Gregory. *The Shape of the Liturgy*. London: Dacre Press, 1945; new edition with additional notes by Paul V. Marshall, New York: Seabury, 1982.

———. *The Theology of Confirmation in Relation to Baptism*. Westminster: Dacre, 1946.

Douglas, Winfred. *Church Music in History and Practice: Studies in the Praise of God*. New York: Scribner's, 1937.

Ellard, Gerald. *Men At Work At Worship: America Joins the Liturgical Movement*. New York: Longmans, Green and Co., 1940.

———. *The Dialog Mass: A Book for Priests and Teachers of Religion*. New York: Longmans, Green and Co., 1942.

———. *The Mass of the Future*. Milwaukee: Bruce Publishing Co., 1948.

———. *The Mass in Transition*. Milwaukee: Bruce Publishing Co., 1956.

Foster, Roland. *The Role of the Presiding Bishop*. Cincinnati: Forward Movement, 1982.

Garrett, T.S. *Worship in the Church of South India*. Ecumenical Studies in Worship, No. 2. Richmond, Va.: John Knox, 1958.

Gray, Donald. *Earth and Altar: The Evolution of the Parish Communion in the Church of England to 1945*. Norwich: Canterbury Press, 1986.

Hatchett, Marion J. *Commentary on the American Prayer Book*. New York: Seabury, 1980.

———. *The Making of the First American Book of Common Prayer, 1776–1789*. New York: Seabury, 1982.

Hebert, A.G. *Liturgy and Society: The Function of the Church in the Modern World*. London: Faber and Faber, 1935.

———. *The Bible From Within*. New York: Oxford, 1950.

———, ed. *The Parish Communion: A Book of Essays*. London: S.P.C.K., 1937.

Holmes, David L. *A Brief History of the Episcopal Church*. Valley Forge, Pa.: Trinity Press International, 1993.

Hughes, Kathleen, ed. *How Firm a Foundation: Voices of the Early Liturgical Movement*. Chicago: Liturgy Training Pubs., 1990.

Jagger, Peter J. *Bishop Henry de Candole: His Life and Times, 1895–1971*. Leighton Buzzard, Beds.: Faith Press, 1975.

———. *A History of the Parish and People Movement*. Leighton Buzzard, Beds.: Faith Press, 1978.

Kennedy, Robert J. *Michael Mathis: American Liturgical Pioneer*. American Essays in Liturgy 5. Washington, D.C.: Pastoral Press, 1987.

Ladd, William Palmer. *Prayer Book Interleaves: Some Reflections on How the Book of Common Prayer Might Be Made More Influential in Our English-Speaking World*. Greenwich, Conn.: Seabury, 1942.

The Lambeth Conference 1958: The Encyclical Letter From the Bishops Together With the Resolutions and Reports. London and Greenwich, Conn.: S.P.C.K. and Seabury, 1958.

Lampe, Geoffrey W.H. *The Seal of the Spirit: A Study in the Doctrine of Baptism and Confirmation in the New Testament and the Fathers*. London: Longmans, Green, and Co., 1951; 2nd ed., London: S.P.C.K., 1967.

Leonard, William J. "The Liturgical Movement in the United States." In *The Liturgy of Vatican II: A Symposium in Two Volumes*, pp. 293–312. Edited by William Barauna. Chicago: Franciscan Herald Press, 1966.

Marshall, Paul V. *Prayer Book Parallels: The Public Services of the Church Arranged for Comparative Study*. 2 vols. New York: Church Hymnal, 1989, 1990.

Marx, Paul B. *Virgil Michel and the Liturgical Movement*. Collegeville, Minn.: Liturgical Press, 1957.

McMichael, Ralph N., Jr., ed. *Creation and Liturgy: Studies in Honor of H. Boone Porter*. Washington, D.C.: Pastoral Press, 1993.

Mitchell, Leonel L. *Baptismal Anointing*. London: S.P.C.K., 1966.

———. *Praying Shapes Believing: A Theological Commentary on the Book of Common Prayer*. Minneapolis: Winston, 1985.

Moorman, John R.H. *The Anglican Spiritual Tradition*. Springfield, Ill.: Templegate Publishers, 1983.

Northup, Lesley A. *The 1892 Book of Common Prayer*. Toronto Studies in Theology, Vol. 65. Lewiston/Queenston/Lampeter: Edwin Mellen, 1993.

O'Connell, Marvin R. *The Oxford Conspirators: A History of the Oxford Movement, 1833–1845.* New York: Macmillan, 1969.

Palmer, William. *Origines Liturgicae; or, Antiquities of the English Ritual; and a Dissertation on Primitive Liturgies.* Oxford: University Press, 1832.

Parsons, Edward Lambe, and Jones, Bayard Hale. *The American Prayer Book: Its Origins and Principles.* New York: Charles Scribner's Sons, 1937.

Prichard, Robert W. *A History of the Episcopal Church.* Harrisburg, Pa.: Morehouse, 1991.

Procter, Francis, and Frere, Walter Howard. *A New History of the Book of Common Prayer with a Rationale of Its Offices.* London: Macmillan, 1905.

Robinson, John A.T. *Liturgy Coming To Life.* London: A.R. Mowbray, 1960; 2nd ed., 1963.

Shands, Alfred R. *The Liturgical Movement and the Local Church.* London: SCM Press, 1959.

Shepherd, Massey Hamilton, Jr. *The Living Liturgy.* New York: Oxford, 1946.

——. *The Liturgical Movement and the Prayer Book; The Twenty-ninth Annual Hale Memorial Sermon.* Evanston, Ill.: Seabury-Western Theological Seminary, 1946.

——. *The Oxford American Prayer Book Commentary.* New York: Oxford, 1950.

——. *The Worship of the Church.* Greenwich, Conn.: Seabury, 1952.

——. *The Reform of Liturgical Worship: Perspectives and Prospects; The Bohlen Lectures 1959.* New York: Oxford, 1961.

——. *Liturgy and Education.* New York: Seabury, 1965.

——, ed. *Worship in Scripture and Tradition: Essays by Members of the Theological Commission on Worship (North American Section) of the Commission on Faith and Order of the World Council of Churches.* New York: Oxford, 1963.

Simpson, James B., and Story, Edward M. *The Long Shadows of Lambeth X: A Critical Eye-Witness Account of the Tenth Decennial Conference of 462 Bishops of the Anglican Communion.* New York: McGraw-Hill, 1969.

Skardon, Alvin W. *Church Leader in the Cities: William Augustus Muhlenberg.* Philadelphia: University of Pennsylvania Press, 1971.

Stevenson, Kenneth. *Gregory Dix—25 Years On.* Bramcote, Notts.: Grove Books, 1977.

Stevenson, Kenneth, and Spinks, Bryan, eds. *The Identity of Anglican Worship*. Harrisburg, Pa: Morehouse, 1991.

Stuhlman, Byron D. *Eucharistic Celebration 1789–1979*. New York: Church Hymnal, 1988.

Sydnor, William. *The Story of the Real Prayer Book, 1549–1979*. Wilton, Conn.: Morehouse, 1978; revised ed., 1989.

Taylor, Michael J. *The Protestant Liturgical Renewal: A Catholic Viewpoint*. Westminster, Md.: Newman, 1963.

Thurian, Max. *The Eucharistic Liturgy of Taizé*. London: Faith, 1962.

Tuzik, Robert, ed. *How Firm a Foundation: Leaders of the Liturgical Movement*. Chicago: Liturgy Training Pubs., 1990.

Underhill, Evelyn. *The Mystery of Sacrifice: A Meditation on the Liturgy*. New York: Longmans, 1938.

White, James F. *The Cambridge Movement: The Ecclesiologists and the Gothic Revival*. Cambridge: University Press, 1962.

White, Susan J. *Art, Architecture, and Liturgical Reform: The Liturgical Arts Society (1928–1972)*. New York: Pueblo, 1990.

———. *Christian Worship and Technological Change*. Nashville: Abingdon, 1994.

Magazines and Articles

"Bishop Paul Moore, Jr., . . . " *The Daily*, 15 October 1970, p. 1.

Donovan, J.P. "Were Our Own Liturgists Afoul?" *Homiletic and Pastoral Review* XXXIX (1949): 750–751.

Ellard, Gerald. "Non-Catholic Liturgical Movements." *Thought* XVIII (September 1943): 451–468.

———. "The Liturgical Movement in Catholic Circles." *Religion in Life* XVII (Summer 1948): 370–381.

"Episcopal History Made." *The Boston Globe*, 4 October 1969, p. 1.

The Episcopalian. 1967–1979.

The Living Church. 1967–1979.

Moriarty, Michael. "William Palmer Ladd and the Origins of the Episcopal Liturgical Movement." *Church History* 64 (September 1995): 438–451.

"Rev. Dr. Ladd Dies; Educator, Author." *The New York Times*, 2 July 1941, p. 21.

Scott, R. Taylor. "The Likelihood of Liturgy: Reflections Upon Prayer Book Revision and Its Liturgical Implications." *Anglican Theological Review* 62 (1980): 103–120.

Shands, Alfred R. III. "What Sunday Morning Is Coming To." *The Episcopalian* 133 (November 1968): 8.

Shepherd, Massey H., Jr. "The Berakah Award: Response." *Worship* 52 (July 1978): 299–313.

——. "The Dimension of Liturgical Change." *Anglican Theological Review* 51 (October 1969): 241–256.

"South Bend—AWOL air force man . . . " *The National Catholic Reporter*, 10 September 1969, p. 1.

Taylor, David L. "The Order of St. Luke and *The Versicle*; A Resume: 1946–1961." *Doxology* 3 (1986): 48–56.

Unpublished Sources

Garner, Joel P. "The Vision of a Liturgical Reformer: Hans Ansgar Reinhold, American Catholic Educator." Ph.D. Dissertation, Columbia University, 1972.

Madden, Lawrence. "The Liturgical Conference of the United States of America: Its Origin and Development, 1940–1968." Ph.D. Dissertation, Trier, 1969.

Meyers, Ruth A. "The Renewal of Christian Initiation in the Episcopal Church 1928–1979." Ph.D. Dissertation, University of Notre Dame, 1992.

West, Samuel E. "Episodes Towards a Recorded History of Associated Parishes for Liturgy and Mission." 1987.

Woolverton, John F. "William Reed Huntington and Church Unity: The Historical and Theological Background of the Chicago-Lambeth Quadrilateral." Ph.D. Dissertation, Columbia University, 1963.